PRIMARY SCIENCE

Education at SAGE

SAGE is a leading international publisher of journals, books, and electronic media for academic, educational, and professional markets.

Our education publishing includes:

- accessible and comprehensive texts for aspiring education professionals and practitioners looking to further their careers through continuing professional development

- inspirational advice and guidance for the classroom

- authoritative state of the art reference from the leading authors in the field

Find out more at: **www.sagepub.co.uk/education**

PRIMARY SCIENCE

A GUIDE TO TEACHING PRACTICE

Edited by

Mick Dunne and Alan Peacock

Los Angeles | London | New Delhi
Singapore | Washington DC

Editorial arrangement and Introduction
© 2012 Mick Dunne and Alan Peacock
Chapter 1© Alan Peacock and Mick Dunne 2012
Chapter 2 © Alan Peacock 2012
Chapter 3 © Richard Watkins 2012
Chapter 4 © Dave Howard, Ashlee Perry,
Malcolm Smith, Liz Flintoft and Robert Collins 2012
Chapter 5 © Tara Mawby 2012

Chapter 6 © Leigh Hoath 2012
Chapter 7 © Natasha Serret and Sarah Earle 2012
Chapter 8 © Mick Dunne and Dave Howard 2012
Chapter 9 © Tara Mawby and Mick Dunne 2012
Chapter 10 © Leigh Hoath and Tanya Shields 2012
Chapter 11 © Dave Howard and Ashlee Perry 2012
Chapter 12 © Alan Peacock and Mick Dunne 2012

First published 2012

SAGE Publications Ltd
1 Oliver's Yard
55 City Road
London EC1Y 1SP

SAGE Publications Inc.
2455 Teller Road
Thousand Oaks, California 91320

SAGE Publications India Pvt Ltd
B1/I1 Mohan Cooperative Industrial Area
Mathura Road
New Delhi 110 044

SAGE Publications Asia-Pacific Pte Ltd
33 Pekin Street #02-01
Far East Square
Singapore 048763

Library of Congress Control Number: 2011923830

British Library Cataloguing in Publication data

A catalogue record for this book is available from the British Library

ISBN 978-0-85702-505-0
ISBN 978-0-85702-506-7

, Chennai, India
Books Group, Bodmin, Cornwall
ble resources

CONTENTS

ACKNOWLEDGEMENTS

The editors and publisher would like to thank the following for permission: Alan Peacock and Ailie Cleghorn, *Missing the Meaning*, Palgrave Macmillan, 2004. Reproduced with permission of Palgrave Macmillan.

THE EDITORS

Mick Dunne is Head of Teacher Education at the University Centre, Bradford College. Working in secondary and middle schools for ten years he took on a number of roles, including subject responsibility for science, ICT, and mathematics, before moving into teacher education as a senior lecturer in science education. He has been a member of several editorial boards both in the UK and abroad, has actively supported the Association for Science Education, and also undertaken a wide range of other work, including managing and coordinating both TEMPUS and Comenius 2.1 pan-European science and environmental education projects. His research interests within primary science include children's perceptions, out-of-classroom learning and environmental education, with his passion being the marine biology of rocky shores. He has published in a variety of texts and recently completed a doctorate on the subject of learning outside the classroom.

Alan Peacock is Honorary Research Fellow at the Graduate School of Education, University of Exeter, and until recently he was Editor of the journal *Primary Science* for six years. He has worked in teaching, training, and research in science education for over forty years, in various regions of the UK and overseas. He has carried out primary science consultancy work for the British Council, UNESCO, the EU, The National Trust, various environmental groups, and numerous NGOs in Africa, including in Kenya, South

Africa, Namibia, Botswana, Senegal, and Mozambique. His publications include *Science Skills: A Problem-Solving Activities Book* (Taylor & Francis); *Science in Primary Schools: The Multicultural Dimension* (Routledge); *Opportunities for Science in the Primary School* (Trentham); *Teaching Primary Science* (Macmillan Education), and *Eco-literacy for Primary Schools* (Trentham). He recently chaired the UNESCO working group on *Guidelines for enhancing quality education through textbooks.*

NOTES ON CONTRIBUTORS

Robert Collins is a lecturer at the University of Strathclyde's School of Humanities and Social Sciences. He has published extensively focusing primarily on student teacher development and on the use of ICT in school settings. Robert is a committee member of the Scottish Educational Research Association, one of the science advisor team to the Glasgow Science Centre and an active member of the Editorial Board of the Association for Science Education's journal *Primary Science*.

Sarah Earle is currently Science Subject Leader for Elmlea Junior School in Bristol and visiting lecturer on the PGCE Primary course at Bath Spa University, where she previously completed her Master's in Science Education. She has published articles in the ASE's *Primary Science* and is currently Reviews Editor for this journal.

Liz Flintoff has worked in ITE for five years specialising in ICT pedagogy. She has considerable school experience including as the subject coordinator for ICT in several different primary schools. She graduated from Sheffield Hallam University with a BEd specialising in primary science, and later Huddersfield University with an MSc in Multimedia and E-Learning. Her particular interest is using different subjects, particularly science, as a vehicle for effective embedding ICT.

Leigh Hoath spent eight years working in two secondary schools before becoming science education lecturer at the University Centre, Bradford College. Her research interests lie particularly in science pedagogy and learning in non-traditional settings and she is currently studying for her EdD. Leigh represented the Association for Science Education at the New Zealand ASE 2009 national conference, where she delivered a range of workshops on Questioning in Science. She is a regular contributor to *Primary Science* as well as other science education journals.

Dave Howard was a primary class teacher for sixteen years including five years as a deputy before moving into teacher training. For the last few years he managed education and professional studies colleagues before becoming Head of Primary ITE at Bradford College. His academic interests include children's self-assessment, the inclusive practice of ITE tutors, and the transition from class teaching to lecturing in ITE.

Tara Mawby started teaching in 1995, becoming a consultant for Warwickshire Local Authority in 2002. She is currently a consultant for Primary Science with a number of Black Country authorities, focusing on Science Enquiry, and also edits the ASE's *Primary Science* journal.

Ashlee Perry is a Lecturer in Science Education and Leader of the Physics Enhancement Course at University Centre, Bradford College. After gaining a PhD in biochemistry from the University of Leicester he spent several years as a research scientist before completing a PGCE and becoming a secondary science teacher. He is new to ITE where his research interests lie with Gifted and Talented learners and the transition between KS4–5.

Natasha Serret was a primary school teacher in inner London for six years. She joined King's College, London, in 2001 as the senior researcher for the primary Cognitive Acceleration through Science Education (CASE) project and is one of the main authors of *Let's Think Through Science!* Her PhD thesis explores the relationship between classroom talk and cognitive development. She is now senior lecturer on the BA in Primary Education course at Nottingham Trent University.

Tanya Shields is an independent consultant who works with both primary and secondary professionals. She is also a Professional Development Leader for CIEC at the University of York, providing CPD for the Science Learning Centres. Her previous work includes teaching and the development of resources for use in the primary classroom.

Malcolm Smith was a senior lecturer in the Department of Teacher Education at Bradford College, specialising in ICT within all the primary ITE courses and being course leader for the PGCE Secondary ICT course. Over the last ten years he became interested in pedagogies associated with online learning which led to involvement with a number of European Universities researching and developing strategies to maximise this rapidly emerging resource both within the classroom and for the professional development of serving teachers.

Richard Watkins is Senior Learning Adviser for primary science for three local authorities in North Wales. He previously worked in a primary school where he spent time on secondment working for Liverpool John Moores University and the University of Liverpool. Before moving into education Richard worked in the oil industry. He is a member of the editorial board of *Primary Science* and has recently contributed material to NGfL and the Geographical Association publication, *Primary Project Box*.

INTRODUCTION

This is a *'Yes, you can!'* book. Novice primary teachers, NQTs, recently qualified teachers, and student teachers are always on the lookout for practical help to make their early experiences of teaching easier and more satisfying – and never more so than when preparing to teach science. Our aim is to support you in this but it would be misleading to give the impression that good science teaching is easy. Report after report on primary science teaching has emphasised teachers' anxieties about subject knowledge and their lack of confidence and the situation is not helped by the emphasis (some would say over-emphasis, especially in England) on the constant requirement for testing learners' knowledge of science ideas. By the end of primary school, in many contexts, children are already beginning to be turned off science, and sadly this decline can continue into secondary school. It may sound like a daunting task to reverse this trend. But many teachers before you have shown that it can be done.

The main way to shore up a lack of confidence over the years has been to focus on teachers' continuing professional development in two main areas, namely science subject knowledge and practical enquiry skills, with each of these closely related to the requirements of national curricula. These approaches – often delivered via excellent programmes run by local authorities or science learning centres – tend to treat science as a self-contained subject within a centrally-controlled primary curriculum. Published materials, both official and commercial, also tend to reinforce this treatment of science as a stand-alone, tested discipline. This book, however, takes a different line.

The contributors – all with a wide professional experience of teaching, training, and advisory work within primary science – are very aware that truly effective science learning arises out of children's curiosity about the world around them and that many of the questions they will ask, and want to explore, will not fit readily into a single school subject. Nor will a teacher's science knowledge, however extensive, always be up to the job of answering such questions with definitive answers, since increasingly there are no conclusive answers to many of the big questions that puzzle them. Fobbing children off with test answers, thereby reducing science to a kind of trivia quiz, will only serve to alienate them further.

This book therefore is written with the sole purpose of supporting you, the novice teacher, in dealing with these concerns. It is not a book that will give you lots of 'bright ideas' for a Monday morning lesson that you haven't had time to prepare; what it will do is develop your repertoire of skills and approaches for fostering children's curiosity, encouraging their questioning, getting them talking and arguing about the big ideas that science can help them deal with. It aims to help you see the connections with other areas of learning, to build on common skills relating to the gathering and use of evidence for example, and to help children build theories and test ideas of their own. In other words, we are focusing on helping you develop children who are able to become genuinely 'science literate' and keen to learn science.

In finalising the content of this book, our first task was to find out what novice teachers actually wanted it to include. In order to do this we set up focus groups of trainees in four training institutions, gave them each a rough list of chapter headings, and asked what they would want to see under each heading. Some chapters disappeared as a consequence, or became integrated with others, while some new chapters emerged.

Each of these, as a consequence, has a short section which shows how the authors responded to what we have called 'Student Perspectives'. Authors also set out key ideas, linked these to theory, and provided examples of how all this had worked out in actual practice in real classrooms through case studies and vignettes. The first two chapters focus on putting the issue of science learning into context, looking at how science education has evolved historically and how we can learn from practice in diverse settings and cultures. Chapters 3–5 focus on the relation between science learning and other areas of knowledge – particularly numeracy, ICT, literacy and geography – and draw from these some valuable examples of effective curriculum linking.

The second half of the book then addresses other concerns raised by the focus groups, specifically learning science outside the classroom; helping children communicate their science learning effectively; teaching tricky topics using metaphors, analogies, and models (always the same few difficult areas!); teacher assessment in science; and inclusion and transitions between phases. There is no chapter specifically about foundation and early years' science; our focus groups preferred this to be tackled within the other chapters, which is what authors have attempted to do. And apart from the 'tricky topics' chapter, we have not tried to deal systematically with science knowledge, partly because the curriculum requirements differ increasingly from country to country within the UK, and partly because we feel that to have several big chapters devoted to teaching science knowledge would give the book an emphasis that was out of line with our view of good science learning.

Our final chapter attempts to sum up our philosophy and approach in three ways: first, by drawing out from all previous chapters a digest of where we think primary science stands today, in 2011, second, by considering what we think works and why; and finally, by developing the editors' ideas about a possible way forward – not a way for policy makers, test setters, or administrators, but a way forward that is feasible for you, the novice teacher. We hope that, by the end of Chapter 12, you will agree with us. High quality science education provision has never been more important, which necessitates those delivering it to be willing to go beyond that which is being currently prescribed. Teaching is a profession. Professionalism is characterised by many things but we have placed particular value on the best professional educators being responsive, critical, flexible, imaginative, and creative practitioners. Enjoy the book.

CHAPTER 1

HOW SCIENCE HAS EVOLVED

Alan Peacock and Mick Dunne

Chapter Overview

This initial chapter focuses on the relevance of an understanding of the evolution of science and science education to primary teachers, at a time of what seems like perpetual change in the curriculum, approaches to teaching it, and the training of teachers. It traces the origins of much of what we know as science back to roots in China and the Islamic world, acknowledging some of their accomplishments we now take for granted in astronomy, chemistry, medicine, papermaking, ceramics, and many other fields. It also draws attention to what we now call Inquiry-based Science Education (IBSE) which has been at the root of scientific advances for centuries, such as the importance of observation, hypothesising, and the testing of ideas against evidence. The chapter then focuses on something that lies at the heart of this book – that science acknowledges uncertainty, rather than certainty, as its starting point. It is not about 'right answers' but about enquiring minds and the skills to handle evidence and postpone certainty. This has been the basis of work by all the great scientists, from Galileo and Newton through to Darwin, Einstein, Heisenberg, and Hawking. The only science knowledge we possess is that which emerges from such enquiry.

The chapter concludes by tracing the development of resources for primary science teaching from the 1960s onwards in the UK, including Nuffield Junior Science, Science 5–13, the SPACE research reports, and a wide range of commercial science schemes. This leads into the advent of the National Curriculum, the status of science as a core subject, and the controversial and often contradictory recent reviews that have set out to guide future developments. It concludes by asking you to consider where you stand in relation to some key questions about the future of primary science teaching.

Key Ideas

If you are a trainee, or an inexperienced primary teacher confronting science for the first time, you are probably opening this book expecting to find answers to some big questions like *'What is science?'*, *'Why should we teach it?'*, *'What is good science education?'* and *'How do children learn best in science?'* And so you may wonder why the focus of this first chapter is relevant: what you'll have to teach is laid down in the curriculum isn't it? How will searching back through history help?

You may feel like this because your previous experience has conditioned you to expect answers in the form of definitions – the kind that start off *'Science is ...'* or *'As a teacher of science in primary schools, you should ...'* – the clear-cut statements that tell you what to do to conform with official expectations. But the authors of this book, all of whom are and have been closely involved in training and developing teachers of science for primary schools, do not believe in that approach. And we have gone to great lengths to consult with 'Focus Groups' of trainees, in different parts of the country, on what exactly ought to go into 'your' book on Primary Science.

The reason for this is that science and the way it is taught have been in a constant state of flux for a very long time and remain so, as this first couple of chapters will try to show. And there are reasons why things constantly change. So the way in which you teach science will need to be adapted to the situation you find yourself in – which means to the children you teach, the environment of your school, the current concerns of society, government policy, and to technological change, to name only a few factors. To be effective as a teacher of science, therefore, you can't just trot out the tried-and-tested ideas of the past; you need to be a thinking, reflective teacher who can weigh up alternatives and makes up your mind on the basis of the best evidence, sound advice, and what suits your own personality.

The following chapters will therefore provoke discussion and debate rather than tell you what to think. Such discussion will inevitably draw on many of the key qualities of effective scientific enquiry and show how these concerns relate to classroom practice. This will start by exploring how the characteristics of science, and science enquiry, have evolved, leading in recent years to their application in a primary classroom context. We aim to balance historical perspectives with a clear focus on the present climate for primary science education. And most importantly, we will always be helping you find an appropriate balance between the characteristics of scientific activity and science as a body of knowledge.

Where did Science Start?

It's likely that science began when our ancestors first made stone tools, used fire and water to cook, or utilised skins and wood for clothing and shelter. But they certainly didn't think of themselves as scientists; in fact the term 'scientist' was only coined in 1833 by William Whewell at the request of poet and philosopher, Samuel Taylor Coleridge, who needed a word to describe the group of active experimenters who were making such huge advances in 'Natural Philosophy', as it was called, at the end of the eighteenth century. Thousands of years ago the people of the Nile valley made observations of when the river flooded so they could predict when best to plant their crops. The Mayans of South America were remarkable astronomers who made such accurate observations of the sun, moon, and planets that their calendars were virtually as accurate as ours are today. One way in which they did this was by digging deep, well-like pits in the earth and lying at the bottom; by doing so, they could observe a tiny portion of sky from which all extraneous daylight was excluded. They recorded, without any instruments, observations of stars which are now no longer visible to the naked eye!

Observe, suggest explanations, test them, expand knowledge, and then apply it – this is what people have done for millennia, a process of 'Coming to Knowing' about the world and the universe. What those very early ancestors were doing is something which is still at the heart of much science and technology, namely the search for understanding and ways to make work and life easier. Try asking children or your fellow non-science students what science is; they will probably say things like, *'how the world works'* or *'understanding the world around us'* – but they might also tell you *'physics, chemistry and biology'* because that has been their main experience, science as school subjects. And it's here that we face the first way in which science has evolved, because even these 'subjects' are quite recent inventions. For example, Humphrey Davy, the famous Cornish scientist and inventor of the miners' safety lamp (as well as investigating anaesthetics), claimed in his first book, in 1797, that *'Chemistry has arisen from the ruins of Alchemy'*. But even he didn't claim it should be taught in school! Geology and geography were new disciplines in the nineteenth century and today you will find university departments for things like socio-biology, geo-chemistry, paleo-archaeology, neurosciences, and many others. Yet all these new branches of science basically use the same underlying approach.

We have to go a long way back beyond Davy to see where science began in earnest and this happened not in the famous universities of Europe but in China and the Islamic world. In the ninth century Jabir ibn-Hayyan was preparing strong acids and alkalis using scientific methods, well before these techniques became common in the West. Jabir is believed to have written;

> The first essential ... is that you should perform practical work and conduct experiments, for he who performs not practical work nor makes experiments will never attain the least degree of mastery.

This is something we are still encouraging learners to do over a thousand years on.

Such 'scientists' were capable of great scientific accomplishments in astronomy, medicine, and algebra in the Muslim 'Golden Age' of 800–1200 AD, contrary to some current ideas that Islam opposes the scientific method or the advances of scientific understanding and the application of technology. The Prophet Muhammad urged individuals to be curious and to reason about the knowledge to be found in the natural world and this amazing research and development work carried out in the Islamic world can best be seen on the '1001 Inventions' website (http://www.1001inventions.com/) which describes the invention of various things we now take for granted, like soap, shampoo, fabrics, perfumes, fountain pens, toothbrushes, carpets, clocks, coffee, and the camera.

The Chinese were active too, long before their counterparts in Europe, in creating paper, printing, porcelain, the compass, medicines, and gunpowder. In Africa the people of Benin were creating beautiful and incredibly detailed bronze castings. All these developments by skilled artisans were based on principles and procedures that resemble what we now call 'the scientific method' of observation and experimentation. Aristotle had propounded some of these ideas as early as the fourth century BC by emphasising the importance of the experience of the senses – what is sometimes called Empiricism – and these ideas lasted and were refined over many centuries by famous names like Roger Bacon, Copernicus, Galileo, Francis Bacon, Newton, Descartes, Dalton, Darwin, Davy, Faraday ... the list is endless, of course. A quick 'Google' will tell you as much as you wish to know about all of these and many more.

Another more recent shift in thinking about science was Karl Popper's understanding that scientific theories could not be proved, they could only be falsified; in other words, no matter how much evidence you produce to back up an idea, it is still always possible that someone may find evidence to prove you wrong – and once you do find this falsifying evidence, the whole theory will collapse and you will have to start again. Thus science proceeds by falsifying, not by proving; even with young children science can be seen as testing their ideas against the evidence of their senses.

From a twenty-first century point of view specific ideas are not the most significant things. What matters is that frequent huge shifts in science-related thinking have taken place. Galileo and Newton changed the way we see our universe and the forces that make it work; Darwin changed our view of ourselves and our origins as a species; and in the past one hundred years, Einstein, Bohr, Heisenberg, Feynman, Hawking, and others have altered the way we think about matter, what it is, and how it can be transformed. But all these came into conflict with other, often religious, beliefs, particularly Galileo and Darwin, and even today the argument between evolutionary biologists and creationists who promote 'intelligent design' rages on in many countries.

Change and Uncertainty

Gradually, therefore, our understanding of what science is and how it works is changing. During the nineteenth and twentieth centuries, it became commonplace to believe that science and technology could control nature; we were 'harnessing' it to produce energy or grow more food. But in recent years, tsunamis, earthquakes and volcanoes have reminded us that even with the most sophisticated technology there are things we can't control. Native peoples in the Americas, Australia, and Asia have always known this and are aware of the need to live with nature and not try to control it. Yet many science professionals still do not regard their ideas (on natural remedies, for example) as being 'proper' science. David Peat in his (1995) book *Blackfoot Physics* explores these ideas at great length and other eminent scientists such as Fritjof Capra have made a huge effort to emphasise the links and similarities between the ideas of physics and ancient belief systems, such as those of eastern mysticism. Capra opens his (1975) book *The Tao of Physics* with this quote from Werner Heisenberg:

> It is probably true quite generally that in the history of human thinking the most fruitful developments frequently take place at those points where two different lines of thought meet. These lines may have their roots in quite different parts of human culture, in different times or different religious traditions: hence if they actually meet, that is, they are at least so much related to each other that a real interaction can take place, then one may hope that new and interesting developments may follow. Capra, F. 1975.

So science also progresses by making links with ideas from other disciplines and thought systems and in his other groundbreaking book, *The Hidden Connections* (2002), Capra demonstrates how we need a unifying system that can help understand the network of connections between science and such fields as economics, ecology, the mind, and social realities. In 2011 we are highly aware of the impact of global capitalism on all we do and these connections have been made forcibly by James Lovelock using his Gaia Principle, which sees our planet as a living entity in itself which will always find its own equilibrium, regardless of what we do to it (or even whether we are here or not!).

One further big change is the relatively recent realisation that our understanding of everything is beset by uncertainty, as proposed by the same Werner Heisenberg in his Uncertainty Principle. Scientists in the early twentieth century developing the quantum theory of matter realised that you could not observe very small, sub-atomic particles without changing them – a realisation that has had profound effects. We can only now talk about an electron probably being here or there, this or that; we cannot say for certain, and never will be able to. Hundreds of millions of dollars are being spent on investigations, such as that currently going on using the Large Hadron Collider (LHC) in Switzerland, in an attempt to find the 'ultimate' particle – but how will we know it is the ultimate? Probes with high-res cameras are also being sent to the edge of our solar system, but we are unlikely to be able to test the probability that, given the unimaginable number of galaxies and planets, there is life elsewhere.

At this point I can sense you are thinking, *'Hmm, maybe this book isn't for me, after all...'* but please stay with it! Uncertainty is everywhere and as teachers we have to recognise this. Nobody was certain where the volcanic ash cloud was heading in April 2010, despite the incredible technology available to the Meteorological Office, and while new species are being discovered all the time (over 100 in Borneo this year, I read) others like the tiger have an uncertain future. We are uncertain how fast the climate is actually changing, uncertain about how fast the Greenland icecap will melt, because it is impossible to have enough data to know for sure. We have to accept that our understanding is beset by inadequate data and the need to live with probabilities, as we do all the time when watching the weather forecasts on TV.

So developing young minds to think scientifically means first of all not preparing them to expect certainties, not wanting to know what the 'right answer' is, because despite the years of testing you have probably endured in school so often there will be no right answers. Of course if you jump off a building there's a high probability that you will fall and hit the ground; some probabilities are quite high! Ironically, of course, we have better 'gear' for enquiry and investigation than ever before. In school I used a Bunsen burner, test-tubes, balances, and (rarely), a microscope; now there is a huge range of digital technology at your disposal to help you do and see things that were impossible twenty years ago. And there are still a myriad things in your environment to enquire into, things probably unique to your school's surroundings.

Take the humble dandelion, a plant probably found around every school in the country, and consider how many investigations into its growth, size, seed dispersal, place in the food chain, etc. you could carry out. Simply investigating how the seeds move in the air could fascinate children for hours (what happens if ... you cut the parachute shorter, for instance?). Or take a bowl of fruit and think of the observations, predictions, and theories you could come up with by just considering the link between their size, colour, skin, and the seeds inside each fruit. We will suggest more simple activities like these in subsequent chapters.

The Emergence of Resources for Science Teaching

However, this kind of thinking about science as enquiry penetrated primary schools only recently. Until the mid-1960s, the closest that younger children got to a science activity was through nature walks and a nature table in the classroom. This might involve collecting frogspawn in spring, bringing it to the classroom and watching the eggs develop; or by collecting wild fruits and seeds in autumn and planting them in soil; or making systematic observations of the weather on a class chart. Of course much of this depended on whether your class teacher had the knowledge and understanding and even an interest in this sort of work. The physical sciences were rarely tackled. In the late 1960s, however, the Nuffield Foundation introduced *Nuffield Junior Science*, a scheme which had the deliberate intention of encouraging a practical, sensory experience of physical phenomena for children. Those who experienced this new approach clearly relished the chance to do practical activities even though there was little in the way of a clear link between this and their concept of learning.

There was at that time still no National Curriculum in Britain, so it was entirely up to individual schools and teachers to decide if and how to deal with science learning. However there was in existence an organisation called the Schools Council, an independent body which drove much curriculum change, and as each of its project teams was at least 50 per cent made up of teachers, their initiation of a programme for science was based on what teachers felt was needed. Out of this came *Science 5–13*, a project based at the University of Bristol, which had a much clearer basis in the understanding of children's learning, introducing the idea that 'science skills' were central to effective learning, as well as new ways of looking at a wide range of science content. Its publications included the ground-breaking introductory book, *With Objectives in Mind*, setting out the essential skills and concepts needed for an understanding of science. This was organised using three developmental stages and adopted Jean Piaget's ideas about intellectual development. Crucially it also tackled the physical sciences, with units on topics such as Structures and Forces, Working with Wood, Science from Toys, and Metals. The scheme also coined the now-familiar concept of Minibeasts. Happily, these excellent resources (developed, in the main, by teachers) are now becoming available again this time online.

Science 5–13 was highly influential amongst teachers and especially teacher trainers at the time. And it illustrated how, as our understanding of science changes, so too do our ideas about the way it is taught. Its impact was in some ways a precursor to the government's publication in the mid-1980s of *Science for All*, a first attempt not only to create a basis for good practice but also to insist that all primary school teachers should be teachers of science – something that had existed systematically in few classrooms up to then.

The Arrival of the National Curriculum

Sadly, however, ideas about science teaching have sometimes been steered and influenced by considerations that were quite remote from what could be called 'good science practice'. In particular when the government of the day centralised control of school education in the early 1980s, removing it from being the responsibility of local authorities, political interference in teaching led in the late 1980s to the emergence of the first National

Curriculum (NC) for Science and the standard testing of children's science knowledge, which has since become increasingly controversial. This was never the intention of those experts who devised the NC – they wished to develop a system that would balance the testing of knowledge with examining enquiry skills through practical investigations. But cost and logistics, alongside the politicians' wish to simplify, gradually led to an abolishing of practical tests and a reversion to paper and pencil exams. This in turn has led too many teachers away from science as a process and towards a narrower view of science education (as represented by *'Posh science words to know',* something I saw on one classroom wall). This was a great pity as huge strides had been made by schemes such as those mentioned above to develop science learning that was based on enquiry skills. Primary Science, in a way, was the guinea pig for subsequent NC subjects, as it was the first to be implemented, in 1989, and went through a number of disruptive revisions in the following years.

At this time also international surveys of attainment in basic subjects were being carried out with increasing frequency and the UK's failure to do well in these prompted yet more government intervention. Consequently teachers and other educators had to manage the introduction of a whole new raft of jargon into the way we talk about curriculum, including Programmes of Study (PoS), Attainment Targets (ATs) and Standard Attainment Tests (SATs), all of which arose out of the government's wish to adopt approaches that had seemed to be successful elsewhere especially in the USA and Japan.

Yet parallel to this was some important research being carried out at the universities of Leeds, Liverpool and Kings' College, London, on children's science misconceptions. Until this time it was commonly thought that children's minds, as far as science was concerned, were empty vessels into which 'correct' science ideas could be poured. Research showed powerfully that this was not so and that children on entering school already had their own ideas about science phenomena, even if many of these were at odds with those held by scientists. As a result the *Science Process and Concept Exploration Project* (SPACE), systematically explored young children's understanding of science concepts and their development in 12 areas, such as Electricity, Materials, Evaporation, Growth, etc. and built on earlier research from New Zealand and by the late Rosalind Driver in Leeds (whose (1983) book, *The Pupil as Scientist,* exemplified much of what was known about children's learning in science). The results led to the publication of eight major research reports and then to the development of a set of curriculum materials – *Nuffield Primary Science* (1994) – which quickly developed a national and international reputation. This new scheme aimed to establish and communicate the ideas which primary school children have in particular science concept areas and set out to show ways in which teachers could help children to modify their ideas as the result of relevant experiences, bringing them in line with those of the science community.

Teacher's Professional Development

In the early 1990s, therefore, and following on from these bursts of developmental activity, primary science suddenly took centre stage where the curriculum and teacher education were concerned. The amount of time devoted to science in primary teacher education, and the numbers of trainers involved, increased rapidly. Science was now deemed to be a 'core subject' of the primary curriculum and it began to be treated with greater status in schools. Government schemes of work, such as that from the Qualifications and Curriculum Authority (QCA), flooded into schools and universities and Continuing Professional Development (CPD) programmes proliferated, sponsored by local authorities, universities, and private operators. A bandwagon was thus in motion. Scotland followed its own path, deliberately avoiding the standard testing route, but otherwise all the home countries put science at the forefront of their thinking. For example, many schools were using science-based topics as ways of thematically linking subjects together.

No doubt you will have noticed that all this has now changed. The first major factor in reducing the emphasis on science was the introduction of the National Literacy Strategy (NLS) in 1998, closely followed by the National Numeracy Strategy (NNS). Literacy has always held pride of place in the concerns of many primary teachers and whilst it became increasingly difficult to attract teachers into science CPD programmes those relating to the NLS were usually oversubscribed. Literacy has continued to be the central and probably most controversial aspect of primary teaching ever since. It has been difficult at times to combat the tendency of some advocates to see science as a 'vehicle for literacy teaching', rather than the reverse!

The second major influence on primary science teaching was the change to a New Labour government in 1997. This came at a time when England's performance in international surveys of attainment was still not good and it seemed to many at the time that the education strategies which were soon to be adopted by Prime Minister Blair were directed primarily at improving this state of affairs, at whatever cost. We had to be seen to be 'raising standards', following his claim that his priorities for government were 'Education, Education, Education'. The strategy adopted to achieve this took the form of increased testing of primary age children in particular, tests which served to reverse, in many schools, the move to effective, inquiry-based science (now usually referred to internationally as IBSE). Testing – and thus teaching – continued to emphasise the learning of factual knowledge rather than the acquisition of science inquiry skills which were much harder and more time-consuming to test. Under pressure from Ofsted inspections to improve the (fairly arbitrary) standards, schools and teachers rapidly refined their strategies for 'teaching to the test' in order to improve their schools' standing in the now mandatory league tables of attainment.

Recent Changes

Research, however, stubbornly continued to indicate that early improvements soon levelled off (Royal Society, 2010) and that primary teachers, 97 per cent of which still did not have a post-school science qualification, still lacked confidence when it came to teaching science. One approach to tackling this came with the government's *Every Child Matters* initiative which required teachers, in all subjects, to demonstrate how they were reaching individual children whatever their background and level of attainment. At the same time the emphasis on digital technology and children's need for ICT skills was gaining ground. Having commissioned a new review of the primary curriculum in 2008, headed by Jim Rose, the Brown government made the decision in 2009 to adopt these proposed changes to the curriculum which would give an increased emphasis on ICT, withdraw the core status from science, and make it part of an 'area of learning' characterised as 'scientific and technological understanding' (Rose, 2008). At the same time though, the consultation process had suggested that many in primary science education were not happy with the findings, particularly as another large review headed by Robin Alexander in Cambridge had come simultaneously to quite different and (to primary science people) much more preferable conclusions that took account of teachers' concerns. For example, it highlighted a worry amongst many, after years of teaching to the test, that 'We need permission to innovate. Sometimes it even seems as if we even need permission to think' (Cambridge Primary Review, 2009).

Yet only a matter of months before the Rose Review was due to be implemented New Labour was replaced, in May 2010, by the present coalition government and plans for a revision along the lines of Rose were shelved. A hiatus thus exists at the time of writing in relation to what changes in the primary science curriculum can be expected – if any. Many would probably wish for no change in order to enable a period of consolidation, yet differences between the primary science curricula and the approaches of the four home countries have been growing, to the extent that England alone now persists with a standard testing of science at age 11 and the contents of the four curricula have considerable differences in emphasis, especially where IBSE and curriculum integration are concerned. Creativity in primary science teaching, some would suggest, has been developing more rapidly in Wales, Northern Ireland, and Scotland following their withdrawal from a narrow emphasis on testing knowledge.

We therefore need an authoritative pronouncement based on evidence and fortunately this has been provided recently by the Royal Society's *State of the Nation* report on Science and Maths Education (Royal Society, 2010) and effectively summarised by Wynne Harlen in a recent issue of *Primary Science*. This re-iterates the report's conclusions about what should be done to improve primary science education in schools, as follows:

- Provide every school with access to a science specialist.
- Increase funding for teachers' continuing professional development in science.
- Focus assessment on promoting progress rather than on measuring it.
- Ensure that national policy for science education is based on evidence from research and effective practice.

- Encourage more research into children's development of science knowledge, under-standing and skills.

(Harlen, 2010)

Summary

The Royal Society's report brings us right up to date with the state of play in late 2010. It is, of course, not mandatory in any way and schools will – whilst taking note of it as helpful guidance – be reluctant to make major changes until the dust settles around government policy. But for you, as a trainee or novice teacher, or as one of the many non-science specialists wishing to engage more productively with science, it raises several important questions that you might wish to discuss before moving on to read the rest of this book. Some of these questions could be formulated as follows:

- If you were asked to initiate a discussion about the policy for science in your school, what would be on your agenda and what would your priorities be in order to bring about improvement?
- Taking account of the Royal Society's recommendations, which of these do you think are likely to be implemented under the current climate within education?
- What can you learn from the development of primary science as set out above that could help you arrive at good practice in your own classroom?

These questions will be returned to in our final chapter, in an attempt to summarise what authors from a wide range of perspectives have to say on these issues. They are also relevant in that they signal to those entering the profession, and indeed to more estab-lished colleagues, an acceptance of our need to be able to manage uncertainty and change. Primary education since the late eighties has witnessed a huge number of initiatives from the 'top down': one of the characteristics of being a good professional is the capacity to engage with change but not to do so unquestioningly. Such a person does not function cynically but with a clear sense of being able to identify what is right for the educational context in which they are located. Top-down change has focused, and is likely to continue to focus, primarily on the 'what' and perhaps concentrate less so on the 'when' but not on the 'how'. Decisions about whether or not to do practical work in science should not be determined by curriculum guidance but by the principle of educational fitness for purpose.

Change management will always exercise teachers' professionalism. This book accepts and welcomes the dynamic nature of education in general and science educa-tion in particular. We hope that by engaging with what is being shared you will see that change can be engineered effectively without a consequent loss of quality in educational provision. The authors place a strong emphasis on not providing you with a 'ready reck-oner' for science education but with a resource that will encourage you to think, to not be afraid to exercise your judgements but to know what is high quality science education for our younger learners.

References

Cambridge Primary Review (2008) *Children, their World, their Education.* Available at www.primaryreview.org.uk/
An independent research review with an international perspective that takes a substantial look at the primary curriculum. Essential reading for any primary practitioner.

Capra, F. (1975) *The Tao of Physics.* London: Fontana Paperbacks.
Explores the parallels between modern physics and Eastern mysticism and illustrates the ultimate harmony between world-views of science and mystical traditions.

Capra, F. (2002) *The Hidden Connections: A Science for Sustainable Living.* London: HarperCollins.
Integrates our understanding of apparently disparate fields such as biology, psychology, economics, and eco-design.

CRIPSAT (various dates) *Science processes and concept exploration (SPACE) reports.* Available at www.cripsat.org.uk/publications/space_pub.htm
Summaries of research into children's misconceptions and how to modify their ideas across all content areas of the NC.

Harlen, W. (2010) 'The Royal Society's report on primary school science', *Primary Science*, 115: 25–27.
Summarises the findings of the Royal Society's report and hints at the policy implications.

Holmes, R. (2009) *The Age of Wonder: How the Romantic Generation Discovered the Beauty and Terror of Science.* London: HarperCollins.
Charts various voyages of discovery in astronomy, botany, chemistry and other fields, through fascinating studies of the lives of great eighteenth-century scientists such as Banks, Davy, Herschel, and others.

Nuffield Foundation (1995) *Nuffield Primary Science.* London: Collins Educational. Available at www.cripsat.org.uk/publications/nuffield_pub.htm
A scheme of work with teachers' guides covering the whole of the NC as it was in the mid-1990s and based on the findings of the SPACE reports.

Peat, D. (1995) *Blackfoot Physics: A Journey into the Native American Universe.* London: Fourth Estate.
This is by an eminent physicist and author who spent many years living amongst the native peoples of America in order to learn about their ways of thinking about science and their environment. This book explores the similarities between modern understandings of the universe and the advanced understandings of ancient civilisations such as that of the Maya.

Rose, J. (2008) *Independent Review of the Primary Curriculum: Final Report*. Available at http://publications.education.gov.uk/eOrderingDownload/Primary_curriculum_ Report.pdf
A government-sponsored report that set out to be the basis for a reform of the primary curriculum.
Royal Society (2010) *Science and Mathematics Education, 5–14: A 'State of the Nation' Report*. London: Royal Society.
Schools Council (1972) *Science 5–13*. London: Macdonald Educational. Available at http://openlibrary.org/books/OL16576313M/Guide_to_science_5-13

Further Reading

Okasha, S. (2002) *Philosophy of Science: A Very Short Introduction*. Oxford: Oxford University Press.
This small publication provides a philosophical perspective of some of the ideas introduced in this chapter. It also helps explain what science is thought to be and provides an alternative insight to the history of the development of science.

CHAPTER 2

LEARNING FROM ELSEWHERE: AN INTERNATIONAL PERSPECTIVE ON THE DEVELOPMENT OF PRIMARY SCIENCE

Alan Peacock

Chapter Overview

The chapter begins by taking on board the recommendations of focus groups to give more attention to lessons about professionalism and pedagogy and to concentrate less on the prescribed curriculum. It therefore deals with lessons about widening teachers' repertoire of teaching skills, beginning with the emergence of an emphasis on Behavioural Objectives in the USA in the 1960s and continuing with the subsequent rapid expansion of science teaching ideas within common-wealth countries after the end of empire. A key element to be addressed through-out is the dissonance between teachers' own experiences of science learning and the changing expectations placed on them as emerging professionals.

The chapter then explores the impact of international surveys of science attainment during the 1970s and beyond, in particular the response of governments to these,

(Continued)

(Continued)

leading to the imposition and impact of standard tests (SATs) across the UK along the lines of those in the USA. Parallel to this, however, was the development across Europe and elsewhere of an awareness of the importance of science inquiry to effective learning and especially to learners' engagement with science. This leads to a discussion of various pan-European initiatives such as the POLLEN and FIBONACCI projects.

The chapter ends by examining the gradual divergence of approaches between regions of the UK following devolution and draws attention to reports from such scientific bodies as the Wellcome Trust and the Royal Society on the current state of play. The concerns of these reports are summarised as being about the reduction of prescription and testing; the linking of science to other subjects; sharing ideas and concerns between teachers; the development of resources and improvisation and the kind of planning strategies that will allow these to be built into an enquiry-based approach to science learning.

Key Ideas

For almost one hundred years from the beginnings of compulsory primary education in Britain in the 1870s, science as we now know it was largely absent from the curriculum. From the turn of the last century nature study in the form of 'object lessons' was introduced into elementary schools, which from the late 1940s until the 1960s was characterised by collecting and studying plants (wildflowers, trees) and small animals (tadpoles, mice, chicks …) in their environment, keeping weather records and observing seasonal phenomena. In the 1960s, when science quite suddenly took on greater importance, primary educators began to look for the best way of teaching it to young children, since when we have had forty years of almost incessant change in the curriculum, teaching approaches, and assessment methods.

The previous chapter provided a brief overview of these changes. This chapter will go on to explore in more detail what drove these changes internationally (since the same changes were taking place in many other countries) and which ideas we have taken on board from 'best practice' elsewhere, with examples of these taken from a range of countries and contexts.

Student Perspectives

When asked what they felt about a chapter on the changing curriculum, the students in our focus groups were more concerned with the professional and teaching lessons to be learned from other countries and less concerned with what other curricula might have to offer them. This is probably a consequence of their feeling that curriculum content is, in some ways, out of their hands, and more context-dependent than teaching methods – and in some respects they would be right. However, my own study of curricula in 33 countries in the early 1990s showed that, at that time, science curricula in primary schools had much content in common, with general topics like the natural environment, observation and measurement, physical processes, and human biology being almost universal (Peacock, 1993). Thus one of the questions explored below will be to what extent this situation has changed since then, and if so, why has this happened?

What trainees emphasised in discussions was the importance of ideas about professionalism, approaches to professional development, and alternative ways to foster science learning, such as play-based learning. Hence the sections below will also provide examples of how these have been developed elsewhere, particularly within continental Europe and the developing world, and specifically within the now widely-emphasised notion of Inquiry-Based Science Education (IBSE). Note that we tend to spell the word as 'Enquiry' in the UK, but internationally, the practice is to spell it with an 'I'.

Discussion of Issues: What Drives Change?

The technological revolution and behavioural objectives

The 1960s saw a rapid development in new technology in the fields of nuclear power, electronics, radio astronomy, and new materials, all fostered by the 'Cold War' between the USA and the Soviet Union, which brought about a proliferation of new and more powerful nuclear weapons and a race into space, culminating in the first manned moon landing in 1969. The powerful industrial nations, which included Britain, realised that greater technological developments meant having more scientists. Universities supplied these scientists and took a keen interest in secondary science education, which ultimately raised wider questions both about the requirement for primary science and more and better science teaching in schools. Hence new approaches to teaching science as a subject within the curriculum were initiated, the first of these for the primary phase (in Britain) being Nuffield Junior Science in 1964–66 (see the weblink below) which emphasised practical experimentation and the use of simple and inexpensive apparatus.

The change was not primarily about curriculum content, however. One of the key innovations in the USA had been the way in which technologists and technicians (largely within the military) were now being trained, involving the notion of Behavioural Objectives, described as specifically as possible, to make it easier for trainers to know if learners had been successful. As a result many programmes of training began with lists of precise behavioural objectives, often starting with the phrase, '*By the end of this module, you will be able to ...* '. As a consequence, teachers and teacher trainers were encouraged to adopt a similar approach which opened the door to an initiative from the late 1950s, when researchers in the USA had also come up with a *Taxonomy of Behavioural Objectives* for learning (Bloom et al., 1956), made up of three domains named cognitive, affective, and psycho-motor. The language of this approach was some-what off-putting to teachers, as might be imagined from the titles – in effect, it was a way of classifying objectives in terms of mental skills, attitudes and physical skills – but nev-ertheless it found favour amongst planners and trainers for a while and is still reflected in the way we categorise learning objectives.

One of the outcomes of this in the UK was the *Science 5–13* programme already mentioned, initiated by the Schools Council in 1973 and subtitled *With objectives in mind*. You will recognise the stated objectives of the scheme as being very similar to those currently in vogue here, emphasising as they did the following:

- Developing interests, attitudes, and aesthetic awareness.
- Observing, exploring, and ordering observations.
- Developing basic concepts and logical thinking.
- Posing questions and devising investigations to answer them.
- Acquiring knowledge and learning skills.
- Communicating.
- Appreciating patterns and relationships.
- Interpreting findings critically.

The scheme proved popular with trainers and some teachers, partly because much of the development work came from teachers themselves working within the Schools Council projects. Yet it is important to remember that when this scheme was published we were still fifteen years away from having a National Curriculum. Hence there was no pressure on schools or the local education authorities which still controlled them to teach science at all, never mind in any specific way. One consequence was that in 1978 a report by Her Majesty's Inspectorate (HMI) concluded that few primary schools had effective programmes for teaching science, that in very few classes were science skills taught, and that the most severe obstacle was teachers' lack of knowledge of elementary science (DES, 1978).

Meanwhile big changes were taking place elsewhere, in perhaps rather more unlikely localities.

The end of empire

As the 'winds of change' blew through the British Empire in the early 1960s one country after another sought independence from Britain and this happened rapidly in Africa in particular. Education was one of the fields where all newly-independent states wanted to establish their identity: hence, in the mid-1970s, UNESCO initiated and supported the Science Education Programme for Africa (SEPA) to bring together science educators from these countries to develop new curricula, materials and teaching methods, with its primary focus being on 'the learner and his immediate environment' (SEPA, 1976).

SEPA produced detailed specifications and many new materials supported by some of the best science educators from around the world. Unlike in Britain, however, most of these countries had decided on creating new national curricula from the outset: individual African states therefore took the SEPA ideas and materials and re-developed or republished them to fit their own new curriculum. Many of these materials proved to be excellent, ground-breaking examples of good practice. Kenya developed a primary science curriculum around the idea of *Problem-solving Skills*, and produced a wide range of pupil materials to support this approach. For example, their small book, *Ask the Ant-Lion*, encouraged children to find and observe these small, ubiquitous creatures that lived in sand and to 'ask' them questions (such as, '*Where do you live? What do you eat? How do you catch your prey?*'), which pupils then answered through careful, sustained observation and recording. The curriculum content might be very different – developing countries like Kenya inevitably focused on such topics as soil, water, tools, food, and health – but the teaching approach advocated was very similar to that proposed by *Science 5–13*. This was encapsulated in a book designed for African primary teachers during their initial training, developed from experiences in Nigeria by Beverley Young. His foresight, however, was clear from the opening paragraph of the introduction, pointing out as he did that:

> The division between 'methods' and 'content' in teacher training courses is an artificial distinction which soon breaks down in practice. It is impossible to study methods of teaching a subject without also considering examples of what is taught. (Young, 1979: iii)

Working in Kenya at the time this curriculum was introduced I was impressed by the enthusiasm of learners, yet as a teacher trainer I also soon became aware that most of my students did not have the educational background to be able to adapt to this radically different way of thinking about science. The teaching approaches they had experienced, dominated by those within mission schools, were entirely based on rote learning and repetition, with little spoken language and no discussion. Hence the government's radical and admirable new approach was not being implemented in practice, a situation which could be found all over Africa at that time.

How is this relevant to our situation today you may ask? What can we learn from what happened in Africa 30-odd years ago? The key point here is the mis-match between 'official' expectations of teachers, as set out by ministries, advisers and inspectors, and the background of the teachers expected to implement innovation. And in the UK, where innovations have come thick and fast in recent decades, your experiences of science as a primary pupil may have been, like those of the Kenyan students, very different from what is now being expected of you. This is supported by much research from the UK which, repeatedly over the past twenty years, has exposed the lack of confidence in science experienced by primary school teachers.

~~~   **Points for Reflection**

Consider the current expectations placed on you as a teacher of science and your own science background from your schooling. Are the teaching methods expected of you in science any different from those you experienced as a pupil, and if so, in what way? What are the implications of this for your professional development?

International surveys of attainment

From the mid-1970s onward the International Association for the Evaluation of Educational Achievement (IEA) instigated regular comparisons of attainment in different subject areas across a wide range of countries, with the first major science survey (SISS) taking place in the mid-1980s. Similar studies of Trends in International Maths and Science (TIMSS) took place at four-yearly intervals from 1995 onwards. The timing of these surveys is significant for the UK – SISS came after the damning HMI report of 1978 and after a change of government the pressure on the new Thatcher administration led to a DES statement of policy in 1985. This introduced for the first time a requirement for all primary teachers to teach science and eventually ushered in the Education Reform Act of 1988, which in turn introduced the first National Curriculum in science. Later on the first TIMSS results would emerge shortly before Blair's New Labour government was elected in 1997. England performed quite badly in relation to its 'competitors', which meant that government felt obliged to do something to improve the country's standing in international comparisons of science achievement.

In the first instance, the Conservatives in the mid-1980s were aware of research into children's concept formation and the need to correct their misconceptions about science ideas if they were to perform well on tests of attainment. They would also have been aware of the USA's approach to standard testing. Hence the developers of the new National Curriculum in science – the first subject to be developed in this way – were charged with developing a curriculum of science content and skills and a systematic multiple-choice testing regime based on Attainment Targets (SATs).

It was at this point that a divergence began to occur between approaches in England and those in Scotland in particular, where it was decided not to introduce SATs in science. That divergence has continued to the present day with the other three countries of the UK taking an increasingly different approach to science based on what they saw happening elsewhere, as discussed below.

The government's initial SATs testing regime, which was mindful of the need to teach science 'process skills' as they were then called, included some practical testing of children. However, it was rapidly apparent that these were expensive and time-consuming to administer and so they were soon dropped in favour of pencil-and-paper testing only. Attempts to measure the higher cognitive skills describe in Bloom's taxonomy were also attempted, but these have never gained much prominence: teachers and parents have tended to see the SATs as tests of science knowledge and publishers have responded by producing the kind of revision-and-test books that now dominate booksellers' primary education shelves. Science teaching in the early 1990s therefore saw a retreat from the enquiry-based learning promoted in the 1970s and in recent years all the home countries except England – taking notice of what was happening in the rest of Europe – have abandoned a standard testing of science in favour of more systematic approaches to teachers' informal assessment.

Relevance and fostering pupil enthusiasm for science: recent developments across Europe and the UK

And Europe? You will have noticed there has been no mention of primary science in Europe up until now, for a good reason. This is because, with the exception perhaps of Sweden, science had played little part in the primary education of European countries throughout the 1970s and 1980s. I visited schools and training institutions in Germany and France in 1990 and found little that we in the UK would recognise as science teaching. It did not exist as a subject; what science teaching there was had emerged in programmes of local study or the environment. Trainee primary teachers were taught science knowledge and its verification through set experiments; as a consequence, there was no stress on science investigations in schools. In Eastern Europe there was no science training for primary teachers and an emphasis on 'knowing' with little or no engagement with 'doing'.

European primary education placed much more emphasis on language and mathematics, and in the former, much more emphasis on oracy (speaking and listening) than in the UK (Alexander, 2000). In England, as the 1990s wore on under an increasingly punitive testing and inspection regime led by 'league tables' of school performance, an unease developed amongst teachers about children's attitudes to science. They loved doing science but as they progressed through school the emphasis moved to tests and revision, especially in years 5 and 6, and pupils were increasingly 'turned off' science by the time they transferred to secondary school.

This phenomenon was not confined to England, however, and in France in 1996 a programme called *La main a la pâte* (which translates as 'hands-on') was instigated, not by government dictat but by the Nobel prize-winning physicist Georges Charpak, the astrophysicist Pierre Léna and others, with the support of the French Academy des Sciences (Belay et al., 2007). This initiative led to a programme of European collaboration to develop IBSE called POLLEN, a network for promoting Inquiry-Based Science

Education (see the weblink below). It set out to be a pilot programme that would work with communities to develop a 'hands-on, minds-on' approach to science education in primary schools. The project began in January 2006 and lasted three and a half years, the team being made up of teacher training and scientific organisations from 12 European countries, including the ASE from Britain, and was launched in 12 European cities. The work has now been followed up and superseded by the Fibonacci project (see the weblink below) which aims at the dissemination of inquiry-based science and mathematics education (IBSME) in Europe through universities, teacher training centres, and research institutions that are recognised as having a high status in science education. The project began in January 2010 and will last until February 2013, involving 60 tertiary education institutions throughout Europe. IBSE, in other words, has arrived in the rest of Europe, but how has it affected the curriculum, teaching methods, and professional development here in Britain?

One key change in recent years, as a consequence of events outside England, has been an awareness of the need for more creative approaches to science in order to foster children's enthusiasm. Wales, Northern Ireland and Scotland, as well as the rest of Europe, have already moved in this direction. In Wales, for example, where the 'National Strategies' of England have not been applied, the emphasis is now more on 'thinking and learning skills' and the independence of the teacher. This has been achieved through making science testing no longer compulsory, thereby allowing teachers to counteract a narrowing of the curriculum that has been evident in England as a consequence of 'teaching to the test'. Learning skills for science have been gradually introduced as part of the Welsh curriculum, backed up by a teacher-developed assessment promoted by their Assessment Review Group. Such initiatives clearly promote more teacher autonomy and demand effective professional support, both of which have been demanded by teachers across the UK.

Points for Reflection

A large research programme in your area finds that whilst creativity in science teaching has increased, pupil attainment on standard testing has gone down. How would you respond to this? What evidence would you wish to see that could help you adapt the way you teach science?

Wales has also looked to Northern Ireland and its earlier moves into curriculum change. Unlike in England, Northern Ireland never separated technology from science, simplifying the curriculum content into just two areas, *Investigating and Making* and *Knowledge and Understanding*, an approach that has proved popular with teachers. Schools are left to organise the elements in inventive ways, incorporating a good deal of practical construction and testing. And whilst children do take examinations before the transfer to secondary schools, this testing process does not include science – yet again freeing teachers to be more creative in their teaching approaches.

One aspect of this is the creation of a learning area entitled *The World Around Us*, which aims to foster links between science, history, geography and technology where appropriate, all the while encouraging teachers to make connections. In order to sustain this, the statutory content of the curriculum has been reduced, allowing for flexibility and a stronger focus on skills and IBSE. A clear outcome of this has been the variety of ideas and real enthusiasm for innovation apparent amongst teachers and trainers in the province (Kerr, 2009).

In Scotland changes in national government separated science from cross-curricular approaches by the 1990s through the implementation of the new 5–14 *Curriculum Guidelines*. This change was characterised as the *Environmental Studies (ES) 5–14 Unit Study* (see the weblink below) which effectively replaced teacher choice within a thematic approach that was generated by a lack of practitioner subject knowledge in science. This, plus a heavy programme of assessment and recording in classrooms, a lack of preparation time and adequate subject-specific resources, all affected primary teachers' confidence to implement the proposals.

In 2009 however, the Scottish government introduced a key change to the way education in Scotland would be implemented. Outlined within this new *Curriculum for Excellence* (see the weblink below) was a desire to de-clutter existing approaches and content and to replace these with a more child-centred approach. The 'Sciences' component was the first to be conceptualised, modified and published, so that work within schools in respect of its content is now among the first to be piloted and embedded as part of a move towards more child-centred teaching and an integration of history, geography, mathematics, and science.

Yet since the introduction of the new Curriculum for Excellence in 2010 'science' is now a discrete component in its own right and has been given a key role in respect of its ability to act as a catalyst for child-centred, collaborative, active, and interdisciplinary approaches within the primary school. The CfE's approach also highlights the promotion of children's own experience, alongside learning outcomes, and presents these in terms of broad aspirations for their learning, prefixed by '*I can …;*' and '*I have …;*'. The CfE not only promotes the teacher's mediating role in the classroom, it also encourages them to adopt a holistic approach towards children's cognitive, emotional, and social development when planning programmes of work.

∿   Points for Reflection

In a small group, brainstorm reasons why it makes sense to be aware of developments in other countries as described above. Then list possible constraints on the effective transfer of ideas and methods from one country or culture to another and consider how these might be overcome.

The Impact of International 'Best Practice'

So how have all these initiatives impacted on practice? We in England have given the world Newton, Darwin, Faraday, Rutherford, Whittle, Crick, Watson and the rest, and this can often give the impression that we have much to offer other countries but little to learn from them – yet at present this seems not to reflect the situation in primary science at all. (We also gave the world football, cricket and rugby, but Spain, Brazil, Pakistan, India, South Africa, and New Zealand are now teaching us a thing or two about how to play!).

It would seem that before looking at what we can learn from elsewhere it is worth summarising the problems we need to tackle. A recent seminar for top scientists organised by the Wellcome Trust came to the conclusion that, in recent years, the mistranslation of what (the National Curriculum) originally intended had resulted in:

- Many teachers feeling disempowered to teach in a manner appropriate to their students and circumstances.
- A strong sense of over-prescription in terms of the content of the curriculum.
- Increased pressures to 'teach to the test' at all levels.
- Frequent, apparently piecemeal, changes to the curriculum in order to fix shortcomings and meet top-down policy changes.
- Tests and examinations dominating not just what was taught but also how it was taught.

(Wellcome Trust, 2010, weblink)

Hence, best practice elsewhere can provide the following lessons.

Reducing prescription, testing and inspections

Frequent change is demoralising for hard-working teachers, especially in an area like science where many still do not feel that confident. Countries like France and Japan make relatively infrequent changes to their curriculum or to their prescriptions for how to teach. In the past three decades here, however, change has been incessant, and at present there is still uncertainty about what the new coalition government is going to prescribe. Many teachers feel they know how to teach science better, but are deterred from doing so by the pressure brought to bear from national science testing and punitive inspections. Finland, for example, which consistently out-performs us on international comparisons, has abandoned these as not being cost-effective as a means to long-term improvement in teaching and learning. At the same time the retreat from testing in Wales, Scotland and Northern Ireland in recent years, as mentioned above, is already leading to more confidence and creativity amongst teachers and those involved in their professional development.

Subject integration

In many countries science is not taught as a discrete subject but is linked instead to other areas of knowledge. An awareness of a need for science to be relevant to learners' lives has meant that teachers are more concerned with topics like climate change, renewable energy, poverty, food and health, clean water and biodiversity, and tackling these involves not only science and technology but also an awareness of factors arising in geography, history, economics, social policy and religious beliefs. Sub-Saharan African countries, for example, have placed a big emphasis in primary schooling on HIV/AIDS education as a major issue for schools, with many pupils and teachers having been affected by the disease.

Enabling teachers to share

Across Africa and Europe there has been a positive impact on teachers from being able to meet and share their experiences, ideas, and concerns about science teaching. This may be through face-to-face group meetings taking place locally on a regular basis, with an 'expert' as the catalyst, or increasingly through using email and the internet. Knowing you are not alone with your problem, and hearing how others have tackled a difficult concept or topic, can lead to a growing repertoire of ways to teach – in other words, to enhanced Pedagogical Content Knowledge (discussed in more detail in later chapters) as well as greater self-confidence. In Britain, where only about 3 per cent of primary school teachers have a post-school science qualification, such opportunities are essential. Any effective system of professional development should provide such opportunities for discussion and safe practice, rather than being dominated by PowerPoint presentations that 'tell'. It is one of the planks on which the POLLEN and Fibonacci projects sharing of science expertise amongst teachers across Europe has been built.

IBSE as the approach to teaching science

On his recent appointment the new President of the Royal Society, Nobel Laureat Sir Paul Nurse, was asked in a TV interview what advice he had for improving science teaching in this country. He mentioned just two factors: making science exciting to young people and treating it as a process rather than as a body of knowledge – for which IBSE is the internationally-acknowledged focus. The mere fact that this acronym is less common in the UK is a clear indicator that other countries have taken science enquiry more seriously. Of course, as this chapter has already pointed out, there have been moves within the science education community to make this the centre of our teaching strategy for the past forty years yet support for this from policy makers and successive administrations has been half-hearted, with a growing emphasis on testing science as a body of knowledge. This is not the case in many other countries. For example Chile – following the lead of British Columbia – teaches a course on research skills to all primary school children.

Materials, resources, and improvisation

Since we have never had central government control over school textbooks, this country has probably published more science schemes and pupils' materials than any other in the past three decades. Yet research worldwide indicates that most of these materials are either misused or under-used by teachers in the classroom (Peacock & Cleghorn, 2004). This is even more likely to happen here where frequent curriculum change soon renders materials out-of-date. Part of the reason for this over-production of reading materials in England especially may arise from our obsession with literacy in primary schools, a battleground that is still fought over by experts and teachers. Yet many countries do not start to teach reading and writing until much later than the UK, reflecting a feeling that the best way to learn science is not through reading, recipes and recording, but through children's questions, active enquiry, and their discussion and exploration of their own ideas, often through play in the early years.

There is also a strong tradition, across the world, of encouraging pupils to improvise the materials they can use to carry out their own investigations. In Kenya I worked alongside a primary teacher whose Year 6 class had all made their own toolbox and set of tools (hammer, screwdriver, saw …) from a huge pile of scrap metal, wood and plastic that had been collected in the school grounds. Plastic bottles are widely used to make a range of vessels, germinators, wormeries, etc., and a wonderful microscope can be made from nothing more than a matchbox, Sellotape, some Vaseline, and a drop of water (Peacock, 2003: 85–88). Children enjoy nothing more than making and using their own science equipment.

Incorporating these ideas into your planning

There is not much you can do about the prescribed science curriculum, except hope that it reduces in size and gives more freedom and flexibility to you as a teacher. However, it is possible for you to take control of some of the other aspects mentioned above. For example, *collaboration* between teachers from your local cluster of schools, preferably with the support of some outside expertise, can provide a huge boost to confidence and to the repertoire of science teaching skills amongst the group, many of whom are unlikely to be science specialists (see subsequent chapters). Planning for sessions of mutual coaching, for instance, has also proved to be very effective as a professional development tool, both amongst practising teachers and trainees paired in a classroom (Monach & Bryant, 2009).

Incorporating enquiry-based activity from the earliest stages is vital if the habit of enquiry is to be established throughout science in the primary phase. The movement towards play-based learning in the UK is strong and it is a very small shift from thinking of children's science activity as play to thinking of it as enquiry. When starting a new science topic, even with postgraduate trainees, I will usually put out the materials we are likely to use before they arrive and then watch what they do when they enter. Almost always this involves playing with the materials to establish their potential – what can we do with these? Such play inevitably raises questions – which represent the beginnings of any science enquiry. Science is about learning to test your ideas against the evidence provided by your senses and the only science knowledge we have is the science that has been done through this approach. So in order to understand science the children in your class must do science and think scientifically. Nothing less than this is worth doing.

Materials need to be carefully assessed and used sparingly rather than being depended upon: they will often not be entirely appropriate to your situation and adapting them can create as many problems as it solves. You can assess their appropriateness as part of your planning using the Index of Text Demand (see Peacock & Cleghorn, 2004: 216–217) which was trialled in the UK and Canada with trainees. And in addition you can, as part of your planning, become a collector, a hoarder, of things that can be used to *improvise*. Whole books have been written on this topic which is too broad to go into here.

The Index of Text Demand (ITD)

You should first select a page or double-page spread of a science book for primary children, and considering the pupils you might use it with, answer the following questions with either 'yes' or 'no':

Conceptual demand

1. Are any of the ideas on the page new to them?
2. Are any of the concepts abstract?
3. Do the concepts need to be understood in order to progress?

Language demand

4. Do the words occupy more than 50 per cent of the page?
5. Does the page contain new vocabulary?
6. Are the sentence structures long and complex?

Visual demand

7. Does the page contain pictures/photographs?
8. Does it contain a table, chart or graph?

(Continued)

(Continued)

9. Does it contain a <u>cross-sectional diagram</u>?
10. Does it use <u>symbols such as arrows or icons</u>?
11. Does it use illustrations which need to be <u>linked sequentially</u>, such as a cartoon, or stages in a process?

Format

12. Is the format <u>unfamiliar</u> to your pupils?
13. Do the words and sentences cut <u>across the page</u>, rather than following on down the page, as in narrative text?
14. Are words and visuals <u>not explicitly linked (e.g. by captions)</u>?

Message

15. Are <u>instructions ambiguous</u> and in need of teacher mediation?
16. Are there <u>practical obstacles to doing the prescribed activities</u> in the classroom?
17. Are the instructions <u>inconsistent</u> with your teaching style?
18. Is the text written or published in <u>another country or culture</u>?

To estimate Text Demand: count number of 'yes' responses.

0–6	Low demand
7.11	Average demand
12+	High demand

Summary

The development of science in primary schools has not followed a straight line and in many ways we are still going round in circles. Other countries have in the past admired our pioneering approach; consequently, there has been a reluctance, in England, to accept that much could be learned from elsewhere. Happily that is now changing, as practice in the home countries diverges following devolution, and as collaboration within Europe becomes more prevalent. Recent developments, such as Emergent Science for example, are focusing on children's early observations and, the development of understanding in an international context (Johnson, 2010). Yet the change of government has thrown what looked like a new approach based on 'areas of understanding' back into the melting-pot, along with Cambridge Review. The key point to take from all this, we propose, is for a new teacher like yourself to keep an open mind, have faith in your skills and knowledge, seek out whatever ideas are available, and then accept the challenge of taking responsibility for being a creative, enquiring teacher who can inspire children, as Sir Paul Nurse emphasised, to find science exciting. The remaining chapters of this book are intended to provide you with the support that will bolster your self-assurance.

References

Alexander, R. (2000) *Culture and Pedagogy*. Oxford: Blackwell.

Belay, R., Jasmin, D. and Léna, P. (2007) '*La main à la pâte*: a programme to renew science education in primary schools', *Primary Science Review* 99: 18–19.

Bloom, B. (ed.) (1956) *The Taxonomy of Educational Objectives: The Classification of Educational Goals, Handbook I: Cognitive Domain*. New York: Susan Fauer.

Department of Education and Science (DES) (1978) *Primary Education in England: A Survey by Her Majesty's Inspectors of Schools*. London: HMSO.

Johnson, J. (2010) 'Learning from the Early Years', *Primary Science*, 111: 9–11 (whole issue on science in the early years).

Kerr, K. (2009) 'Dealing with change: a Northern Ireland perspective', *Primary Science*, 110: 21–22.

Peacock, A. (1992) 'What can we learn from other countries about teaching science investigation skills to young children?' *Evaluation and Research in Education*, 6 (2–3).

Peacock, A. (1993) 'A global core curriculum for primary science?', *Primary Science Review*, 28: 8–10.

Peacock, A. (2003) *Teaching Primary Science*. Oxford: Macmillan.

Peacock, A. & Cleghorn, A. (eds) (2004) *Missing the Meaning: The Development and Use of Print and Non-print Text Materials in Diverse School Settings*. New York: Palgrave Macmillan.

Monach, J. & Bryant, C. (2009) 'Unlock your potential with coaching', *Primary Science*, 110: 34–36.

Schools Council (1973 onwards) *Science 5–13*. London: Macdonald Educational.

SEPA (1976) *Handbook for Teachers: Science Education Programme for Africa*. Accra, Ghana: SEPA.

Young, B.L. (1979) *Teaching Primary Science*. London: Longman Group.

Weblinks

Fibonacci project: http://fibonacci.uni-bayreuth.de/

Nuffield Junior Science: www.nationalstemcentre.org.uk/elibrary/collection/461/nuffield-junior-science

POLLEN project: http://www.pollen-europa.net/?page=CLDGDJVwskY%3D

Scottish 5–14 curriculum guidelines: http://www.scotland.gov.uk/Topics/Education/Schools/curriculum/5to14

Scottish Curriculum for Excellence (CfE): http://www.ltscotland.org.uk/
Wellcome Trust (2010) *Leading debate: 21 years of the National Curriculum for Science.* http://www.wellcome.ac.uk/stellent/groups/corporatesite/@msh_peda/documents/web_document/wtx063344.pdf

Further Reading

Harlen, W. (ed.) (2006) *ASE Guide to Primary Science*. Hatfield, ASE Publications.
Chapter 6 by Peacock, Symonds, & Clegg provides a brief but useful overview of international perspectives on science education.

http://www.upei.ca/~xliu/multi-culture/home.htm
This site contains various links to information about scientists throughout history. It looks at specific contributions to the development of knowledge and understanding in biology, physics, chemistry, astronomy and engineering.

http://www.al-bab.com/arab/science.htm
This site is a very useful source of Arabic science and its contribution to contemporary scientific knowledge and understanding.

CHAPTER 3

LINKING SCIENCE TO THE WIDER CURRICULUM

Richard Watkins

Chapter Overview

The chapter begins by considering a range of planning models and how these might be used to make links between science and other curriculum subjects. It focuses on the essential elements of relevance and contextualisation and provides criteria for assessing which planning models are most appropriate for ensuring effective links. Example units are provided in detail in order to illustrate how to make sure key concepts are built in and coverage is maintained. Detailed examples that illustrate the commonalities between science and geography are provided, and the chapter moves on to examining how enquiry skills are developed via learners' own explorations, using a nationwide Spring Bulbs Project as a successful way of engaging learners in data capture, analysis and sharing. The chapter closes with an examination of how planning links can focus learners' attention on both the detail of skill and concept development and the bigger picture reflected in topics of relevance and general concern.

Key Ideas: Curriculum Planning

This chapter defines a variety of curriculum planning models and discusses how to plan for science in primary schools most effectively. The relative merits of these methods of curriculum planning are then examined, particularly the use of cross-curricular links in developing science enquiry skills and scientific knowledge and understanding. Examples of cross-curricular planning from schools will be utilised to examine ideas and resources to draw effective links to science skills and knowledge. Yet whilst geography and earth science are used as the main examples for this, the same principles for creating cross-curricular links will apply to links between science and other subjects such as history or the creative arts. As will be emphasised below, geography and science have much in common in the way they rely on evidence about our environment that is gathered by observation and experiment.

Assessment *for* learning has proved a powerful force for good in UK classrooms over recent years. Not only has this triggered a permanent shift in the philosophical outlook of teaching professionals across primary and secondary settings, it has also delivered tangible benefits for the quality and depth of learners' experiences. The challenge today, however, is to ensure that curriculum planning models are fit for purpose. Many existing science schemes of work are based on a knowledge-driven curriculum and, therefore, reflect a more transmissionist pedagogy. We must now ask ourselves two key questions: do existing science schemes of work offer adequate opportunities to promote more independent learning, and secondly, are these schemes based on the principles of assessment *for* learning and constructivist pedagogy?

Student Perspectives

A regular response from focus group students was to emphasise the importance of this area of curriculum planning. They were clear that they needed to understand ways of broadening their approach, through strategies such as role-play and integration, in order to be able to demonstrate that, as one student said, they were not simply reproducing an externally-imposed way of doing things, but were able to take on 'the mantle of the expert' in thinking through the best way of approaching science learning in relation to the rest of the curriculum.

Curriculum Planning and Pedagogy – Developing Relevance and Contextualisation

Arguments about curriculum planning and the merits of different models have been well rehearsed since the inception of the National Curriculum in England and Wales. For many years schools followed published schemes such as that provided by the Qualifications and Curriculum Authority (QCA, 1998). Subject-based schemes such as this can provide a very valuable starting point for the non-specialist primary teacher and develop conceptual knowledge and understanding for pupils at an appropriate pace throughout the various units. These materials also contain a wide variety of activities that allow pupils to undertake practical enquiry work. However, this scheme also has several critical limitations:

- It lacks relevance for learners as activities often lack contextualisation.
- The units can be overly long and lead to learner disaffection.
- Although some units incorporate some form of diagnostic assessment, assessment for learning and thinking skill strategies do not feature prominently.
- A greater focus is needed on mapping out systematic science enquiry skills across age ranges.
- It lacks any cross-curricular links or references to the development of generic skills for lifelong learning that modern curricula demand, such as in the skills framework for Welsh schools (DCELLS, 2008).

In many primary schools, pre-National Curriculum planning was often characterised by the use of topic work or integrated studies, where subjects with distinct identities were brought together under a common theme. Although anecdotal memories perceive this to have been a nearly universal feature of primary classrooms in the 1970s and 1980s, records indicate that 30 per cent of teaching during this period was actually subject based. The reality was that curriculum planning took many forms:

- Model 1 – Fully integrated, with all subjects taught under a theme.
- Model 2 – Team teaching using a theme.
- Model 3 – Partially integrated, with some topic work and some subject teaching.
- Model 4 – Separate teaching with occasional linkage.
- Model 5 – Separate subjects in an integrated day.
- Model 6 – Separate subjects in a timetabled day.
- Model 7 – Separate subjects and teachers (*cf.* a secondary school model).

Since the 1989 National Curriculum, and with the pre-eminence of the QCA scheme of work, science has traditionally been delivered as a separate subject with cross-curricular links (Models 4 and 6), although some schools have continued to adopt partial integration through topic work as a preferred style (Models 1 and 3).

With the devolution of educational provision to the home countries of the United Kingdom, curriculum re-organisation has led to increasing freedom for teachers to plan and deliver science that reflects more closely the needs of the learners and the skills of teachers. This has inevitably led many schools to reflect again on the merits of thematic or integrated studies. In doing so serious consideration has to be given to the frailties of this mode of curriculum delivery as outlined in the landmark 'Three Wise Men' report of 1992 (Alexander et al., 1992), which offered a stinging rebuke on the efficacy of thematic approaches and criticised the lack of depth and skill development that characterised much of the pre-National Curriculum topic work at that time. This report went on to highlight that 'subject coherence can be lost in the attempt to subsume too much into the grand theme' and that '[pupils] must be able to progress from one level of knowledge, understanding and skill to another within the subject'. This last point remains a key problem when developing thematic or integrated schemes of work: how, for example, do teachers map skill progression across subjects within a themed unit? And, secondly, how do we ensure progression across year groups?

Table 3.1   Comparing the planning of science as a discrete subject or as part of a theme

Aspect of Learning	Subject-based Planning	Thematic/Integrated Planning
Science content knowledge	Allows a clear and traceable progression in science content knowledge across year groups (including key concepts and ideas).	Knowledge and understanding can be readily mapped out across science-led themes. However, issues arise with non-science themes as it is not always possible to make meaningful links with the remaining science content to match the given theme. Some form of discrete teaching of science may be necessary.
Science skills (including generic lifelong learning skills)	Allows clear and traceable progression in science process skills, e.g. science skills ladders. Subject leader has clear overview of science planning in one document.	Can be difficult to plan for and deliver skills efficiently. Accountability may prove very difficult as skills may occur in cross-curricular evidence. Year groups planning in isolation may lead to omission of skills.
Progression in learning	Easy to ensure progression via one set of science curriculum documents. Science subject leaders can readily assess the breadth and balance of learners' experiences and, if necessary, make adjustments to the science scheme.	Given that year groups may plan themes independently, potential problems exist in ensuring progression between year groups. Science subject leaders must actively monitor schemes of work to ensure progression.
Relevance and contextualisation	Can sometimes lack relevance for learners and meaningful context alongside other subjects. Can be catered for through the imaginative use of contextualised 'entry points' or 'big questions' that will form the stimulus for activities and challenges.	Offers very relevant contexts and meaningful links between bodies of knowledge. Likely to engage pupils' interest and promote more independent learning. Also allows pupils the opportunity to utilise relevant skills, including number, communication, ICT and thinking.
Cross-curricular links	Relatively straightforward to draw simple links between geography, design technology, numeracy and literacy.	Excellent opportunities for this, but some effort may be required in order to avoid repetition and/or tenuous even tokenistic links.
Mixed age classes	Yearly cycles can allow for complete coverage with no repetition for Year 3/4 and Year 5/6 classes. Difficulties with Year 3/4, 4/5 and 5/6 class structure, although this can be solved by utilising common science units across year groups in each cycle (to avoid repetition and/or prevent omission of knowledge).	Can be very difficult to adapt thematic planning to mixed-age classes. Termly themes in these settings require extensive differentiation and careful consideration of progression in both content and skills.

Whatever style of curriculum planning schools select it must:

- Provide relevance for learners.
- Trigger questions to set a cognitive conflict and/or contextualised 'entry points' into activities.
- Provide opportunities for pupils to construct their own learning via carefully sequenced learning activities.
- Give diagnostic and formative assessment tasks linked to commonly held misconceptions.
- Include a focus on the development of specific science process skills.
- Supply opportunities for pupils to carry out a range of science enquiry types (see the AKSIS website: the URLs for websites mentioned here are listed at the end of the chapter).

Paradoxically, even when these factors are taken into consideration, it may be possible to *plan* for progression in conceptual understanding and/or skill development without actually *enabling* effective learning to take place. Creating schemes of work without due regard to these six principles means disregarding the fundamental issue at stake: we need to *enable* leaners to *learn.* A scheme of work that merely details *what* and *when* to learn is unlikely to enable learners to make sense of fundamental scientific ideas, whether there are simple or increasingly abstract in nature. Such schemes are also likely to result in learners being passive participants and not actively involved in constructing

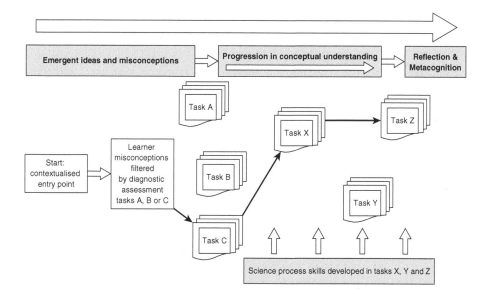

Figure 3.1

their own understanding. They are unlikely, therefore, to be given an opportunity to make *sense* of these new ideas and concepts as the scheme of work races along from one knowledge-based objective to the next.

It may be that the school has planned for expected outcomes from national curricula and assessment level criteria without due regard for the starting point of their learners – they are being taken down a learning pathway that they either don't require (as they already understand the concepts/ideas) or that is conceptually too demanding for their stage of development. Another failing of conventional subject-based schemes is that these often simply list (albeit in great detail) a series of tasks and/or activities that pupils must undertake with little reference to skill or conceptual progression. Many such schemes, including a number of commercial ones, also fail to reference commonly held misconceptions as starting points for teachers. In short, many science schemes are not based on constructivist principles (where each learner's ideas are placed at the heart of the learning process) and pupils are not allowed to co-construct their learning experiences.

Science subject leaders and/or science graduates are likely to be aware of science misconceptions and to use these to structure and guide learning according to constructivist principles (Selley, 1999). Schemes of work centred round commonly held misconceptions are an invaluable tool for the non-specialist primary teacher. Existing schemes have failed these teachers; they need alternative schemes that not only detail the activities to undertake and knowledge to impart but also, crucially, give ideas for diagnostic assessment, addressing misconceptions, and allowing time for learners to reflect on experiences and process new ideas. This process is summarised in Figure 3.1 above.

Making Effective Cross-curricular Links: Science and Geography

The 2008 Welsh curricula covering the *Foundation Phase*, *Key Stage 2* and *3* are all underpinned by a common philosophy: they afford schools the opportunity to plan and deliver a more learner-centred, skill-based curriculum. The aim is for schools to provide a curriculum that is stimulating and relevant for pupils. Schools use a set of transferable cross-curricular skills essential for successful lifelong learning. These include:

- Thinking.
- Communication.
- ICT.
- Number.

A group of schools from Flintshire, North Wales, has created a set of exemplar half-term planning units in an attempt to develop a more integrated, holistic curriculum. This links subjects in order to provide a broad and balanced delivery of knowledge and skills, with relevant and exciting learning experiences for primary pupils. This is a holistic approach that strengthens all aspects of a pupil's life – academic, physical, personal and emotional (see Figure 3.2 below).

Ready Steady Recycle

RESOURCES

Green Poems collected by Jill Bennett
ISBN 0 19 276198 6

KS2 Scientific Enquiry Materials
Recycling, Unit 3
ISBN 978 0 9557200 1 7

KS2 Optional Assessment Material
Paper and Recycling, Unit 7
ISBN 0 7504 8923 5

A3 English sheets.

Junior Voiceworks 2 by Kevin Stannard -
ISBN 978-0-19-335574-3

Art in a box written by Sarah
Richardson ISBN 1 85437 536 9

WEBSITES

www.esd-wales.org.uk
www.oup.com
http://www.ngfl-cymru.org.uk
http://www.climatechoices.org.uk
http://www.recycling-
guide.org.uk/schools.html
http://www.recyclenow.com/schools/
http://www.ecofriendlykids.co.uk/Rec
yclingSchool.html

TELEPHONE NUMBERS

Possible trip to 'Plas Power
Environmental Education Centre'
Tel No. 01978 757524

KEY WORDS

Environment	trees	litter
recycle	nature	water
reuse	fly tipping	waste
packaging	rubbish	compost
landfill sites	collage	pollution
sustainable	materials	noise

Subjects included

Science – how humans affect the local environment and a consideration of what waste is and what happens to local waste that can be recycled and that which cannot be recycled.

Geography – living in my world: caring for places and environments and the importance of being a global citizen.

English – Argument and Discussion (year 6, term 2, unit 2) & A Range of Poetic Forms (year 6, term 3, unit 2)

Art – Create a piece of art work using recyclable materials.

Music – Song: 'Water don't waste it.'

ICT – Use ICT sources of information. Store, retrieve and present information.

D&T – Investigate simple products and evaluate use (suitability) of materials.

Numeracy – Estimating/measuring quantities. Identifying different types of data; different ways to use this data. Correct mathematical language.

PSHCE – personal, spiritual, moral well-being. Active citizenship. Decision making. Stewardship.

(Continued)

(Continued)

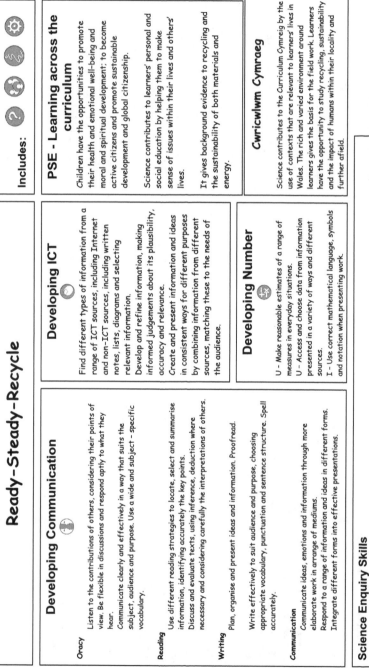

Ready-Steady-Recycle

Includes: ○ ○ ○ ○

Developing Communication

Oracy

Listen to the contributions of others, considering their points of view. Be flexible in discussions and respond aptly to what they hear.

Communicate clearly and effectively in a way that suits the subject, audience and purpose. Use a wide and subject-specific vocabulary.

Reading

Use different reading strategies to locate, select and summarise information, identifying accurately the key points.

Discuss and evaluate texts, using inference, deduction where necessary and considering carefully the interpretations of others.

Writing

Plan, organise and present ideas and information. Proofread.

Write effectively to suit audience and purpose, choosing appropriate vocabulary, punctuation and sentence structure. Spell accurately.

Communication

Communicate ideas, emotions and information through more elaborate work in arrange of mediums.

Respond to a range of information and ideas in different forms. Integrate different forms into effective presentations.

Developing ICT

Find different types of information from a range of ICT sources, including Internet and non-ICT sources, including written notes, lists, diagrams and selecting relevant information.

Develop and refine information, making informed judgements about its plausibility, accuracy and relevance.

Create and present information and ideas in consistent ways for different purposes by combining information from different sources, matching these to the needs of the audience.

Developing Number

U – Make reasonable estimates of a range of measures in everyday situations.

U – Access and choose data from information presented in a variety of ways and different sources.

I – Use correct mathematical language, symbols and notation when presenting work.

PSE - Learning across the curriculum

Children have the opportunities to promote their health and emotional well-being and moral and spiritual development; to become active citizens and promote sustainable development and global citizenship.

Science contributes to learners' personal and social education by helping them to make sense of issues within their lives and others' lives.

It gives background evidence to recycling and the sustainability of both materials and energy.

Cwricwlwm Cymraeg

Science contributes to the Curriculum Cymreig by the use of contexts that are relevant to learners' lives in Wales. The rich and varied environment around learners gives the basis for the field work. Learners have the opportunity to study recycling, sustainability and the impact of humans within their locality and further afield.

Science Enquiry Skills

- Communicate clearly by speech, writing, drawings and diagrams using relevant scientific vocabulary.
- Search for, access and select relevant scientific information from a range of sources including ICT.
- Pupils turn ideas suggested to them, and their own ideas, into a form that can be investigated.
- Evaluate outcomes against success criteria.
- Describe how they have learned and identify the ways that worked the best.
- Link their learning to similar situations within and outside school.

Figure 3.2 Ready Steady Recycle

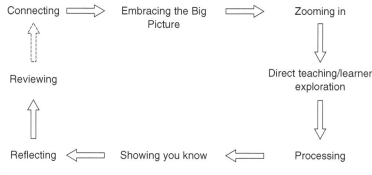

Figure 3.3

The traditional notion of curriculum and pedagogy as mutually exclusive components of education is limiting. Thinking skills and assessment for learning principles are integrated into this planning framework. Rather than teaching about the skills, students are afforded opportunities to practise them in active ways. Skills do not compete against knowledge for curriculum time; the units provide the contextualised backdrop for the development of skills and the acquisition of knowledge. This focus on the development of learning-to-learn capabilities has necessitated a change in both classroom practice and the nature of curriculum planning.

In these exemplar units the pupil is placed at the heart of the learning process. The resultant curriculum planning reflects the principles outlined in Figure 3.1, namely both a Constructivist and more learner-centred approach. Each unit follows a sequence that allows teachers to uncover pupils' misconceptions and ideas, followed by activities that promote more independent learning placed within a contextualised setting. There remains, however, a specific focus in the planning for those occasions when teachers recognise they may need to intervene in direct learning and/or deliver specific knowledge and skills. This focus on the detail of science process skills and the delivery of key concepts and ideas in science was often absent in earlier thematic work. The planning sequence follows the principles of the Flintshire 'Aspirations for Learners' policy.

Once at the reviewing stage learners have the opportunity to consolidate their conceptual knowledge and understanding (both scientific and other subject specific concepts) that were inter-connected within the larger context being used as the focus. Hence the use of the arrow back to 'connecting' in this otherwise linear process.

Science and geography share many areas in common with regard to subject knowledge and also enquiry skills. They are therefore are an ideal base from which to explore integrated planning units. The principal areas of overlap include those listed below in Table 3.2:

Table 3.2

Science in the 2008 Welsh Curriculum requires pupils to study:	Geography in the 2008 Welsh curriculum requires pupils to study:
Through fieldwork, the plants and animals found in two contrasting local environments.	Fieldwork to observe and investigate real places and processes. Study: living in Wales – their local area and an investigation of at least one aspect of the geography of the whole of Wales.
The interdependence of living organisms in those two environments and their representation as food chains. The environmental factors that affect what grows and lives in those two environments.	How is this place the same or different from other places/environments and why?
How humans affect the local environment, e.g. litter, water pollution, noise pollution.	How have people affected this place/environment? How can I and other people look after this environment?
A consideration of what waste is and what happens to local waste that can be recycled and that which cannot be recycled.	Living in my world: caring for places and environments and the importance of being a global citizen.

Problems with Coverage – Planning for Discrete Science

A common fault with many earlier thematic or integrated schemes was the issue of forced links between subjects and/or knowledge. Paradoxically, in an effort to make increasingly relevant links for learners many schemes resulted in weak or tenuous links being forged in a desire to attain an absolute curriculum integration. The folly of this approach is self-evident, and, although such mistakes are rarely made today, there is a need to exercise caution when planning for an integrated curriculum. In a subject-based National Curriculum, schools became experienced at drawing out meaningful cross-curricular links where these occurred naturally in the learning process. Today this has been taken a step further in the examples from the Flintshire integrated planning units (see Figure 3.2 above). Schools can now identify and plan for integrating shared knowledge and/or skills, as with geography and science, but crucially can also plan for and deliver science as a discrete subject where relevant links cannot be made. This method is both pragmatic and preserves the integrity of pupils' scientific experiences.

Developing Science Process Skills: Direct Teaching and Learner Exploration

According to the AKSIS (2010 online) findings, pupils need to encounter a range of science enquiry types in school, including:

- Exploration.
- Fair testing.
- Classifying and identifying.
- Pattern-seeking.
- Investigation models.
- Making things or developing systems.

Since the introduction of the National Curriculum, schools have made significant advances in the delivery of a range of science enquiry skills. However, as the AKSIS study highlighted, an imbalance stills remains towards exploration and fair testing enquiries. Geography and earth sciences provide important opportunities for pupils to undertake classification and pattern-seeking enquiry. (Pattern-seeking enquiries differ from fair tests in that no variables are directly controlled by the pupils. Learners identify the dependent variables that they consider important and choose to observe these in order to identify the patterns or relationships between them. Pattern-seeking activities are often triggered by the identification of an outcome or effect, e.g. *are smaller pebbles always found nearer the water's edge?*)

Periods of *direct teaching* and/or *learner exploration* (see Figure 3.3) need to feature prominently in thematic planning. These are occasions where teachers can plan for and actively ensure that pupils are able to practise essential science enquiry skills. This may necessitate either the *direct teaching* of process skills (e.g. using equipment, making observations and drawing conclusions) or a more independent *learner exploration* that allows pupils the opportunity to develop specific science process skills. Learner exploration is only effective, however, if process skills are identified clearly in teachers' planning. This task is assisted greatly by the use of science skills ladders.

Spring Bulbs for Schools Project – processing and showing you know

Since October 2005, primary school scientists across Wales have been part of a long-term study looking at the effects of climate change on the average flowering times of spring flowers across the principality (see the SCAN website, also Cowell and Watkins, 2007). The study of annual and seasonal cycles in the natural world (phenology) allows pupils to participate in authentic science enquiry work. Not only are they engaged in collaborative studies gathering daily rainfall, temperature and growth data, the project has also produced some fascinating all-Wales data on:

- Average temperature.
- Average hours of sunshine.
- Average flowering dates for daffodils and crocuses.

Table 3.3

	Average flowering date				
	2006	**2007**	**2008**	**2009**	**2010**
Crocus	25 February	16 February	16 February	13 March	6 March
Daffodil	19 March	6 March	14 February	7 March	24 March

Such projects are an excellent example of how pupils can be offered relevant and contextualised challenges that also reflect how real science works. Gathering data over a long period of time, and as part of a collaborative exercise, demonstrates to pupils the importance of exploration and pattern seeking as enquiry methods. With respect to the 'big picture' of climate change, it mirrors the methodology of more serious research-based projects in this area. Crucially, it also highlights key principles of science that are difficult to engage with in a primary classroom: that science is a *process* as well as a *body of knowledge* and also that scientific knowledge and understanding is *conditional* in nature. Young children (and some teachers too!) need to be aware that science has no finality or absolute answers, but does offer us a systematic method for recording and presenting findings from which we can attempt to draw conclusions using the current knowledge we possess. On a more concrete level, pupils are able to practise a number of science process skills:

- Communicating using an appropriate scientific vocabulary.
- Making observations and recording measurements.
- Using ICT to make measurements (e.g. using a data logger for either real time readings or for logged data).
- Using basic equipment (e.g. a rain gauge, thermometer).
- Making comparisons and identifying trends.
- Explaining findings and making informed decisions.
- Linking their learning both within and outside school.

Pupils have access to a web-based archive of results that offers opportunities to develop data handling skills. In the Spring Bulbs project, pupils *process* ideas and explain their results in the context of any significant weather-related events for that year and the impact this may have had on the average flowering dates. They may choose to create a weather fact file card, poster or a true-false card game based on their findings. During the *showing you know* phase schools may elect to use focused summative assessment tasks (such as the suite of Optional Assessment Materials provided to Welsh schools) from which teachers can record the level characteristics exhibited by pupils. The Spring Bulbs for Schools project may allow pupils to identify more long-term trends in the UK's weather and also enable them to link their learning to the 'big idea' of global climate change.

There are also significant variations related to local geography, (e.g. coastal versus inland, rural versus urban). A range of fascinating activities and information for studying phenology can be found on the Woodland Trust's Nature's Calendar project (see the website). The Association for Science Education's Primary upd8 resources offer pupil similar opportunities to undertake focused exploration and pattern-seeking activities, including the British Bluebells and the Evolution Megalab Project as described by Moon and Oldershaw (2010). A number of interesting weather-related analogies and illustrations can be found in the joint Edinburgh City Council, Scottish Earth Science Forum and Royal Meteorological Society publication, *The Science of Weather* (Aldridge et al., 2005). A range of informative ideas and suggestions from the Geographical Association demonstrate best practice in teaching and learning, particularly with aspects of dialogic teaching, assessment for learning and developing more learner-centred enquiry (see the website).

Science and geography: connecting/embracing the big picture

Children harbour wonderful ideas about the earth, from imaginative misconceptions about its creation, structure and place in the solar system through to challenging questions about its longevity and emergent ideas about plate tectonics. Addressing these questions may be a challenging task for non-specialist teachers, but it is necessary to do so in order for children to construct their own understanding of these big ideas based on scientific knowledge. Curriculum content and pupils' pre-existing ideas are often at odds. However, effective planning and pedagogy are needed in order to mediate the two and help them build up a sound conceptual understanding. Schemes of work must allow pupils to *connect* with the subject matter in order for emergent ideas and misconceptions to be addressed by learners. This is particularly important when they encounter more abstract ideas and adult constructs, including, for example, concepts surrounding gravity and current flow. *Connecting* can be achieved by the selective use of a number of formative assessment strategies outlined in resources such as Active Assessment (Naylor et al., 2004) and Northern Ireland's 'Active learning and teaching methods' (see the website). Effective strategies include:

- KWL grids (**K**now, **W**ant to know and have **L**earned).
- Mind maps and/or graffiti boards.
- Ideas posters.
- Concept cartoons.
- True-false card sort activities.

Once pupils have been given sufficient time to connect with the subject matter, teachers can plan for a phase of contextualisation where future tasks and activities are given relevance – *embracing the big picture*. For example, in the recycling unit in Figure 3.2, pupils are challenged to audit recycling opportunities both in schools and at home in an effort to enable them to identify the key issues and problems that could merit further investigation. In this case learners need to discuss issues surrounding fly tipping and the location of waste recycling centres. It is the responsibility of the teacher to guide them through their chosen enquiry path, ensuring the delivery of key science process skills.

If pupils' pre-existing ideas are not challenged in the *connecting* phase, then they are likely to be retained into adulthood. What is clear from traditional units of work such as the QCA unit on Rocks and Soils (QCA, 1998) is that many such misconceptions are not addressed or even explored. Pupils may learn about process skills of exploration, classification and recording rock types from this unit, but they may well have no basic understanding of the fundamental nature of the world they stand on.

If geography offers clear cross-curricular links with science, then earth sciences offer a wealth of similar opportunities in the primary classroom. As described by Ford (2009) and many others, the study of simple geological principles allows teachers to develop a number of science process skills and, in particular, gives them the opportunity to undertake exploration and pattern-seeking activities. Opportunities for pupils to become involved in extra-curricular earth science activities are available from the Geologists' Association *Rockwatch* project, which aims to encourage and foster young geologists (see websites).

Science and geography: zooming in and reflecting/reviewing

Once they have *connected* their learning, pupils need to be provided with a focused task in order to develop science enquiry skills and, if possible, to provide an opportunity for them to construct their own understanding of concepts or ideas. In the cross-curricular unit in Figure 3.2, pupils are challenged to create a recycling questionnaire and/or plan and carry out an interview with a council recycling officer. In this *zooming in* phase, strategies such as placemat activities help to encourage collaborative work and enable learners to form considered opinions. When engaging pupils in more traditional fair testing or pattern- seeking activities, teachers may elect to utilise modified concept cartoons or card sort activities (see Table 3.4) in order to create a contextualised entry point into practical work.

In north east Wales, the Loggerheads Geodiversity Education Pack has been developed to allow schools to study earth science; geodiversity in this sense includes not only the rocks and fossils but also the heritage and industrial history of the site. The resources

Table 3.4

Card Sort Activity
(Pupils challenged to sort cards and identify key variables associated with a shadow puppet investigation)

Distance of puppet (from screen)	Height of puppet
Thickness of puppet	Shape of puppet
Distance of screen (from puppet)	Type of torch
Brightness of light	Colour of puppet
Size of torch	Type of screen

are based on practical fieldwork and allow teachers to create relevant opportunities for pupils to *zoom in* on contextualised problem solving. Although geology and geography are the main subject areas, the resources are cross-curricular and include many aspects of maths, English/Welsh, history and art. The pack (available from www.newrigs.org) outlines a series of enquiry activities that focus particularly on exploring, recording and drawing conclusions from observable features – all essential skills for earth scientists. The geodiversity trail can be used as a vehicle to develop pupils' thinking, communication, number and ICT skills. It also allows teachers to develop *Y Cwricwlwm Cymreig* (developing learning through the culture and history of Wales).

The learning process culminates in *reflecting* and *reviewing*. Here, pupils are encouraged to consider the work they have undertaken and reflect on the new knowledge they have gained and the skills they have developed during the unit of work. Significantly, they should be encouraged to *reflect on how* they learn most effectively, using strategies such as self-and peer-reflection. Learners also need time to *review* the new knowledge and skills they have acquired. This final phase of the learning process – metacognition – may involve learners re-visiting initial mind maps/KWL grids or reviewing further examples of concept cartoons in order to consolidate their new ideas and place them in the context of their own earlier misconceptions. This is a prerequisite phase in order for any model of curriculum planning to be effective.

Summary

In this chapter we have seen how the nature of curriculum planning plays a pivotal role in the quality and depth of learning experiences and how geography and earth science provide valuable opportunities for pupils to undertake a range of science enquiry types. A range of models can be identified in schools, ranging from subject-based through to fully-integrated thematic work. Whatever vehicle a school may adopt to deliver learning experiences, effective planning needs to:

- Provide relevance and contextualisation.
- Utilise assessment for learning principles to foster active learning.
- Match knowledge and skills closely to learners' needs.
- Deliver focused science process skills.
- Allow learners to experience a range of enquiry types.

Relevant cross-curricular opportunities exist to develop science and geography. Schools should also make maximum use of the outdoor classroom. Subject linkage must neither be forced or by itself a means to an end. Schemes of work should be contextualised and skill-focused and allow for a progression in conceptual understanding. Whether schemes of work are subject-based or integrated, teachers need to focus more time on planning for diagnostic and formative assessment opportunities rather than spend time labouring over cross-curricular links. For without the former, effective learning is unlikely to take place.

References

Aldridge, V., Meldrum, G. & Ross, H. (2005) *The Science of Weather: A Primary School Resource*. Edinburgh: The City of Edinburgh Council.
A useful resource bank of ideas and activities based on the theme of the weather.

Alexander, R., Rose, J. & Woodhead, C. (1992) *Curriculum Organisation and Classroom Practice: A Discussion Paper*. London: Department for Education and Science.
One of the seminal academic papers commenting on some of the issues associated with thematic work that still stands as a warning against the inadequacies of weak thematic planning.

Cowell, D. & Watkins, R. (2007) 'Get out of the classroom to study climate change – the 'Spring Bulbs for Schools' project', *Primary Science Review*, 97: 25–28.
Short article outlining Welsh schools' participation in a national phenology project.

DCELLS (2008) *Science in the National Curriculum for Wales*. Cardiff: Department for Children, Education, Lifelong Learning and Skills.
Science curriculum orders for Wales for Key Stages 2 and 3.

Ford, A. (2009) 'Rocks, fossils and evolution', *Primary Science Review*, 107: 31–33.
Information about pupils learning about geology from the Jurassic coast in southern England.

Moon, M. & Oldershaw, C. (2010) 'British Bluebells Primary upd8 activity', *Primary Science Review*, 112: 33–35.
An overview of a fascinating project that helps pupils develop exploration and pattern-seeking enquiries.

Naylor, S. & Keogh, B. (2000) *Concept Cartoons*. Sandbach: Millgate House Education.
A must for every primary classroom. These cartoons assist in diagnostic assessment and challenge learners to reflect on their understanding of a wide range of scientific concepts.

Naylor, S., Keogh, B. & Goldsworthy, A. (2004) *Active Assessment: Thinking Learning and Assessment in Science*. Sandbach: Millgate House Education.
This is an excellent source book providing both a paper-based and digitally a wide range of different techniques for AfL in science. These techniques can also be easily adapted for other subjects.

QCA (1998) *A Scheme of Work for Key Stages 1 and 2*. London: Qualifications and Curriculum Authority.
Still the basis for science schemes in many schools, this remains a very useful source of ideas and activities for teachers. Most topics are covered twice across Key Stage 2.

Selley, N. (1999) *The Art of Constructivist Teaching in the Primary School: A Guide for Students and Teachers*. London: David Fulton.
An accessible account of constructivist pedagogy outlining the fundamental principles of this teaching style and its application to different subjects.

Weblinks

AKSIS: www.kcl.ac.uk/schools/sspp/education/research/projects/aksis.html (accessed September 2010).
A very valuable resource that provides definitions and examples of enquiry types as well as information on what characterises best practice in science education.

NEWRIGS: www.newrigs.org/ (accessed September 2010).
Website of the North East Wales Regionally Important Geological and Geomorphological Sites, containing a downloadable Key Stage 2 geodiversity education pack.

Northern Ireland 'Active learning and teaching methods': www.nicurriculum.org.uk/key_stages_1_and_2/index.asp (accessed July 2010).
A very useful source of formative and thinking skill strategies.

Primary upd8: www.primaryupd8.org.uk/ (accessed September 2010).
An excellent subscription-based resource that provides relevant and stimulating activities for pupils.

Rockwatch: www.rockwatch.org.uk/ (accessed August 2010).
The Geologists' Association junior club who run events and offer advice to budding collectors. There is also an online 'ask the experts' and weblinks to recent earth science stories in the media.

SCAN: www.museumwales.ac.uk/en/scan/schools/ (accessed September 2010).
Website of the National Museum Wales containing activities and ideas for developing education for sustainable development, including the Spring Bulbs for Schools Project.

Further Reading

The Geographical Association: www.geography.org.uk/eyprimary
This popular subject association website offers many ideas for planning and delivering geography in primary schools and also includes links with science.

Wallace, B., Cave, D. & Berry, A. (2009) *Teaching Problem-Solving and Thinking Skills Through Science*. Abingdon: Routledge.
This is a very useful outline of some strategies to develop more independent learning through science. Gives detailed and interesting examples of classroom practice.

Woodland Trust: www.naturedetectives.org.uk/
An informative site providing a great bank of ideas on how to begin to study phenology in the primary classroom.

CHAPTER 4

LINKING SCIENCE TO NUMERACY AND ICT

Dave Howard, Ashlee Perry, Malcolm Smith, Liz Flintoft and Robert Collins

Chapter Overview

This chapter builds on the discussion of teaching science across the curriculum set out in Chapter 3 and explores ways in which science can be linked with Numeracy and ICT as a means to promote science learning. The authors draw on enquiry-based pedagogies to provide an insight into ways to support effective science education. Section (a), contributed by Dave Howard and Ashlee Perry, focuses on developing science through links with numeracy, whilst section (b) from Malcolm Smith, Liz Flintoft and Robert Collins, develops the extensive opportunities within ICT for links to the acquisition of science concepts and skills. From a pedagogical perspective, science in the wider curriculum can benefit children in developing understanding across subjects through the use of meaningful real-life contexts and genuine engagement, exploiting their natural curiosity and stimulating their imagination.

The chapter suggests ways to enable teachers to plan learning experiences based on the needs of learners, the curriculum's demands and flexibility. Specific skills and concept acquisition are identified at various stages in the model that will support planning, teaching and assessment. This emphasises that ICT should not take over the science curriculum nor should it replace hands-on science taking place in the nursery or classroom, but should be used instead as a tool to enhance science teaching and learning experiences.

Section (a): Linking Science and Numeracy

By the end of this section you will be clearer on the links between science and numeracy and the pedagogical principles that underpin them. Practical examples are provided that demonstrate classroom-based activities that can be used from early years up to KS3 (Y7) to effectively enhance both scientific and mathematical knowledge, understanding and skills development. The content of this chapter is underpinned by pedagogy and practice rather than being shaped by formal curriculum pressures.

The clear synergy between science and numeracy can be used to boost learner understanding of key concepts and skills by enabling children to make connections between discrete 'bits' of knowledge that are too often perceived to be located in and limited to subject areas. The cross-fertilisation of ideas is strengthened by an application of skills and knowledge in contexts which span both subjects. Such an approach is not constrained by reference to a national curriculum or government initiatives. The developmental model described will allow teachers to select an appropriate strategy for their own class, but also retain the underlying principles that will be evident in any effective curriculum and approach to teaching and learning.

The definition of pedagogy we are using throughout is this:

> The act of teaching together with its attendant discourse. It is what one needs to know, and the skills one needs to command, in order to make and justify the many different kinds of decisions of which teaching is constituted. (Alexander, 2004: 11)

This highlights the distinction between teaching and learning, the role of the teacher and the significance of teachers intentionally choosing to act in particular ways for particular purposes, i.e. pedagogical fitness for educational purpose.

> ## Student Perspectives
>
> In a large undertaking such as linking curricular subjects together, it is important to recognise the key role of the subject specialist whilst helping the generalist novice teacher to gradually acquire the mantle of the expert. Many strategies can be adopted to achieve this, including for example the collaborative development of science skills within 'big' topics that cut across several subjects. There is also an important need for teachers to explore the downside as well as the upside of such a linking of subjects. Effective resource use can play a crucial role in this, as will be emphasised below.

Key principles of effective practice

These principles are well established, evident in primary classrooms, discussed and explored in Initial Teacher Education programmes, espoused by advisers and education consultants, and iterated in educational literature. For this reason we will not provide a detailed analysis, but will highlight the pertinent issues related to a cross-curricular approach involving science and numeracy, namely:

- Engagement.
- Collaborative working.
- Valuing the process itself not just the outcome.
- Facilitating the role of the teacher and other adults (including scaffolding and modelling).
- Teacher subject knowledge.
- Use of resources.
- Differentiation.
- Assessment.

We feel that this approach to teaching and learning can be adopted for any curriculum or scheme of work.

Statements in the left-hand column in Figure 4.1 relate to general pedagogical principles underpinning the children's learning; they can also be seen as discrete elements as well as a hierarchical progression depending on the context of learning. Statements in the right-hand column relate to specific scientific approaches, methods and processes. There are strong connections between each pedagogical principle and its corresponding scientific method and process. This model will enable a teacher to integrate any subjects (in our example science and numeracy) for any class at any level. The teacher's expertise and experience will determine how the model can be adapted to any subjects. Barnes says '*active involvement in any subject can be*

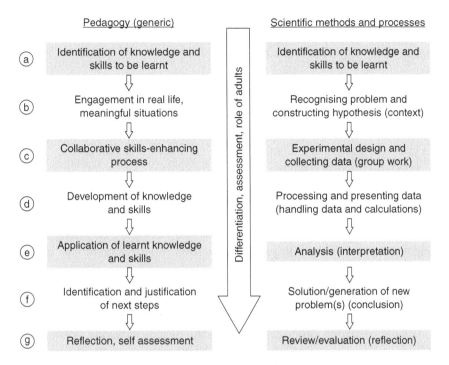

Figure 4.1   Pedagogical principles embedded in a scientific mode

suitable for cross curricular learning' (2008: 164). Differentiation and the role of the teacher and other adults are key elements of effective practice and run through this model – hence their central position. By following such a structure teachers can embed sound pedagogy in their practice across subjects and encourage 'deep' learning in learners.

Examples of Activities Modelling Good Practice

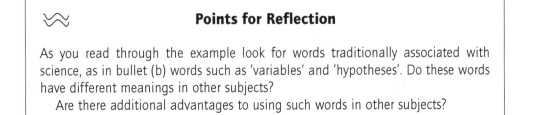

Points for Reflection

As you read through the example look for words traditionally associated with science, as in bullet (b) words such as 'variables' and 'hypotheses'. Do these words have different meanings in other subjects?

Are there additional advantages to using such words in other subjects?

Our first example will be readily recognised by many primary practitioners; our intention here is to illustrate how our model can be applied to meet the needs of all learners and is not age specific. The context is a car survey:

(a) The teacher identifies *counting* as the focal point of the activity at the planning stage.

(b) Our problem, stated as a question, is 'Will a walking bus affect the amount of traffic near our school?' This represents an engaging real-life situation leading to group and class discussions, the identification of variables impacting on the context, and the generation of hypotheses.

(c) The teacher groups the children, according to ability or other factors, to design a way of capturing relevant data. (Particularly through stages c-g above, differentiation and on-going assessment – see Chapter 8 – become more important in guiding the children in their task.) The children conduct the car survey, recording their results using their agreed method; this may involve some 'on-the-spot' modification of their method.

(d) Back in the classroom the children, still in their groups, sort and present data before beginning their analysis.

(e) Links will be made to their original hypothesis; where there is discord with the data the teacher or 'expert other' will facilitate the next step. Blythe (1998) comments that generative topics and challenging experiences provide the motivation to question, problem solve and find answers.

(f) The original question can now be reconsidered in light of the empirical evidence that has been generated. That these data are genuinely their own and are both meaningful and relevant is highly significant. There are many possible outcomes at this stage of the *investigation*; for example, acceptance of the original hypothesis, the generation of new questions, a need to collect more data, and adaptation of the original experimental method.

(g) As the teacher you will create opportunities for children to self- and peer-assess both outcomes related to the original question and their methodological approaches to addressing it. You can use this information not only to complement their own assessment judgements but also to inform future planning and teaching.

⌇⌇   Points for Reflection

Where's the mathematics in this example?

This example, 'counting', has been chosen as the focus for nursery and reception age children. It is unlikely that many will proceed to the other stages (a-c). However, a KS1 teacher could target sorting and classifying and a simple collection and analysis of data (stages a-e). The learning outcomes for KS2 children could be related to averages, validity of data collection methods, use of ICT to present data and recognition of types of variables (stages a-g).

The dialogue below represents some interaction between the teacher and the children in a reception class at stages (b) and (c) in our model. The teacher initiated the discussion by asking the class how they travelled to school (b).

    T: Ten of you walk to school. Who do you come with?

    C1:   I walk with mum.

    T: Is it just the two of you? (Child nods)

    C2:   I come with mum and Johnny.

    C3:   I come with Sarah and Samira.

    T: Who comes with you?

    C3:   Our mummies.

As this discussion unfolded it emerged that several of the children walked to school together with their mothers (only one came with their father). The teacher explained the notion of a 'walking bus'. Children were excited by the phrase, saying things like 'How can a bus walk?' and 'How can we be a bus?' The teacher then modelled a walking bus with the children. (The school had already decided to investigate the feasibility of a walking bus; gathering evidence would add to the strength of their case.)

In the next phase of the project the children, in ability groups, talked about traffic outside the school. The teacher intervened with prompts to direct them towards the need to collect data (c).

    T: What sort of traffic passes the school?

    C1:   Cars.

    C2:   Motorbikes and buses?

    T: How many pass the school?

    C2:   Lots.

    T: How can we find out how many?

    C1:   Count them.

    T: Great; how will we count them?

From this, several approaches to collecting the data were suggested. The teacher then organised one adult for each group to conduct the survey (c).

〰️   **Points for Reflection (links to theory)**

Evident from the example is the influence of both Vygotskyian and Piagetian ideas; for example, the intervention of an 'expert other' in facilitating progress as well as the social dimensions of learning including the importance of speaking and listening. 'Discord' or 'challenging experiences' equate to Piaget's notion of disequilibrium and the modern idea of 'creative tension' or cognitive dissonance. The role of the teacher and other adults is *vital in facilitating access to the planned provision* through a range of differentiated approaches based on individual need identified through assessment.

Our second example will be less familiar to primary practitioners. The context is racing snails:

(a) A teacher identifies *calculating speeds* as the focal point of the activity at the planning stage.

(b) Our problem stated as a question is 'Who is the fastest person on the planet?' This represents an engaging real-life situation (Olympics context), leading to group and class discussions regarding what speed is and how it is measured and generating suitable hypotheses about speed and the units of measurement. (The idea of using snails is to engage the children and adopt the well known principle of 'chunking down', starting from smaller units and building up to larger ones. The children can be encouraged to consider the most suitable unit of measurement in this context. Units such as mph and even m/s can be suggested even though two variables are being addressed – *distance and time.*)

(c) The teacher groups the children, according to ability or other factors, to design a way of capturing relevant data. The experimental design could involve many different variables such as the use of light, temperature, the enticement of food and the size of the snails. The children will discuss suitable distances to measure and units to use at this stage.

(d) Back in the classroom the children, in their groups, will sort and present their data before beginning their analysis.

(e) Links will be made to their original hypothesis; where there is discord with the data the teacher or 'expert other' will facilitate the next step. For example, the children's hypothesis could be that snails will travel more quickly towards food; if the experiment does not confirm this the 'expert other' can assist them in moving to the next step. This could involve identifying other possible explanations such as how well snails see, what food they 'like' and whether they are hungry.

(f)   The original question can now be reconsidered in light of the empirical evidence. Having calculated the speed from measuring distance and time this can be extrapolated to sprinters to address the question. This could then lead to a further investigation involving their own speeds and then making comparisons, through research, with those of professional sprinters.

(g)   The teacher will create opportunities for children to self-and peer-assess regarding the original question and their approaches to addressing it. The teacher can use this information to help triangulate their own assessment judgements. These will inform future planning and teaching.

Points for Reflection

Where's the mathematics in this example?

This example, 'calculating speeds', has been chosen as the focus for upper KS2 children who will proceed through all stages a-g. Depending on the nature of the cohort other aspects could be introduced, such as discussions about reliability and the validity of the experimental method including controlling variables and accurate use of measuring instruments. At KS1 children could collect simple data such as the time taken for the snails to cover a given distance; this could be graphically represented with simple analysis made (stages a-e). Young children could measure the snails using non-standard units (stages a-c). This would arise from asking the question 'Which is the fastest?' and designing an appropriate experiment to answer this.

The snails' example engages children, addresses the creative needs of the teacher, meets curriculum objectives and includes opportunities for assessment. This example is dependent on the availability of snails which are quite easy to find, inexpensive if purchased and reasonably robust animals; some children (and teachers) however may be apprehensive about using them. Snails do not travel in straight lines so using tracks or lamps may help to address this. Woodlice, worms or maggots could be alternatives to snails and despite possible difficulties the benefits far outweigh the disadvantages.

Points for Reflecton (links to theory)

The model is flexible so that the teacher can chose at which stage they enter and exit depending on the teacher's intentions, children's responses and any learning opportunities that may arise (planned and/or spontaneous). In terms of engaging

(Continued)

> *(Continued)*
>
> children both variety of activity and teaching approach are critical in enhancing intrinsic motivation and natural curiosity; differentiation will mostly be addressed by the nature of the task and by support. Here there is also satisfaction in resolving a problem which is a particular feature of both science and mathematics. There are rich opportunities for children (and teachers) to review and evaluate learning: working in a group, approach to task, development of subject knowledge and understanding and its application in a range of contexts.

Application across Areas of Numeracy

The two examples above detail how the model can be applied in two specific contexts – counting and calculating speeds. Other investigations could include:

- Baking buns – amounts and weights of ingredients; changing states; units of measurement; recording time.
- Melting chocolate – recording time and temperatures; experimental design; analysing results; changing variables.
- Measuring heights – unifix cubes, use of string graphs (non-standard measures); use of measuring instruments such as trundle wheels, callipers and clinometers (for trees).
- Energy saving – collecting rainwater (measurement); energy-saving devices (units of measurement); pollution detection and measurement; recycling (household numbers and amount) and types of waste (handling data).

Section (b): Science and ICT

Key ideas

The fact that you will have found a reference to Information and Communication Technology (ICT) in other chapters in this book gives a good indication of how important this curricular area is. It is also the one which is developing most rapidly. As well as hardware such as digital cameras, microscopes and data-logging equipment, etc. we have various software packages such as the ubiquitous Microsoft Office suite (or freeware equivalents) as well as specific science-based software packages. Interactive Whiteboards (IWB) have become the norm within the classroom environment and while this technology has the potential to really engage pupils with their learning, it is often only used as a glorified projector. The use of so-called 'Cloud computing' (see below) became a realistic possibility within the last four years or so. Virtual Learning Environments (VLEs) and e-Portfolios are also finding their way into many primary schools and can add yet another dimension to pupils' learning and your teaching, not just of science but across the curriculum.

Such rapid evolution presents challenges for textbook writing. Information on software and hardware is soon outdated, superseded or no longer relevant, and it is therefore imperative to consider the philosophy underpinning its use in supporting best practice teaching and learning within the classroom. A secure underlying philosophy will continue to have its place in the future, regardless of those changes yet to materialise. It is essential to remember that it is not just the use of ICT that is important, it is also how ICT can be used effectively and with purpose.

It would be remiss not to include safety issues related to the use of ICT by pupils, especially those linked to the use of the internet. Safeguarding pupils from more unsavoury internet sites is an important duty of not only the classroom teacher but also of the school as a whole.

This section, while emphasising how ICT can be used to support the teaching and learning of science, will also explore these other important aspects so that you – whether in a classroom or other setting – can make informed decisions not only about how to use ICT effectively to support high quality science education but also, and just as important, about when not to use it! As can be seen, ICT is a dynamic and exciting addition to your armoury as a primary teacher and like science it has its own language and acronyms. Some trainee teachers will embrace these with gusto, however most will not! It is not our intention to burden you with these unnecessarily – rather to use and explain the ones that are important for you to know.

Why Use ICT in Primary Science?

ICT as a curriculum subject is rapidly becoming a means to facilitate learning in other subjects including science. Suggested changes to the National Curriculum in 2009 made clear that ICT should not only be taught discretely but also embedded within all of the subjects, with a strong emphasis being placed on the latter mode of delivery (Rose, 2009: 54).

Using ICT in the teaching and learning of primary science is a statutory requirement. At Key Stage 2 in England the science programmes of study Sc1 (scientific enquiry, investigative skills) states *'make systematic observations and measurements, including the use of ICT for data logging'*. Statement 2h directs teachers to ensure learners *'use a wide range of methods ... and ICT, to communicate data in an appropriate and systematic manner'*. Furthermore, the Breadth of Study section states that those teaching science should be *'using a range of sources of information and data, including ICT-based sources'* (NC, 1999: 83). Other ways in which ICT can be used or how the different curriculum areas can be linked are identified within the ICT Programme of Study. However, since the introduction of the National Curriculum in 1988 ICT has developed significantly in two key areas, namely its relationship with other subjects and the expansion of newer technologies on the market. Primary science often provides an authentic context for developing children's ICT skills, knowledge and understandings while simultaneously aiding the development of science knowledge, understanding and skills.

ICT can be particularly effective in supporting the learning of scientific process skills and concepts. It has the capacity to enhance children's questioning, thinking and decision-making skills (Murphy, 2006) but is particularly powerful at enabling learners to explore areas of science that otherwise would be difficult to access such as Earth in space; for example, the NASA website (www.nasa.gov) contains a whole host of images, podcasts, vodcasts and videos as well as a Twitter feed, all of which can usefully contribute to teaching science.

Making the Most of ICT in Science

The use of ICT must be carefully planned and directly linked to the intended learning outcomes: when being used in science tasks and activities, it is vital to remember that the science must be the priority (Harlen and Qualter, 2004: 223).

The internet and good simulation software can enable pupils and teachers to access and observe experiments (and data) that would not otherwise be viable (cost, time, safety) in the classroom. More importantly utilising ICT can ensure that the collection of data, through the use of data logging and digital video, is more accurate and valuable time is saved (McFarlane and Sakellariou, 2002). These authors also believe that the most powerful use of ICT within the science curriculum is to support and/or replace practical work: and further, that the use of multimedia software and the internet are of primary importance for the development of scientific reasoning. They go on to suggest that simulations can allow pupils to concentrate more on the analysis and data interpretation than on the mechanics of the practical.

When considering the role of ICT in the teaching of science it is necessary to place this in the context of the pedagogical model adopted as the vehicle for curriculum delivery. The investigative approach embedded into the science curricula of countries in the UK requires teachers to use ICT within their teaching. This model promotes the learning of both 'scientific theory and process simultaneously' with various uses of ICT including scientific experiment simulations and interactive models (McFarlane and Sakellariou, 2002: 220).

Computers can also be used to model or simulate a concept that would be difficult to do in the classroom. Investigations that would have been too time consuming, dangerous, or difficult to do in the classroom have now become accessible to primary school children (Newton, 2000: 167).

Using ICT in the Scientific Classroom

The following subsections will discuss many of the different areas of ICT and how they can be used to enhance the science curriculum.

(a) The internet

With the advent of the internet a whole new world has become accessible to both teachers and learners alike. The internet can be used as preparation for an educational visit as many locations such as museums and galleries now have excellent websites. Many will explain what they offer to schools and provide follow-up activities that can be done in the classroom after the visit. Teachers can also choose which areas they may want to focus on during the visit, thereby enabling them to prepare worksheets or other materials to support this (Williams and Easingwood, 2003: 121).

The majority of the information found on the internet is constantly updated. Children now have access to weather reports, live satellite streams and even astronomical telescopes. They can link with other schools and compare climates in different regions or in different parts of the world (de Boo, 1999: 155). Many schools also subscribe to educational websites that children can access from both home and school. However, it is important that access should be limited to 'safe' sites and that communications are carefully screened (Ball, 1998: 173). The internet has opened up a variety of new ways for children to present and share information. They can design web pages or pod casts (see later) which can be uploaded for the whole world to see. Learners are also able to access up-to-date news using secondary sources like the internet and multimedia software, but they must also be taught how to be critical of information they find on the web. Many sites contain biased and misleading information and both teachers and pupils should always look at the URL in order to try and ascertain the validity of the information provided. For example sites ending .gov.uk or .ac.uk are more likely to be accurate compared with those ending with less official endings, such as .com, .tv or .net.

One particularly valuable use of the internet has been for student-teachers, NQTs or RQTs and their more experienced colleagues to access support materials. These resources can be used to aid teaching and learning provision but they can also serve teachers by helping them develop their scientific knowledge and understanding. The 'Fear of Physics' website (www.fearofphysics.com/) is particularly useful as it helps to explain some inherently difficult concepts such as those related to matter, forces, energy and Earth in Space. This resource has its limitations but is interactive and particularly helpful in supporting those of us who are still uncertain about some aspects of physical science.

Databases

There are many specific primary school software packages on the market and most will fulfil the needs of a specified age range. One such piece of software is TextEase (www. textease.com) – it has both a branching database and a more traditionally laid out database, with the latter allowing children to enter data they have collected from a scientific investigation into a database and using this to plot graphs, produce tables and make simple keys (see Figure 4.2).

Encouraging children to design their own databases enhances their scientific questioning and observational skills and also requires them to think carefully about which information they need to include. Databases can also allow work to be added to and compared over a longer period of time (Byrne and Sharp, 2002: 17). For example, Y5 pupils have carried out a survey of what is growing in a wild area and produced a database of their findings which is stored electronically. The following year a different Y5 class completing the same task can now compare their data with the previous year's, providing a valuable authentic extension to the basic task.

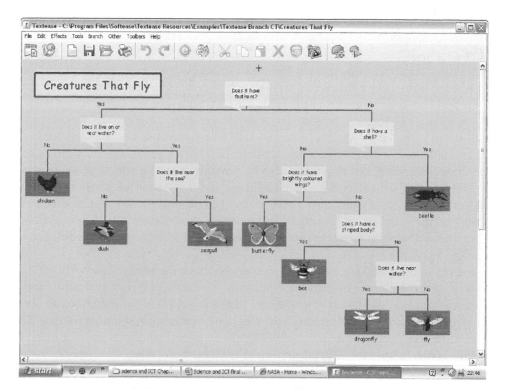

Figure 4.2

Branching databases can be used to group, sort and classify a range of inanimate objects or animate beings. The differentiation of this work is not necessarily due to the complexity of the software but more to do with the scientific vocabulary used (which is better, 'see through' or 'transparent'?). How the software is used within the science lesson is also dependent on the age and ability of each learner. A database can be designed, created and led by the teacher with younger/lower ability learners, yet older children can consolidate their understanding of the scientific concepts taught by designing and creating their own databases, and/or interrogating more complex databases created by others including their peers.

> How can branching-databases be used within the EYFS to help children to sort animals or objects that float or sink?

(b) Data loggers

Data loggers allow pupils to measure and analyse variables in experiments and investigations and are most often used to record temperature, sound, light and speed, although they can also measure and record many more different physical parameters. They play a useful part in science investigations by allowing recordings to be taken over a period of time, or at times that would be impractical, such as the temperature and noise of the classroom at different times of the day and night (Ball, 1998: 172).

Data logging can assist in the recording of results, the production of results tables and the plotting of graphs. While it is important to recognise that children need to learn procedural skills such as plotting and drawing graphs, using a thermometer or recording data, it is not necessary for children to perform these tasks every time they carry out an investigation. If graphs are drawn using a computer, then they can spend more time interpreting and analysing the data rather than the huge amount of time usually required for creating the graphs. This allows children to develop higher order thinking skills as they predict, interpret, discuss and hypothesise.

When data logging sensors are used graphs can be drawn automatically in real time, allowing the children to discuss and predict what they think is happening or will happen (Williams and Easingwood, 2003: 82). Results produced by data loggers can be displayed on an IWB as a stimulus for whole class discussion (Byrne and Sharp, 2002: 22). Used well, sensors will add depth, challenge and substance to the work and any measurements taken will be more accurate. Data loggers can be used to show and hopefully challenge scientific misconceptions as are typically encountered when studying falling objects. For example, which object will fall the fastest – a 10g mass or a 50g mass (both masses are circular discs of metal)? It is only by using a light gate that the data can be gathered (accurate to within 100th of a second) to answer this; an excellent example of best practice use of ICT in science.

(c) Control technology

Control technology can be an area of the ICT curriculum that is often avoided and frequently poorly taught. However there are many opportunities where control technology can enhance the curriculum, particularly in science. Today several different control turtles are available and one that is particularly popular in early years setting is the Bee-Bot by TTS (www.tts-group.co.uk). Bee-Bot has removable shells that can be decorated to fit into differing science themes such as mini-beasts. Habitats can be created so the youngest children can use the control element to guide the Bee-Bot to the correct habitat. In Key Stage 1 as children begin to develop their knowledge of electricity and light and dark a more sophisticated turtle, such as Roamer, can be used alongside the external sound, light and noise sensors. This can then be developed further in Key Stage 2 when the input and output devices (sensors) can be used to create series and parallel circuits which will work alongside the sensors. Turtles have wheels and can be easily employed to investigate the effect of, say, steepness of slope or surface conditions.

Control technology can be used to explore many everyday life experiences such as crossing a road using a pelican crossing. Important but simple safety issues can be tackled with younger pupils using a model crossing but this can easily be extended to what manages the changing sequence of lights, for older students. LOGO – a more mathematically-based form of control technology – has been and continues to be used to enhance the teaching and learning of science; the instructions on the left of Figure 4.3 are all LOGO statements.

(d) CD-ROMs

CD-ROMs can provide a wealth of information for children to access. Unlike books these often contain video clips, animations, sounds and simulations. Many also contain different areas which the children have to navigate through in order to find the information they require, all the while developing deeper questioning skills as they do so (Harlen et al., 2003: 182). A talking encyclopaedia can allow younger pupils to access information where previously they could not. One of the limitations of using CD-ROMs is that often the information can become rapidly outdated, whereas the internet would keep the same information more readily up to date. One advantage of using CD-ROMs rather than the internet is that children can retain the independence of searching for

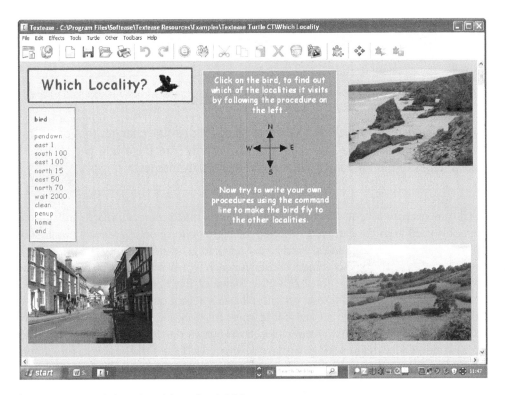

Figure 4.3   A web-based activity using LOGO

information using their own key words, yet are not exposed to any potential e-safety issues (see below).

(e) Digital media

Digital cameras can be used to record events over time, such as changing shadows, growing plants, mould growth or changing seasons. They can also be used to record what has happened in investigations and the images then produced as a discussion tool for follow-up work. When children use cameras themselves they have to consider how the image is going to be utilised, which will lead to them deciding which image they want to capture (Byrne and Sharp, 2002: 44).

Effective use of digital media can also be an excellent way of removing some of the barriers to learning. Pupils can use digital video as a presentation tool to show others what they have found out, which could be in the form of a documentary, advertisement or news report. This allows children to express themselves creatively and avoids an over-reliance on creating a written record, something which all too often can divert learners away from the science being studied.

Points for Reflection

A PGCE student used such technology to show children the changes that occur in the metamorphosis of a caterpillar into a butterfly. Are there any pedagogical advantages to this approach? What about any disadvantages?

Digital cameras have recently become widely available, much more affordable and are now commonly used from the early years through to higher education. Early years pupils show little fear of new technology and are often very quick to grasp the rudimentary principles of how this functions. The type of camera chosen for each type of setting will be dependent not only on cost but also on the suitability of its range of functions. Younger children need cameras that are tough and forgiving yet can still take a decent quality picture and the associated software must be simple enough for learners to easily and speedily see their pictures and print these as required. In this way children will quickly develop a strong sense of ownership and pride. Older children will have more developed ICT skills and be able to use cameras with additional features and more advanced software so they can edit and manipulate images. The areas of science that digital cameras can be adopted for are numerous and listed below are just a few ideas. These images can be produced by both teacher and pupil alike:

- Use images in pupils' presentations.
- Use images to record the different phases of an investigation.
- Use images as a record of their results.
- Produce a photographic record illustrating a scientific concept e.g. a melting ice lolly, a changing shadow, how fruit decays, the growth of seedlings …
- A photographic record of plants found in and around the school.
- Images of habitats at different times throughout the year.
- Images of different materials found in school.
- Photographic record over time of waste in school.
- Use images out of sequence to test pupils' knowledge of a scientific process, e.g. filtration, the life cycle of tadpoles …

(f) Digital microscopes

Digital microscopes can open up a whole new world of things that are too small to be seen with the naked eye. They are much easier to use than traditional light microscopes and have the added advantage of allowing a whole class or groups of children to view the magnified image. When this image is displayed on an IWB a range of educational tools can be applied so this becomes even more educationally powerful; we have heard student teachers and teachers alike gasp in wonder at some of the images they have produced. Many digital microscopes also have the facility to take still images that can be saved for later use (Williams and Easingwood, 2003: 148). All primary schools will have been given a digital microscope but all too often these will be confined to KS2. Evans and Dunne (2006) have challenged this perception and described highly effective work with the digital microscope, driven by learners' curiosity, in an early years setting.

(g) Interactive Whiteboards (IWB)

Many of the uses of ICT would not be as accessible to a whole class without an IWB. The IWB can be used as a conventional whiteboard or to display what is on a computer screen. Images collected from a camera or digital microscope can be presented and its interactive tools will allow images and text to be moved around. The IWB can be used for brainstorming sessions at the beginning of a topic; the work can then be saved for later use or easily change as the children's ideas are developed (Meadows, 2004: 26–27). It is interesting that while Interactive Whiteboards have become an essential teaching tool in many primary classrooms little is known about their effects on teaching and learning (Cogill, 2002).

Some of the possible educational uses of an IWB within a science lesson are:

- Presenting educational resources in a highly interactive way that is suitable for whole class and small group settings. Pupils with special needs can particularly benefit from the presentation of multimedia content on a large screen as this often supports both information processing and retention. Optimal use of an IWB involves both the teacher and learners being able to use it in a classroom situation. It should not be relegated to being the equivalent of a projection screen.
- Presenting student work more publicly.
- Showing video clips that explain difficult concepts.
- Supporting visually impaired pupils.
- Displaying internet resources in a teacher-directed manner.
- Creating handwritten drawings, notes and concept maps during class time, all of which can be saved for future reference.

IWBs can provide an enhanced level of access to digital teaching and learning resources and consequently can also help to expand the number of participants as far as learning style preference is concerned. In addition they will ensure that the whole audience is able to see the materials rather than gathering around a large text, or using individual materials where the learner has the potential to 'get lost' and not know where abouts in the text the teacher is referring to. The IWB gives the teacher the opportunities to engage the whole class by using a range of materials including animations. One limitation of the IWB is that they do not cater for individual learning because their primary purpose is for teachers to use them in whole-class situations: therefore the major effects are on whole-class teaching, whole-class interactivity and the confidence and competence of teachers (BECTA, 2003: 52). Interactive whiteboard developers have taken younger learners into consideration with their newer technology and now some boards are height-adjustable so they can move up and down to meet pupil and teacher needs. The main benefit of being lower is that children are able to access all of the IWB's features.

Recent and new developments

Many of the new developments in ICT share a common feature – the use of so called Web 2.0 technologies. This chapter rightly focuses on the effective use of technologies in supporting teaching and learning in science and so it is not appropriate here to discuss what is meant by Web 2.0. In any case as Tim Berners-Lee (credited with creating the World Wide Web) says '*I think Web 2.0 is, of course, a piece of jargon, nobody even knows what it means.*' However, Web 2.0 technologies can be used by you and pupils to effectively support teaching and learning. Some of the following examples will clarify matters.

(h) Using the 'cloud'

We are sure that all who read this chapter will have come across the search engine 'Google'. However, this company has developed many other useful applications that can be employed in both schools and daily life with Google Earth being just one example. A less well known set of tools are Google docs which include word processing, spreadsheets, etc. and are all available as online applications. In other words, these applications are not installed and will run on your computer like, for example, Microsoft Word. In this type of application the processing involved – such as producing a spreadsheet – is carried out online (effectively on servers based on the internet).

Google docs use an idea called Cloud Computing. This means you are not tied to a single computer because everything is based 'in the cloud'. The advantage is that you can access this anytime and anywhere provided you have an internet connection and, given access permission, so can anybody else. For example, you can use Google forms (part of the Google docs suite) to very quickly develop a questionnaire that can be completed online by your pupils. This questionnaire could be revision questions, a survey of interests or perhaps a survey of the class to establish a range of physical characteristics such as pupil height, hair colour, eye colour and so on. This form – located 'in the cloud' – is filled in by the children online and once completed is returned once again to that cloud where the teacher can access it. However, the real power of this type of technology is that the answers provided by pupils are automatically included in a spreadsheet. This then enables you or the pupils, with very little effort, to manipulate the data to calculate averages, trends, and so on.

As this work is done online pupils do not need to be in school to complete or manipulate the data produced so learning can easily be extended beyond the classroom. It is also easy for them to collaborate online since Google docs include a share facility. This can then be configured to enable a friend or classmate to '*view only*' or '*edit the document*' as appropriate; as with shared writing the possibility of peer support becomes very real. Other web-based applications are available and Microsoft released their Office Web Apps in mid-2010. If you haven't already done so, do have a look at this type of application as it can open up many teaching and learning opportunities to both you and your pupils that would be impossible with traditional pedagogical approaches.

(i) Virtual learning environments (VLEs)

A VLE is a computer-based system that aids learning and is another tool that you can use to support teaching and learning. The use of such technologies has been widespread in Higher Education for some time – indeed you may have used a VLE yourself in your undergraduate and postgraduate studies. Over the past four years or so VLEs have gradually found their way into secondary schools and are now beginning to be found in the primary sector. This new and exciting development offers many opportunities to support the teaching and learning of science not only within the classroom but it also provides the opportunity for pupils to work away from the classroom on their own and at their own pace. The pedagogy of online learning is a relatively new and very active academic field; however the use of VLEs in primary schools is at an early stage of development and we anticipate a considerable expansion of VLE use in the early stages of schooling. Consequently we have concentrated on how you, as a trainee teacher or NQT, could make use of this new technology without going into a detailed discussion of the underlying theoretical frameworks.

A number of VLE platforms are now available and in use within primary schools. It isn't possible or desirable to look at all the different systems – more useful here is to provide some ideas about how VLEs can support teaching and learning especially when pupils are outside of the classroom. Every VLE requires a pupil to have a login and in most cases the activity of the pupil engagement with the VLE can be monitored. This monitoring is designed to help provide optimal support for each learner. Data about what time a pupil logs in, what resources they visit, the results of any tests or quizzes and so on can also be captured.

As mentioned previously it is important that any use of ICT is integrated within the lesson planning process, something that clearly applies to work carried out using VLEs. Online materials could be provided as a starter activity or they could be developed to reinforce learning or to revise content that has already been covered. Activities could be provided to extend the learning for those who are more able. Many of the programs and resources you are already familiar with can be easily adapted and used within the VLE. For example, PowerPoint slides can be utilised to develop learning resources that are easily accessed through the VLE or Microsoft Word documents can be added and downloaded by pupils. The key aspect is that these materials must engage them; they need to be active online learners.

Most VLEs offer the facility to develop online tests or quizzes which also provide automatically calculated results. The more sophisticated ones can allow the provision of formative feedback; do make use of these, as children react very positively to the immediacy of response that needs to be provided. Often tests can be completed more than once, which again can be a powerful motivator as pupils observe their scores improve. As you can imagine, all this can be very time consuming and for a hard pressed trainee or NQT it can be a daunting prospect. However, help is at hand! Many educational suppliers provide learning materials designed specifically for use with VLEs. Check to see if your school has these. In many cases this service will be provided as part of the 'package' supplied by the company providing the VLE. Check with your ICT coordinator to see if these resources are available. So how do you know if what you provide online is appropriate and engaging? You may remember we previously mentioned the ability to monitor pupils' activities within the VLE. One way of establishing the usefulness of your hard work is to quantify pupil-use of the VLE extensively. Central to this is ensuring that all ICT activities are integrated within your lesson plans and that these serve a specific purpose in relation to identified learning outcomes. Do not fall into the trap of simply populating the VLE with worksheets, weblinks and so on, with little regard to their structure or purpose.

Using ICT in Science: A Vignette of Practice

Using an online learning platform

GLOW is an online environment available throughout Scotland that combines many of the tools found in traditional VLEs. It is used not only by pupils but also by teachers as a way of sharing resources and good practice. Olivia Wexelstein uses GLOW with her P4-P7 group to investigate the solar system. The following is taken from the 'Cook books' section which showcases teacher and pupil use of the platform. (http://cookbooks.glowscotland.org.uk/blog/2010/12/19/embedding-glow-in-daily-learning-and-teaching/)

The topic started with some brainstorming to discover what pupils knew about the solar system and what they wanted to find out. Photos of the pupils at work, discussing and drawing up mind maps, have been uploaded to a Picture Library as a record of pupils' understanding and learning experiences. At the conclusion of the topic, similar mind maps will be recorded to show how the pupils' understanding has progressed. They are leading the learning on this rich task. They have set themselves a challenge, brainstormed a list of key questions to be explored, and decided upon activities. One day pupils were delighted to receive a surprise visitor to the classroom – Spud Lightyear! They have enjoyed interacting with Spud and designing activities for him.

Pupils clearly feel a sense of ownership and are highly engaged in their exploration of the topic. The challenge, questions and activities are all prominently displayed on the 'Solar System' page so that pupils can refer to these whenever they wish. Throughout this topic Olivia has again found Glow an excellent tool, as it allows her to bring together a wide range of content and activities that are easy for pupils to find and use.

Blogs are a new feature within GLOW, introduced in August 2010. Olivia has integrated these into the P4-7 Glow Group, with each member of the class having their own blog. A blog – described by one pupil as a 'personal diary' – allows the user to add text, images, audio and video. The Wellwood pupils are using their blogs to write about what interests them and share this with an audience both within their class and beyond. The blogs include creative writing and descriptions of school trips, along with posts about school holidays and likes and dislikes. Pupils have been keen to use their blogs at home during evenings and weekends, as well as in class. Olivia is delighted with their responses, seeing even previously reluctant writers keen to update their blog. This motivation and increased confidence with writing is paying dividends with the quality of written work in the classroom.

(j) e-Portfolios

e-Portfolios are a relatively new and rapidly developing area within primary schools. With pupils' increasing use of the electronic environment they inevitably generate lots of files that need to be stored in a manageable and systematic way and tend to be stored on schools' servers in individual pupil accounts. However, these files don't really provide any indication of the learning journey travelled by the pupil. Nor is it easy to provide feedback on their work when confronted with a simple collection of files. e-Portfolios enable this learning journey to be evidenced more easily as well as offering the opportunity for pupils to make use of a much wider range of digital media. Feedback provided by the teacher is embodied within the work and not as some sort of separate entity: as a result, learners are encouraged to reflect on their work.

The simplest e-Portfolio is a collection of files arranged in order; usually chronological or task specific. However, as with a traditional paper-based portfolio, an e-Portfolio needs to be able to showcase pupils' work. This showcasing is made much easier if the information is more widely available on the internet. To be truly effective an e-Portfolio needs to integrate all forms of digital media text files, video, sound and so on since learners should be encouraged to use the most appropriate medium for the identified purpose. Further, since we are considering a learning journey, the information held needs to be portable so it can travel with each individual from primary phase through to secondary phase and beyond.

There are two main types of e-Portfolio. Some will be integrated within the school's VLE and provided by the vendor as part of a package. This solution is easier to manage and pupils only need to login once to access all their online learning needs. However, this could present difficulties when a child moves from school to school and from phase to phase. Another path is to have a specific e-Portfolio system. These can be used as a standalone e-Portfolio or also linked to the school's VLE. These tend to be more sophisticated but at a cost of ease of use.

Perhaps a more contentious issue is who controls the e-Portfolio. In contrast to VLEs which are controlled and organised by the institution (e.g. the school) e-Portfolios are as much about a pupil's learning journey as they are about meeting specific tasks; they are very much pupil-centred and as such should be controlled by them. Yes, they will need guidance. Yes, they will need to submit their work. But it is our belief that they should control how they use their e-Portfolio and they should also control access to their work. So how can this relate to good teaching and learning in science?

Using an e-Portfolio in Science

e-Portfolios can be used by a pupil to evidence specific topics (e.g. 'Living and Growing') with the use of multimedia as well as traditional text-based files. For example, they may want to show how a cress seed grows. They could use digital images together with a sound file describing the changes that occur or they could write a blog explaining these changes. Instead of digital images perhaps they may be able to use stop-motion animation obtained from a digital camera or even from the digital microscope. It might also include information about how other types of seeds germinate that they have gathered from the internet which is presented as internet links or pictures. The learner may want to share this information with other members of the class to get feedback from them before giving access to the teacher (something which the teacher facilitated).

As a teacher you will wish to provide formative assessment and negotiate (yes, negotiate) access as the task progresses. In most e-Portfolio systems there is a facility to add comments or feedback that will integrate with the evidence a pupil has collated. Using this guidance they will be encouraged to reflect on their science work and ideally such a reflective process will be engineered into the original task given to pupils. What is important here is that they can use what is available and not be limited by traditional reporting techniques.

> ∿   **Points for Reflection**
>
> A philosophy – as with any use of ICT you should build online learning into your teaching.
>
> What sort of things can you do? Can it solve problems? Do online resources support all areas of learning equally well? Do online resources support all learners equally well?
>
> Does it save time?

eSafety

As we have witnessed, the internet can offer exciting and dynamic materials that can both inspire and be used by your pupils to improve and support their scientific knowledge, understanding and skills. Unfortunately there is also a much darker side to this resource and both you and your pupils need to be protected from this aspect. Tanya Byron, commissioned by the government to review the risks associated with internet use by children, made a number of recommendations to improve the safety of pupils while using online resources (Byron, 2008, see websites). She suggested the discussion should move away from the harmful effects of this technology to how adults and teachers can enable pupils to manage risks and make their digital world safer. This move was supported by recent findings from OFSTED who found that:

> Pupils in the schools that had 'managed' systems had better knowledge and understanding of how to stay safe than those in schools with 'locked down' systems. Pupils were more vulnerable overall when schools used locked down systems because they were not given enough opportunities to learn how to assess and manage risk for themselves. (OFSTED, 2010)

Some recommendations were aimed at raising the profile of eSafety and providing mechanisms to support schools as use of the internet within classrooms becomes commonplace, the UK Council for Child Internet Safety (UKCCIS) being one such example. Other instruments concerned the policing of school policies in this area and from 2009 OFSTED have been including this in their inspection frameworks. Information was provided to ITE providers to support trainee teachers and this was reinforced by incorporating aspects of eSafety within the skills tests. Information suggests that 77 per cent of NQTs feel they have the necessary knowledge and understanding of eSafety issues regarding the risks to young people (TDA, 2009).

Byron stressed that eSafety should be woven throughout the primary curriculum and not just seen as an ICT or PSHCE specific issue. When planning to use the internet in your science teaching you need to ensure that pupils are aware of the risks and of how best to minimise these when accessing internet-based resources. To help you in this, the school will have an eSafety coordinator and a detailed eSafety policy (including an acceptable use agreement for pupils to follow), outlining the school's vision and approach to eSafety. This will include how different technologies and facilities are going to be used safely, procedures for responding to incidents and sanctions for misuse. As a trainee teacher or NQT you must both know who is responsible for eSafety and have a copy of the school's eSafety policy.

Following on from her earlier review, Byron completed and published a further review in 2010, 'Do we have safer children in a digital world?', which examines the progress made since the 2008 Byron Review. This identified that the key aspect of raising public awareness had been successful, with one of the most noticeable features being the development of the succinct 'Zip it, Block it, Flag it' code (Byron, 2010: 13), developed as part of the 'click clever, click safe' campaign by UKCCIS.

Use the Code when you talk to your pupils about the internet – it will help keep them safe online.

Keep your personal stuff private and think about what you say and do online.

Block people who send nasty messages and don't open unknown links and attachments.

Flag up with someone you trust if anything upsets you or if someone asks to meet you offline.

Figure 4.4

Another recommendation from the 2008 Byron Review was a 'one stop shop' for digital safety information for children. This has now been realised and the Child Exploitation and Online Protection Centre (CEOP) hosts this. The centre has developed the click CEOP button seen on many social networking sites where young people can quickly access online help if they feel under threat.

Summary

This chapter has provided insights from different subject perspectives into ways to support effective science education across the 3 to 11 age range. From a pedagogical perspective science in the wider curriculum can benefit children in developing their understanding across subjects through the use of meaningful real-life contexts and a genuine engagement, exploiting their natural curiosity and stimulating their imagination. The model is underpinned by established learning theories (Constructivism and Social Constructivism) and accepted 'best practice'. It enables a teacher to plan learning experiences based on pupil need, the curriculum's demands and flexibility. Specific skill and concept acquisition can be identified at various stages in the model that will support planning, teaching and assessment.

The use of ICT in science should promote a better learning of science and not just contribute to the National Curriculum for ICT. ICT should not take over the science curriculum nor should it replace hands-on science taking place in the nursery, classroom or laboratory but should be used instead as a tool to enhance science teaching and learning experiences. This is best practice and often there are synergistic educational benefits to this approach. The suggestions are offered in the hope that you will not be tempted to 'jazz' up a science lesson with technology, as such tokenism contributes nothing to high quality science provision.

References

Alexander, R. (2004) 'Still no pedagogy? Principle, pragmatism and compliance in primary education', *Cambridge Journal of Education*, (34).

Ball, S. (1998) *'Science and Information Technology'.* In R. Sherrington (ed.), *ASE Guide to Primary Science Education.* Cheltenham: Stanley Thornes.

Barnes, J. (2008) *Cross-Curricular Learning 3–14.* London: Sage.

BECTA (2003) *ICT Research Bursaries: A Compendium of Research Reports: A report on the ICT Research Bursaries 2002–03.* Coventry: British Educational Communications and Technology Agency.

Blythe, T. (ed.) (1998) *The Teaching for Understanding Guide.* San Francisco, CA: Jossey-Bass.

Byrne, J. & Sharp, J. (2002) *Using ICT in Primary Science Teaching.* Exeter: Learning Matters.

Cogill, J. (2002) *How is the Interactive Whiteboard being Used in the Primary School and How does this Affect Teachers and Teaching?* London: King's College, University of London.

de Boo, M. (1999) *Enquiring Children, Challenging Teaching.* Buckingham: Open University Press.

DfES (2002) *Framework for Teaching Science: Years 7, 8 and 9.* London: Department for Education and Skills.

Evans, S. & Dunne, M.J. (2006) 'The digital microscope: that belongs in KS2, doesn't it?', *Primary Science Review,* 93: 4–7.

Feasey, R. & Gallear, B.(2000) *Primary Science and Numeracy.* Hatfield: ASE.

This practical, well organised guide supports the development of cross-curricular links in science, offering thematic material and ideas for activities and teaching strategies as well as examples of children's work.

Harlen, W., Macro, C., Reed, K. & Schilling, M. (2003) *Making Progress in Primary Science.* London: RoutledgeFalmer.

Harlen, W. & Qualter, A. (2004) *The Teaching of Science in Primary Schools.* (4th edition). London: David Fulton.

Lakin, L. (2006) 'Science Across the Whole Curriculum'. In W. Harlen, (ed.), *ASE Guide to Primary Science Education.* Hatfield: ASE.

This chapter considers science across the curriculum, identifying a range of skills that can be applied by the learner to make connections between subjects and to broaden and deepen understanding of the world.

McFarlane, A. & Sakellariou, S. (2002) '*The role of ICT in science education*', Cambridge Journal of Education, 32 (2): 219–232.

Meadows, J. (2004) *Science and ICT in the Primary School.* London: David Fulton.

Murphy, C. (2006) *Literature Review in Primary Science and ICT.* Available at www.futurelab.org.uk/resources/documents/lit_reviews/Primary_Science_Review.pdf (accessed 18 December 2010).

Newton, L. (2000) *Meeting the Standards in Primary Science.* London: RoutledgeFalmer.

QCDA (2010) *The National Curriculum Primary Handbook.* Coventry: QCDA.

Rose, J. (2009) *Independent Review of the Primary Curriculum: Final Report.* Available at http://publications.teachernet.gov.uk/eOrderingDownload/Primary_curriculum_Report.pdf (accessed 15 December 2010).

Training and Development Agency for Schools (TDA) (2009) 'Results of the newly qualified teacher survey 2009'. Available at www.education.gov.uk/ukccis/index.cfm (The UK Council for Child Internet Safety).

Williams, J. & Easingwood, N. (2003) *ICT and Primary Science.* London: RoutledgeFalmer.

Weblinks

Berners-Lee, T. (n.d.) developer Works interviews
www.ibm.com/developerworks/podcast/dwi/cm-int082206txt.html

Byron, T. (2010) *Do we have safer children in a digital world?*
http://media.education.gov.uk/assets/files/pdf/d/do%20we%20have%20safer%20
children%20in%20a%20digital%20world.pdf (accessed December 2010).

Byron Report (2008)
www.education.gov.uk/ukccis/userfiles/file/FinalReportBookmarked.pdf(accessed
December 2010).

http://www.nasa.gov/ (accessed December 2010).

The National Curriculum for KS1&2
http://curriculum.qcda.gov.uk/key-stages-1-and-2/ (accessed December 2010).

http://www.textease.com/athome/ (accessed December 2010).

www.tts-group.co.uk/shops/tts/Default.aspx (accessed December 2010).

UK Council for Child Internet Safety
www.education.gov.uk/ukccis/ (provides useful background about e-safety including the
'zip it, block it, flag it' code).

Further Reading

Allen, J., Potter, J., Sharp & Turvey, K. (2007) *Primary ICT: Knowledge, Understanding
and Practice.* Exeter: Learning Matters.
While not totally up to date with e-safety this is a very useful book. The relationship
between ICT and other subjects is examined closely as are the applications and
technologies of ICT.

Hayes, D. (2007) *Joyful Teaching and Learning in the Primary School*. Exeter: Learning
Matters.
This book offers additional insights into the 'inter-weaving' of different subjects such as
science and geography or maths and the physical world.

Wilson, A. (2005) *Creativity in Primary Education.* Exeter: Learning Matters.
A useful and accessible publication. The value of cross-curricular teaching in delivering
meaningful teaching and learning experiences in science is explored. Creativity is not
typically associated with science.

CHAPTER 5

SCIENCE LITERACY

Tara Mawby

Chapter Overview

This chapter distinguishes science literacy from the literacy of the National Strategies, developing its meaning in terms of good science practice and why it is important for both individual learners and society. The emphasis is on learning to make increasingly well-informed choices and judgments. The chapter goes on to discuss progression in levels of science literacy and how to assess this, using everyday examples such as television advertising. The final sections discuss the creation of positive environments in which science literacy can be developed, with examples of activities that promote this and ways to build science literacy into a creative curriculum.

Key Ideas

During this chapter we shall consider the meaning of 'literacy'. This is not the literacy of the National Strategies (that were), or the literacy of the 'literacy hour', or even the ability to read and write. Obviously all these are part of literacy, but we shall be considering the bigger picture and not being straightjacketed by either our own experiences or the need for our children to be good at two of the three R's. The literacy we want to draw upon is that which makes us able to understand the world around us and explore it. This is the literacy that a 3 year-old has of being able to articulate their ideas, as well as an 11 year-old who is able to interpret data from graphs and make informed choices.

The following chapter will pose questions and ideas for you to consider in your own teaching so you can develop science literacy not only in yourself but also in learners.

Student Perspectives

Before we consider scientific literacy, perhaps we had better define what 'being scientific' means as opposed to being a 'scientist'.

A scientist is someone who does science for a living – who uses science knowledge and understanding (and learning) to go about their business. Most people think of an image similar to that of Albert Einstein when they think of a scientist; the stereotypical view of the mildly mad professor with wild grey hair, half moon glasses, and wearing a white coat, who is also usually a white male!

Being scientific doesn't mean you have to wear lab coat or glasses, or even have any hair – in fact you don't have to be male either! To be scientific you need to be able to think. To be scientific you need to be curious (about anything and everything!) and open-minded, so that you don't make up your mind before you have gathered all the evidence you need. So before we can be scientifically literate, we have to instil children with that sense of awe and wonder about the world and provide them with opportunities to be curious and think about why things happen.

Why isn't it a sensible idea to stack all your plates in a cupboard as they come to hand from the dishwasher, no matter what size they are? Why do we need to have splayed legs on highchairs for other adults to trip over in the small confined space of our kitchens? Tackling these problems doesn't require any science background but plain common sense, as they are only answered through observation and curiosity and by taking an interest in things. And these can be easily tested in the classroom!!

What is Science Literacy? A Global Definition

There are some conflicting definitions of what 'scientific' literacy actually is, but it is *not*, as it says on the tin, about doing literacy in science! It is about *using* science to come to a reasonable conclusion. PISA (Programme for International Student Assessment) gives this definition:

> Scientific literacy is the capacity to use scientific knowledge, to identify questions and to draw evidence-based conclusions in order to understand and help make decisions about the natural world and the changes made to it through human activity. (OECD, 2003)

We are all familiar with the 'literacy' that the government has put such a high priority on and the emphasis that the Rose Review proposed for linking with other languages. You could think of scientific literacy as another language. It has its own set of terminology to describe things, but as with all languages it is about being able to converse with others in a way that is understandable and clear. It is a means of communicating your own meaning, even if you don't have all the right vocabulary. I'm sure many of us have experienced trying to ask for something in French or another foreign language and finding that we have an inadequate vocabulary but with a bit of time and thought, and particularly patience and encouragement from the recipient of our efforts, we can convey our meaning. Scientific literacy is just the same. Children, especially younger children, can manage to communicate effectively even without this precise vocabulary. Most important to them is to have sufficient thinking time (see Chapter 9 for more on this) and the right environment that encourages them to 'have a go'.

What is Scientific Literacy in Practice?

Scientific literacy is not about being able to talk in scientific 'jargon' that no-one else understands, but much more about being able to interpret ideas that are put in front of you, about the world around you, using as a basis the scientific knowledge and facts you already possess. Some people can talk very knowledgably about football or a soap opera using what they have learned from television. They can use the information provided for them to hold a coherent and cogent conversation about the topic in question. Opinions are formed and arguments engaged in because they are becoming football literate or *Eastenders* literate. This in essence describes the relationship between science and scientific literacy.

Science is not a 'stand alone' subject; it has to have context to have meaning and not just for scientists but for everyone. By making links to anything from toys to tyrannosaurs we have a 'hook' to hang our learning on. Without the knowledge and understanding that come with being scientifically literate it is hard to be discerning about information that comes our way in later life. How many times do we see an advert which claims something like *'8 out of 10 cats prefer ...'* or *'65% of women said they could see the difference* …'? It sounds amazing to have such a success rate, until you consider such features like the sample size. In essence these ads aren't misleading us (even though the data are often subtly presented) but we all need to be scientifically literate to be able to recognise that actually these data simply aren't good enough.

Arguments about whether or not global warming is taking place, the energy crisis, gene therapy and genetically engineered crops are impossible to make sense of without some level of scientific literacy. This is what makes being scientifically literate so important, to be able to use all the information effectively and not just the headline figures that the presenters or reporters or advertisers want us to see. We need to be able to question and evaluate the information we are presented with and by being scientifically literate we are better able to make informed choices about which cat food to buy or even which face cream (if any) will really get rid of our wrinkles!

On a more practical level (because testing anti-wrinkle cream on the smooth faces of students may not be the best scientific test!) you may consider whether all the 'hype' about plastic bags is really true. Are the ones you pay for stronger that the freebies? Do they last longer? Are they biodegradable? Are we parting with extra money when actually there isn't any benefit to us or the environment? This is one real issue that could be tested in the classroom.

Why is a Scientifically Literate Population so Important?

Why do we teach children science, i.e. 'For what purpose or purposes' do we teach it? Many arguments have been presented for why science must be taught based on the nation's economic productivity, a better equipped workforce and the fact that it is part of our cultural identity. There is also a powerful social argument based on the need to have a scientifically literate population who are able to function effectively in an ever-advancing technological and scientific world.

So science is taught because we need a workforce that can think scientifically, and can cope in our increasingly complex world. In the not so distant past (in fact only about fifteen years ago), you could probably 'fix' your broken car, or change the wheel if you needed to, or even top up the oil in it. Today cars are controlled by an engine management system that screams at you if you so much as lift the bonnet and haven't plugged in a computer to do a diagnostic check!

Without the ability to understand ideas and use the information to work out problems or make decisions we could have a population that are more like sheep, in that they will just follow where they are led without asking any questions or proposing any solutions. Being scientifically literate means that we will have some understanding about why we take medicines for example and why we have to follow the pharmacy's instructions. It also means we can make an informed choice about which washing powder to use and allows us to understand why we should save rainforests.

And what about all those old wives' tales that our parents told us? Where did they come from and is there any basis for them? *Eat your carrots and you'll see in the dark; eat your crusts and they'll make your hair curl; eat spinach to make you strong.* Obviously these are all related to eating and might be hard to test in the classroom, but you can observe the weather – does it rain when cows are lying down? Does touching a toad give you warts? What about the saying *If the oak flowers before the ash, we shall have a splash. If the ash flowers before the oak, we shall have a soak*? All of these things can be researched and while they might not be directly related to science this research will require researchers to have scientific knowledge and understanding. Using approaches such as the Spring Bulbs Project described in Chapter 3 could then bring children in contact with others countrywide, for example to share observations about the behaviour of the oak and ash trees in their area.

Points for Reflection

During the Second World War RAF pilots that were flying at night were encouraged to eat carrots. There *is* some scientific reasoning behind this idea. Find out what it is.

April Fool?

Consider also the infamous 'spaghetti trees' in a 1957 April Fool from the BBC's *Panorama* programme (see Figure 5.1 below). Just because there is an important and normally believable figure (in this case David Dimbleby) involved doesn't necessarily make something true. Millions of people believed this story because of something which you might describe as gullibility, but this is possibly better viewed in terms of scientific illiteracy. You can see new footage of this video and check out how convincing it was at http://news.bbc.co.uk/onthisday/hi/dates/stories/april/1/newsid_2819000/2819261.stm

Figure 5.1

What Does Progression in Science Literacy Look Like?

Making sense of the world at an early age requires young children to explore and play not only with meaningful objects but also with their senses too. Very young children's first attempts at communicating are often a parent's most dreaded time because of the constant and repetitive 'Why?' questions they ask. This search for answers to questions needs to be fostered throughout our lives and not just during those formative years because this represents the beginning of our developing a scientific literacy. Exploration, asking questions, and not being afraid to challenge information alone, however, cannot be sufficient here. We don't want a world of people like the ones Ben Goldacre talks about, who are unable to recognise that the media are:

> Conspiring to promote the public misunderstanding of evidence, to actively undermine people's understanding of what it means for there to be evidence that something's is good for you or bad for you. (Goldacre, 2009: available at www.badscience.net/category/podcast/)

We must at the same time acknowledge that different levels of literacy do exist that we need to become familiar with, so we are able to provide the right sort of science teaching and learning experiences that will enable a progression in the development of children's ideas. Rodger Bybee (1997) proposed the following hierarchy of scientific literacy (see Table 5.1).

Bybee refers to this framework as:

> A unique perspective that gives direction to those responsible for curriculum, assessment, research, professional development, and teaching science to a broad range of students. (1997: 86)

Table 5.1

Nominal scientific literacy	This is where students will recognise some of the vocabulary of science, but don't have a clear understanding of all of this and may have misconceptions about some of it.
Functional scientific literacy	This is where students can describe a concept correctly and use relevant vocabulary, but will have a limited understanding of it.
Conceptual scientific literacy	This is where students will have a greater understanding of a concept and can begin to explain it correctly using their science understanding. They also have a greater understanding of enquiry and technological design.
Multidimensional scientific literacy	This is where students can relate their understanding of concepts and processes and the nature of science in the wider context of science technology and society. It includes philosophical, historical, and social dimensions of science and technology.

How can we Tell if we are Scientifically Literate?

Points for Reflection

Is it really possible to be scientifically illiterate? What if you couldn't engage with the world around you? What if you were a member of a native Amazonian tribe transported into a modern European city or a European living in the heart of the Amazon rainforest – what would you have to do to be scientifically literate in each context? What would be common to both examples? Is there a universal model of scientific literacy? Is scientific literacy culturally dependent? Use Bybee's model to describe a scientifically illiterate individual.

Before we can help our students to become more scientifically literate we are going to have to reflect on our own position. Looking at the model of progression above (see Table 5.1) where would you locate yourself? Possibly at the Conceptual level or are you Multidimensional? How can you tell this? Do you know all the terms you need in order to teach science really well? And do you accept things at face value always, sometimes, or never? These are all points we must ask ourselves in order to consider what we need to develop further.

As with most things we do there has to be a starting point as we can't just jump right in at the deep end. Pupils cannot just be given scientific vocabulary in the hope they will be able to use it correctly. They will need to experience and explore first and to communicate in their own developing, often non-scientific language – and then, and only then, can you provide the subject-specific terminology. In other words just as teachers must carefully plan the progressive development of children's scientific knowledge, understanding and skills, the progressive development of scientific literacy requires equal care and consideration. The idea of 'generic levelness' may help with this:

- Level 1   Pupils using their own experiences and 'stating' facts and names.
- Level 2   Pupils considering differences in objects and describing these in very simple terms.
- Level 3   Pupils considering similarities and grouping and sorting things in a variety of ways, as well as describing them in more detail. They are linking cause and effect, using 'because' to explain simply, but not necessarily employing a scientific terminology.
- Level 4   Pupils using a range of correct scientific vocabulary as well as to describe more fully and explain concepts.
- Level 5   Pupils not only using the vocabulary to explain why, but also in order to apply their understanding to other contexts, and make links.
- Level 6   Pupils adopting concepts to reconstruct and use models in order to explain these.

For example, to provide a 5 year-old child with the word 'vibration' is counter-productive. An intelligent child may well accept this word because of the context in which it has been introduced (in this case in a lesson about sound but with little practical experience). They might also be able to state that *sound is a vibration*, however, the child will not have experienced what a vibration is. They will not have been able to describe it in their own terms or observe a range of vibrations or their effects. This word may well become part of their personal lexicon and they may even believe that they 'know' what it means – indeed they could be able to trot out this definition in years to come but it will be based on scant understanding. Unless a teacher or another peer questions their use of this word that is how this will stay.

The important thing we need to do as teachers is to healthily question everything around us, in a similar fashion to a very young child, in order to try to make sense of the world. As we grow up most of us – but fortunately not all – will lose this natural inclination for inquisitiveness and curiosity and so we may need to be reminded about its importance in order to rekindle our use of the question 'Why?'. If we are not inclined to do this ourselves, and if we also present ourselves as poor role models, we aren't going to be as effective at encouraging the appropriate and relevant attitudes and behaviours in our students.

One place to begin could be by really watching and listening to adverts which pop up all over the place, from the newspaper to the internet and those appearing between your favourite TV programmes. Take one of the adverts for Playstation (other games consoles are available!) for example. Watch the advert carefully. What would make you purchase a game? What can you notice appearing along the bottom of the screen and what does this *specifically* tell you about the game? Would this alter your view of whether or not you would buy it?

Another example here is adverts for yoghurt-type drinks that will boost your 'friendly bacteria'? Do they really have names like *Bifidos digestivum* or are the advertisers having us on – this sounds as if it should be authentic as they seem to have adopted a scientific approach in using a classification-related Latinised name? And what about 'boswellox' which sounds more like a swear word? It is actually the active ingredient in a cream which is based on recreating some of the beneficial effects of Botox but is also a very toxic product from a species of bacteria called *Clostridium botulinum*. Perhaps this could be a good place to start asking some 'Why' questions. (Incidentally 'Botox' is now part of our common parlance and regularly seen in a wide variety of magazines. The problem with such everyday use is that it generates complacency in a readership that might not be particularly scientifically literate. How many people would realise this is based on the botulinum family of neurotoxins, all of which have very high levels of toxicity? Botulism kills up to 100,000 wildfowl birds every year, it has been used as the active ingredient in a variety of biological weapons, and its potential for a bioterrorist weapon is still a cause for concern.)

In addition you may also have noticed that in some adverts the science is almost turned into a 'geeky' aside thereby perpetuating the myth about science and scientists. By stating '*Here comes the science bit*' in some adverts we can be left with the feeling that it is being included because it *has* to be rather than because it is *important* to customers or the product or because as mere mortals we simply wouldn't understand it. Yet audiences can indeed make sense of such information *when* they have been educated to do so. It is only through teaching that individuals will be enabled to see through such tokenism and distortion. Ben Goldacre's column in the *Guardian* or online is a good place to begin as here is an example of someone who continually questions what it is that advertisers are presenting to us as well as exploring and examining other ideas from the science community.

And yet when it comes to our students, how can we foster this questioning attitude in them but also ensure that we avoid some of the cynicism that is so often associated with science? Should we wait until they are in Year 6 to start 'teaching' them about scientific literacy or do we need to be encouraging this from the very start?

What Kind of Environment do we Need?

One of the observations above is that the further into our educational lives we go (as students) the more it will happen that our opinions and ideas are neither sought nor even valued. We are filled to the brim with facts and presented with experiments and activities that only serve to 'illustrate' (at best) what we have already been told. Taking any focus within a science-related lesson or activity, one of the first things we should all do is to encourage our students to talk about their ideas both with us and with each other. To do this we need to create the right environment or ethos by allowing time for this talking to take place and also encouraging it by not closing down conversations through our adoption of a simplistic, one word, right/wrong response to pupils' questions, ideas, or other verbal responses.

There are some simple rules to this:

- Provide an opportunity for discussion. Concept Cartoons (see Keogh and Naylor, 1998) do this very well as they allow for alternative ideas to be discussed.
- Give pupils thinking time. The typical 'wait time' for a teacher for an answer is approximately four seconds! After such a short period of time the teacher will answer the question him/herself or will move on to a different pupil or ask a different question. Practise being quiet and patient! This is harder than it sounds, as it is not only our words that children are sensitive to but also our body language which can give them the cue to wait until they can give us the answer they think we want. As teachers, we need to be sensitive about these paralinguistic impacts on learners. A neutral stance and an open face are both useful for promoting pupil responses.

- Make explicit to pupils that their ideas are valued by listening and being positive about their responses.
- Wherever possible provide opportunities for pupils to explore and play prior to questioning them. Remember the Confucian saying, *'I hear and I forget. I see and I remember. I do and I understand'*, which has been quantified into a series of percentages about making learning 'stick': *'20% of what we read, 30 % of what we hear, 40% of what we see, 50% of what we say, 60% of what we do, 90% of what we see, hear, say and do!'*
- Use displays to promote questions or to pose your own for students to discuss; best practice will involve a question board that includes a 'Science question of the week'.
- Provide an independent exploration/play area no matter how old your pupils are.

The best displays for provoking my students have been those that engaged them by encouraging their thoughts and actions rather than passive exhibitions either of students' work or those of a 'decorative' nature. One such idea was used during the 2010 football World Cup. A selection of PE kit from lost property was stapled to the wall to create a 'footballer', with a half-squashed football and an old piece of 'net' for the goal. Across the top of the board were all the flags of the countries involved in the tournament. The board then had a series of questions and places to write answers as well arrows that could be moved around. This display was aimed at upper primary students as the questions were about the forces involved to get the ball into the net and required them to place arrows in the right place. The second part consisted of asking questions about the likelihood of England winning the competition, based on a probability from the number of countries in the tournament and how this altered as time went on and other teams were 'knocked out'. The idea behind this was that children could actually explore the forces by actually considering related information more scientifically on the back of their enthusiasm and interest in England winning the World Cup (see Figure 5.2).

You can and should foster this enquiring and 'scientific' nature in other subjects and not just those of the National Curriculum whichever form it is in. In the National Curriculum for 2000, enquiry is not only part of science but is also written into, amongst others, the programmes of study for history and geography. In fact the prerequisite skills required related to effective enquiry are generic regardless of the subject being taught. Students need to be provided with skills that can be applied in a range of contexts. At a recent conference there was a discussion about 'enquiry' and how every child needed an 'enquiry toolkit' from which they could choose the necessary tool(s) to help make decisions and find out the answers to whatever was puzzling them. The talk was metaphoric of course, but what if we could support students by providing them with these tools and a physical reminder of this, so they could draw on this 'toolkit' and make an informed choice once they have been taught how best to use them?

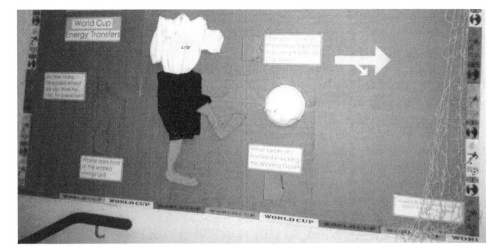

Figure 5.2

What Activities can we do to Support and Develop Scientific Literacy?

As with any activities we plan, they have to start with what the students know and have experienced. You may want them to explain why we must be 'greener' but without exploring what is going on in their own back gardens they will not have internalised the importance of this and are equally likely to be limited to a simple regurgitation of facts. Having created an environment that is question rich, where learners are not afraid to 'have a go', they also require competence in procedural understanding in order to become a better (or even good) critical 'scientific thinker'.

This can be as simple as demonstrating a really bad 'fair test' activity. This doesn't have to be a complex experiment, it can be as simple as racing balls across the floor or playing games such as Snakes and Ladders but 'cheating' as you do so! Students will quickly tell you it isn't 'fair', thereby applying their concept of rules and fairness without being aware of this as a scientific concept and procedure. From this first experience of 'fairness' their ideas about scientific process of fair testing can be further developed. It is interesting that throughout my experience in teaching science some of the best science has emerged when things have gone wrong – not because I manipulated it thus but because of peculiar circumstances. These serendipitous events can prove a rich seam for encouraging a scientific literacy-related involvement on the part of children and teachers. Unfortunately a great many teachers, and especially those who are new to the profession, are often too concerned about always achieving the 'right' results and are under genuine pressure to produce pacey lesson after pacey lesson and so this is often overlooked.

Visual Literacy

Science literacy and 'science and literacy' have often been used confusingly to mean the same thing, so it is probably useful here to dispel a few misunderstandings. One development since the introduction of the National Literacy Strategy (NLS) in 1998 has been the attempt to 'use' science teaching in primary schools as a vehicle for literacy development – which would not be too bad if all aspects of literacy were addressed. However the NLS has concentrated almost exclusively on verbal literacy as found in narrative texts whereas science materials are predominantly also composed of all kinds of visual elements. These include diagrams (many cross-sectional), charts and photographs for example, all of which use a complex and often unexplained set of icons and symbols. Consider arrows, which are used widely in science materials; we found 12 different meanings for an arrow in one Year 3–4 science text alone. Yet the meanings of these arrows are rarely explained, so authors must judge this as assumed knowledge on behalf of the reader.

There is also a widespread assumption that illustrations can help children to understand the related written text but this is commonly not the case. Here is one example: look at Figure 5.3 which is a double-page spread from a Year 3–4 pupils' book, and try to identify problems that it might present.

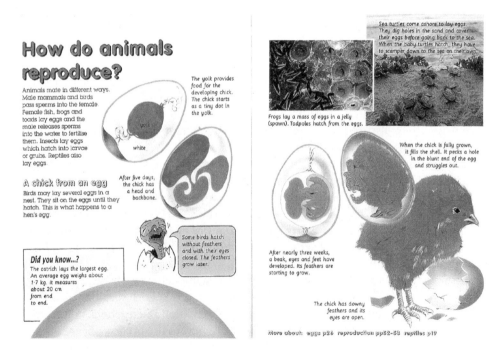

Figure 5.3

One of the key difficulties for learners is simply navigating their way around these two pages – after reading the first sentence, where should they look? When do they turn to the illustrations which do not flow simply down the page, like a storybook, but cut across from one page to the other? Poor layout and complex illustrations can be major barriers to science literacy even though children might be perfectly able to read the words on the page. Another problem here is scale, as the frogs' eggs seem larger than the turtles! There is no other conclusion to be reached here other than we have to teach visual literacy and not fall into the trap of simply assuming children will acquire this without help.

Now compare Figure 5.3 with Figure 5.4 and pose this simple question: '*What science can you see in this image?*' But we don't have to ask a question about science specifically – it might be better phrased as '*What can you tell me about this image?*'

Something that often engages thinking in pupils is when you show you are adamant about something and they will try to prove you wrong. For example, if you begin a lesson with a statement like '*All red cars go faster than any other colour*' the students may or may not agree with you. What it will do is pose a problem for them as they may well believe you but also 'recognise' this as a bit of a sweeping statement. The

Figure 5.4

emphasis is clearly for them to try to work out if the statement is correct or not! Initially the discussion will need to focus on how they can find out and will then be concerned with actually finding out and explaining whether the 'fact' is a fact or not! It is not inappropriate here to pose other questions that will require even more thoughtful engagement such as *'Can a magnet last forever?'*, or what about *'If I only ever see white swans will this mean all swans are white?'* or *'Can hunting be good for conservation?'*, as having a simple right answer defeats the object and challenges narrow perceptions of what science is.

How can we Write Science Literacy into a 'Creative/Thematic' Curriculum?

With all the talk at this time of uncertainty about the need for a 'creative curriculum', we need to consider how we will ensure that scientific literacy doesn't end up being one-off, tokenistic contributions. This has been something teachers have faced before (and perhaps some still do) when doing an investigation or carrying out AfL; such a 'lesson' was rolled out once in a while rather than being embedded within ongoing teaching and learning according to the principles of best practice. Being embedded is key, so whenever you are planning, incorporate links to scientific literacy. The literacy part of the lesson will often reflect the context and can therefore assist with making such learning experiences more creative without these having to be cross curricular.

The NACCE definition of creativity states that an activity has to have purpose, value, originality, and imagination for it to be creative. This doesn't mean it has to be wacky or outlandish. If you want students to find out if it is possible to blow square bubbles then this is fine. Just because it isn't new to you to blow bubbles doesn't mean it isn't original to students. As long as you have a reason for using bubbles and it adds value to the planned learning, then go ahead. In fact we would argue this could be a better vehicle for becoming more scientifically literate because you are *NOT* hung up on the prescribed knowledge that we need students to acquire.

So can you be scientifically illiterate? If we understand science literacy to be the capacity to make sense of the world around us in order to be able to make informed decisions, then a native Amazonian *could* be literate. A professor of theoretical physics who lived and worked amongst Blackfoot and other Native American peoples came to this conclusion:

Knowledge, to a Native person, cannot be accumulated like money stored in a bank; rather it is an ongoing process better represented by the activity of coming-to-knowing than by a static noun. Each person who grows up in a traditional Native American society must pass through the process of coming to knowing, which in turn gives him or her access to a certain sort of power; not necessarily power in the personal sense, but in the way a person can come into relationship with the energies ... of the universe. (Peat, 1995: 55)

Therefore this coming-to-knowing seems to be another way to perceive scientific literacy. It is context dependent, personal, and another way of understanding and respecting ourselves and the environment on which we all depend.

Yet this also raises an interesting question … which you can take on from here.

∿ Points for Reflection

What counts as scientific literacy for you?
Is it about knowledge, attitudes, skills and capacities, or all of these?

Summary

Science literacy here is taken as the ability to explore, understand, and communicate our dealings with the world around us. It is the practical ability to think scientifically and to use science knowledge. It means being able to interrogate information about global and local issues, whether these are climate change, our own eating habits, or the old wives' tales passed down to us. Producing a scientifically literate population is one of the central aims of science education.

From this starting point, the chapter developed ideas about what progression in scientific literacy might mean, identifying four levels – nominal, functional, conceptual, and multidimensional – and the indicators with which these can be recognised in learners, as well as in ourselves, in order to assess our levels of science literacy. This led into a section that set out to show how we can foster the questioning attitudes needed whilst also avoiding some of the cynicism often associated with science.

Crucial to this is the right environment or ethos in the classroom to allow scientific literacy to develop. Some simple rules for this have been developed, including making time and opportunities for exploratory play, valuing children's ideas, providing thinking time, and not closing down discussions too early. Examples of activities were suggested and the importance of visual literacy for making sense of science materials was discussed. The chapter ended with a discussion of how all these ideas can be integrated into a creative, thematic curriculum that could allow children to investigate their own (inevitably cross-curricular) questions and concerns.

References

Bybee, R.W. (1997) *Achieving Scientific Literacy: From Purposes to Practices*. Portsmouth, NH: Heinmann. pp. 82–86.

Harlen, W. (2001) 'The assessment of scientific literacy in the OECD/PISA Project', *Studies in Science Education*, 36 (1): 79–103. Available at http://books.google.co.uk/books?id=wjF0gYoRhn8C&pg=PA49&dq=scientific+literacy+Harlen&cd=1#v=onepage&q=scientific%20literacy%20Harlen&f=false

Keogh, B. & Naylor, S. (1998) 'Teaching and learning in science using concept cartoons', *Primary Science Review*, 51: 14–16.

Millar, R. & Osborne, J.F. (eds) (1998) *Beyond 2000: Science Education for the Future*. London: King's College.

OECD (2003) *The PISA 2003 Assessment Framework – Mathematics, Reading, Science and Problem Solving Knowledge and Skills*. Paris: OECD. Available at www.oecd.org/pages/0,3417,en_32252351_32236102_1_1_1_1_1,00.html (accessed 24 May 2010).
This reference not only links together, maths, literacy, science and problem solving skills, it also provides units that will help to assess these. It is secondary based but still provides good insights into the principles of linking and assessing scientific literacy.

Peat, D. (1995) *Blackfoot Physics*. London: Fourth Estate. (See Chapter 1 for further details on this text.)

Weblinks

www.purduescientificliteracyproject.org/
An American site which has ideas and activities for promoting enquiry and scientific literacy in the early years, or kindergarten as they call it. These aren't a series of lesson plans but approaches.

www.planet-science.com/text_only/sciteach/badscience/index.html
Aimed at older children (14 to 16) but the ideas may transfer to more able children. They are linked to Ben Goldacre's 'Bad Science' column in the *Guardian* newspaper.

Hazen, R.M. (2002) Why should you be scientifically literate?
www.actionbioscience.org/newfrontiers/hazen.html#primer (accessed 24 May 2010).
An interesting and easily readable article on scientific literacy from the USA, with links to lessons and activities to support the ideas discussed.

Milne, I. (2008) What is scientific literacy?
www.sciencepostcards.com/sciencelinks/science_literacy_links/assets/PISP_milne_scilit_08.pdf (accessed 25 May 2010).
An interesting and short article written for a New Zealand website (www.sciencepostcards.com) that offers free resources in the form or stories or postcards. There are links to other articles and resources, including some of the ones already mentioned above.

www.cchsonline.co.uk/school/science/sciliterate.htm
Useful site for a whole school week approach to scientific literacy.

www.conceptcartoons.com/index_flash.html
Concept cartoons from Millgate House Publishing, which provide a useful platform for talk, discussion and ideas.

Further Reading

Ratcliffe, M. & Grace, M. (2003) *Science Education for Citizenship*. Maidenhead: Open University Press.
Chapter 2 of this publication, which considers the value to using socio-economic contexts to develop science knowledge and understanding, is particularly relevant to expanding our ideas about scientific literacy.

Roden, J. (2005) *Reflective Reader: Primary Science*. Exeter: Learning Matters.
This is a highly readable book that integrates theory with practice. Chapter 1 addresses why we teach science and the importance of establishing a scientifically literate population.

CHAPTER 6

LEARNING SCIENCE BEYOND THE CLASSROOM

Leigh Hoath

Chapter Overview

The chapter focuses on all kinds of out-of-classroom environments, from the school grounds to the wider natural environment, and considers both the arguments for taking learning outside as well as the potential obstacles perceived by teachers. It also considers the research leading up to the previous government's manifesto on LOTC, emphasising the importance of using external experts and their specialist knowledge, taking advantage of training opportunities such as non-school placements, and maximising the use of time and spaces away from the classroom. Safety issues are considered as part of the crucial aspects of planning and preparation and there is an emphasis on the appropriate forms of discourse, differing as they must from those of the classroom environment. The chapter ends with a discussion of APP and an assessment of out-of-classroom learning, along with the importance of a constructive, science-based follow up when back in the classroom.

Key Ideas

This chapter will explore ideas of what it means to teach science outside the classroom effectively, rather than simply moving science beyond the classroom. 'Outside the classroom' can mean using the school grounds, or a museum or science centre for example, or indeed going on residential trips. The principles discussed can apply to *any* space which is not the usual classroom; the PE hall and ICT suite, for example, are not excluded. What is important is recognising the changes that can occur as a result of moving pupils away from the traditional primary classroom and its accepted norms of teaching and learning.

There are also ongoing arguments in relation to the management of out-of-classroom experiences, the organisation of off-site visits and accountability that are valid, and these go some way to support teachers in questioning why they should actually undertake such activities. This chapter aims not only to address these obstacles with a sense of realism but also to offer strategies for supporting teaching and learning of science outside the classroom.

In 2006, the *Learning Outside the Classroom* manifesto was presented which aimed to enhance the pupil experience through greater use of the outdoor setting. Research prior to this (Rickinson et al., 2004) indicated that while there was an amount of outdoor learning taking place there were questions that needed to be addressed in relation to ensuring it was to be effective. Teaching and learning in the outdoor setting requires teachers to become familiar both with the use of such an educational space and an understanding of the pupils' interaction with it. Particularly significant is the teachers' role in facilitating learning within this new environment, something that is not simply an extension of what happens within the classroom but which demands different pedagogical approaches being designed to maximise every educational opportunity. It cannot be emphasised too strongly that effective classroom practice is not simply transferable to the out-of-classroom context. Good classroom practice is not synonymous with good out-of-classroom practice; additional pedagogical knowledge and understanding is required for the latter.

Student Perspectives

Amongst students in the focus groups this was felt to be an important area of learning. They emphasised the need to stress links between science learning and the external environment of the school, including what children were able to experience in their home environment. Raising the profile of the richness of such experiences was seen as crucial, not only in terms of science knowledge and skills but also in terms of the wider range of relationships with different 'expert' adults that children would encounter, and the differences in ways of learning and knowing between classroom and beyond. These concerns are reflected in the sections below.

Different Views

The Primary National Strategy, Ofsted and the previous Labour government's *Learning Outside the Classroom* manifesto all encourage schools to provide opportunities for pupils to undertake educational experiences that are in locations such as the school grounds, the local community, further afield rural settings and residential activity centres. The Rose Review (2009 – see the weblink below) also strongly articulated this view and despite the official rejection of that review's recommendations by the coalition government there has been and still continues to be a sound case made for the integration of such activities into the school year.

Points for Reflection

Can you remember an out-of-school experience you had at school? Ask friends or family members the same question. Research tells us that these are likely to be the most memorable events of schooling. Why might this be so?

The QTS Standards demand that trainees are able to identify opportunities for pupils to learn in out-of-school contexts (TDA, 2007: see website). Consequently there are implications for teacher training to ensure that student teachers are fully aware of how to best identify, organise and execute strategies for effective teaching and learning outside of the classroom. Many Initial Teacher Education institutions are now addressing this in a positive manner and embracing the principle that novice teachers need to be prepared for teaching outside of traditional classroom settings. Some are incorporating trainee experiences of working with children in non-school settings as part of their school experience (Peacock and Bowker, 2004).

Some school managers and even teachers will be quick to identify a long list of reasons why they shouldn't become involved with outdoor education – health and safety, bureaucracy, a loss of curriculum time, the threat of litigation, and even union advice. Whilst significant additional demands do exist, especially for out-of-school visits, there is also accessible and helpful support available for the group leader, class teacher and responsible adults. Guidance can be found through the Educational Visits Co-ordinators (EVC) in school, the local authority, some trade unions, the Field Studies Council and the Independent Schools' Adventurous Activities Association (ISAAA). However, ultimately these paperwork demands are there to protect those responsible for this work in the event of any incident. None of these obstacles are insurmountable and ultimately the benefits of undertaking such off-site experiences far outweigh the preparation beforehand. In addition, learning professionals who work in out-of-school settings (e.g. wardens) set very high standards relating to health and safety risk assessments.

Educational Spaces

School teachers and Early Years practitioners manage pupils' transition from home to school or nursery (Aikenhead, 1996). They support pupils in recognising that the 'rules' are different and there are expectations in terms of their behaviour and engagement within the classroom. There is a growing body of knowledge to suggest that when undertaking a visit beyond the classroom pupils require similar support in understanding and making sense of this new space. Will the rules be the same as in school? Are the expectations of them in school transferable to this different setting? What will the buildings be like? Will there be toilets? Can they work with a friend? Where are they allowed to go?

In helping pupils make this transition it is essential that teachers recognise some of the key differences between the contrasting 'cultures' they will experience. The impact of those differences observed and experienced by pupils will be determined to a significant extent by their own history – namely what experience they have had before of the environment they are going into. For example, a pupil going into the countryside for the first time is likely to experience different emotions, anxieties and pleasures compared to a pupil who is familiar with life in a rural setting. Likewise the use of school grounds and surrounding area is able to offer venues for supporting the teaching of science in familiar and 'safe' settings in the pupils' eyes.

There are different views as to how pupils' learning can be maximised when outside the classroom. Some believe that a location or venue offering novelty value can add to their experience and learners are likely to take much more from it. For others the need to fully prepare children for the context in which they will be working is paramount as novelty-related anxieties and concerns will be minimised. What is unarguable here is the need for teachers to be prepared for working in non-traditional spaces. They must have formulated clear ideas of how any transition can be best managed in order to enhance pupils' experiences. All too often the move into these new educational spaces will happen with minimum or no prior planning, preparation and thought being given to the pedagogical approaches required.

Of paramount importance to any trip is the safety of all individuals (this includes staff!) involved. It is for this reason that drawing upon the support of the EVC or LA as necessary is essential and should be seen as a means for helping the staff involved not hindering them. A sufficient and considered risk assessment (again, with support from those with experience and often the training for doing so) and its necessary paperwork (written parental consent, emergency contact details, up-to-date medical information) are there to serve the safety and sound planning of off-site visits. Using museums, specialist centres and locations that are designed for supporting educational visits can often offer additional support in the form of prepared risk assessments and guides for teachers which will in turn minimise the administrative burden. Indeed a collaborative approach between school and venue at this stage can only strengthen the preparation and often result in a much more thorough, detailed and realistic assessment of the location. The documentation supporting teachers in the organisation of trips is usually in the form of *guidance* rather than legislative. There is a tension here in that it would be unadvisable not to follow the guidance and adhere to the recommendations offered to ensure that in the event of any incident due process can be argued as having been followed: however, this should be seen as a minimum requirement rather than being the only aspect of planning, as discussed below.

   Points for Reflection

Some students on an ITE course were taken to the theatre for the first time. Just before the end of the interval their tutor saw them sitting in different seats that someone else had booked. She went to the students to explain that they were only allowed to sit in the seats they had purchased. Why did they move? Should the students have known that they were confined to sitting in their own seats? Does a theatre have its own conventions? How are these learnt? Who teaches them? How do individuals feel when they contravene such expectations?

Identify a situation where you have moved from one particular space where you felt comfortable and secure in terms of what was expected from you (e.g. your home) to somewhere completely new. How were you helped with the transition into this new experience?

Now think of a child settled in the ways of their classroom. This child with little or no preparation is taken on a short residential visit to an outdoor centre. What professionally-related issues should the teacher be aware of? How should the teacher access and develop these?

Planning and Preparation

Beyond these bureaucratic issues teachers also need to plan the trip very carefully in terms of teaching and learning opportunities. But how these will be managed and facilitated when out-of-school can often be overlooked, even though these are the reasons for undertaking the visit in the first place. Most experienced teachers would acknowledge the benefits of providing pupils with such opportunities. They can recognise the potential benefit of making links to school for the curriculum, positive social impact, improved pupil-pupil/pupil-teacher/teacher-pupil interaction, greater collaboration and cooperation and that non-conformist, poorly behaved pupils tend to respond extremely positively in alternative settings. Prior to taking their Year 5 class on a two-day residential, some primary teachers suggested the following varied reasons for undertaking the trip:

* *It fits in with science particularly and the wider geography/environmental side.*
* *They are teaching life skills, science skills ...*

- *I think it's things like teamwork and other experiences that they cannot or are unable to get in their normal everyday lives.*

Often outdoor visits will have to be justified via a rationale that is rooted in delivering a school-based curriculum. It is not unreasonable then to question why there is so little planning put into how these links can be best explored and how teaching needs to be adapted to fully support pupil learning. Those additional benefits (social, personal and behavioural) which seemed incidental at the planning stage, that will happen anyway, are often the most memorable outcomes (for both pupils and teachers). How much greater would the benefits be if this was more effectively managed and supported by teachers? It is only through recognising that different educational spaces cannot all be treated the same way that a teacher's pedagogical content knowledge (PCK: see Chapter 8) is extended and the educational benefits of these experiences become improved.

Points for Reflection

Think about planning, organising and delivering a practical science activity for children working in groups of four in school. Now imagine doing the same but in the school grounds or as part of a day visit to an outdoor centre or a visit to the coast. It what ways would they be the similar? It what ways would they be the different? What would you feel most secure with? Why? You may wish to refer back to the previous box.

Planning and preparation for any educational visit require the teacher to question far more than the logistics of the trip – for example, being reflective and challenging their own position in relation to managing transitions between different spaces, recognising where alternative pedagogical approaches can be used and planning to specifically support pupils' cognitive, personal and social development are all part of the challenge of teaching effectively in the outdoor setting, as is anticipating any potential distractions such as the museum shop.

Discourse

Teachers with experience of taking pupils out of school will offer examples of children manifesting different behaviours in these circumstances compared with those observed in a traditional classroom setting. Recognising these differences is not enough however, as there is an educational imperative to gain as much as possible from the visit; it is not sufficient simply to conclude that the children had a great time which most will anyway! Considering how an educational space 'talks' (the discourse of spaces) to individuals, and the relationship that becomes established within that space, impacts hugely on pupil behaviour. Teachers on visits, especially residential ones, are often more 'themselves' which can have a profound and positive impact upon pupils. It is something which is commonly recognised by the staff and pupils alike:

- *You take off your teacher clothes and put on your jeans or whatever it is and suddenly you are different … it challenges their views of you. (class teacher)*
- *It is really different – well, firstly because the teacher was different and secondly because we didn't have to do numeracy. (Year 5 pupil)*
- *In school he is shouty and strict … here he was jokey and more playful. (Year 5 pupil)*

That teachers often lose their institutional identity presents its own challenges. How can we balance being a teacher (with all its tags, labels and expectations) in this new setting where we are able to function differently as professionals? Not all teachers can manage this successfully which is one reason why good classroom practice does not equate with good out-of-classroom practice. The shift to another different identity resulting in a manifestation of different relationships with pupils requires some thought. How does the novice teacher find this out? Can this be taught and if so, by who, when and where? Indeed should this be taught?

So transitions need to be managed by teachers – but what about pupils? Who brokers such transitions for them? Let's just consider the importance of those rules which are an important feature of schooling. Transiting from a place where there are established rules and expectations to another where different conventions exist may prove challenging. The words of another Year 5 pupil illustrate this nicely:

- *There are rules, but they weren't hard rules … it's somewhere where there was a big adventure.*

Preparing pupils for any contrasting culture they are due to experience must help not least with their ability to make sense of both the physical context and of the rules associated with it. This is just as essential as good planning and helps to bridge the gap between pupils' expectations (and concerns or anxieties) and the reality of the situation that will be faced.

Extending Pedagogical Content Knowledge (PCK)

Most teachers will quite reasonably adopt an institutional identity ('school teacher') and their classroom pedagogy and practice will reflect this institutionalised culture. Teachers teach in certain ways and use pedagogical approaches that are aimed to enhance teaching and learning primary science within the classroom. There is a real danger of assuming that what works well within the classroom will also work well outside of it. Pupils can often respond very positively to 'experts' at centres for educational visits, compared to the way they will relate to their own teachers. Often these individuals will use their first name, are not always formally dressed and perceived by children as being important (because they 'know more') but NOT to have a 'teacher' identity. Their pedagogical relationship with the pupils is often fundamentally different from that of the teacher.

An example of this is taken from two Year 5 pupils on a residential discussing the Education Manager and her approach:

- *She was really good at telling us stuff ... I think she was a bit like a teacher because she was in charge like a teacher ...*
- *She was a lot different to teachers in school and I think Mr H* [their class teacher] *has learned from her because he has been doing what she was doing since we came back to school.*

Teachers need to consider different pedagogical approaches in light of the new culture pupils (and teachers) are working in. Whereas staff in out-of-classroom venues and residential centres will often have a good understanding of effective practice in the primary classroom it is unusual for the reverse to be true for class teachers. There is a tendency for teachers to hand over the responsibility for learning to 'experts' in venues for visits, with teachers supporting pupils in terms of behaviour and to a lesser extent enhancing their knowledge and understanding. To maximise the learning potential, whether conceptual, personal or social, it is essential that teachers organise pre-trip visits to the venue so that an effective collaboration can be planned for.

Points for Reflection

Who should go on a pre-trip visit? When should this be done? How might this help extend a student's or a teacher's PCK? List all the things that you think are important to be found out.

Helping pupils to develop their conceptual knowledge and understanding of science (e.g. through pond dipping) requires some additional practitioner considerations. Whilst some basic principles can be upheld (group work, problem solving, investigation, enquiry) the approach to these will require extending our classroom practice. It is only through adapting and extending the PCK of a classroom teacher (i.e. by helping them acquire content-specific approaches through models, analogies, etc.) that these out-of-classroom educational experiences will become effective. All too often they will accept learning outside the classroom as being incidental with much of the learning described as being socially related. These claims are often based upon a tacit understanding (beliefs rooted in craft knowledge) of how pupils are working and what they are seen to be doing.

Such a strong professional instinct which tells teachers that pupils are making progress will usually lack any real supporting evidence. Assessment for Learning (AfL) including Assessing Pupils' Progress (APP) techniques can capture such data (see below) which will also help strengthen arguments related to the benefits of working in such settings. It is not an onerous task to make a shift with this and be able to have real confidence that pupils are developing and progressing their knowledge and understanding in science.

Assessing Learning out of School

In a time of changing assessment regimes and an increased reliance upon formative assessment this is a prime opportunity for teachers to use additional sources of evidence to support their assessment of pupils' learning. All aspects of teaching outside of the classroom are able to provide assessment evidence for primary science APP. Some examples for pond dipping are included in Table 6.1 below, however these assessment focuses are easily transferable to other science-related activities (e.g. a farm visit, sound trail, building materials survey, investigating types of litter, a minibeast hunt, light and shadow formation, measuring tasks, collection tasks – different types of leaves and so on) and they are also able to support assessment in forms other than APP and exemplify general good practice.

Table 6.1   APP and pond dipping activity

Assessment focus	Examples
AF1 Thinking scientifically	• How will we catch the animals? • Where do the animals live? • What can we do with the animals when we have caught them? • How must we treat the animals?
AF2 Understanding the applications and implications of science	• Will the animals we find be found in other ponds? • Will the animals we find be found in streams and rivers? • What would happen if all the ... were removed from the pond? • What would happen if the number of ... in the pond increased?
AF3 Communicating and collaborating in science	• How will we record what we have found? • Are there different ways to do this? • How can we share what you have found with those back at school? • How well did we work together? • Did everyone have a chance to use the net?
AF4 Using investigative approaches	• How many different types of animals and plants live in the pond? (you do not have to know their names) • Do all the animals live in the same part of the pond? • Are all the plants found in the same part of the pond?
AF5 Working critically with evidence	• Why did some groups find different animals? • Not all the nets were the same. Did this matter? • Even if we hadn't found a frog how would we know this is a good place for them to live?

It is only through careful planning that assessment becomes most effective. Part of the joy of this sort of experience is not being hampered by curricular constraints yet having some thought being applied to intended learning objectives and outcomes. This can be done prior to the visit, and if appropriate, in consultation with venue staff – something that should not limit but enhance learning opportunities.

Points for Reflection

Consider the pond dipping activity and the need for (i) Year 2 and (ii) Year 6 to use identification guides. How would this be differentiated for each age group? Which APP assessment focus(es) would apply? Is any preparation required prior to the visit and use of the guides? If so, what would this be?

What is important here is that teachers are open to the notion of challenging the views they hold of pupils based upon conformity (or not!) within the classroom environment. One teacher describes an experience on a residential trip with a Year 5:

- *My biggest surprise was I think all the preconceived ideas I had about this class just flew out of the window ... so from my point of view just actually seeing them in that situation and in such positive light was brilliant.*

This was mirrored by a member of staff working in a residential centre who said that:

- *We don't have any preconceptions of kids ... we don't know that the day before they did something really awful to somebody or we don't know if that kid never behaves in class ... that gives a sense of freedom to them. It means they can be themselves a little bit more.*

Points for Reflection

Imagine sixteen 10 year-old boys from a primary school on a rock-pooling expedition; it's a fine, sunny morning and they are all excited, since they have never been to this cove before. However, three boys (two of whom are known to have behavioural problems) have come without their Wellington boots. What will happen? Much depends on who is hosting the visit. Their teacher, as well as wanting the children to carry out science observations, make drawings and ask questions, might also be conscious of health and safety issues as well as maintaining behavioural

(Continued)

(Continued)

standards; in effect she is likely to be 'taking the classroom with her', so these three might be asked to sit out the session on the rocks to help them remember their footwear next time.

In this case, however, they are accompanied not by a teacher but by the National Trust Warden (a parent and governor of the school) close to where the school was located. His perception is that they will come to no harm and will be less trouble if fully engaged in the activity, so lets them go into the water in their trainers. He is only able to take this line because of a long-standing tradition of collaboration between himself and the school staff. The boys produce wonderful colour drawings of the shrimps they catch and observe; an example of learning being dependent on the specific context in which it takes place, or the *micro-context* of learning.

Returning to the Classroom

As well as bridging the transit from the classroom to beyond there is a need to plan for pupils returning to it. Educational experiences outside the classroom are often, as previously suggested, not fully prepared for and likewise little consideration is usually given to the impact of moving back into the classroom. A follow-up worksheet, dealing with the visit in science time three days after a visit, or treating this as a discrete event does not support pupils in making sense of the cultural, personal, social or cognitive experiences they have had. Upon returning from a visit to a local science museum, one support assistant suggested that the teacher should forget the planning and give them a visit-based literacy lesson to help the children get the excitement of *what they had done* out of their systems.

Table 6.2 Any outdoor activity e.g. pond dipping (even with a local expert leading this!)

Some Important Do's	Some Important Don'ts
Know what they are likely to find.	Rely on local expert knowledge alone.
Know how to use the basic equipment.	Limit the children's focus.
Participate. Children want to see you involved and enthusiastic.	Limit learning to curriculum-specific goals.
Plan for informal learning opportunities.	Expect learning to simply happen.
Give the children decision-making opportunities.	Assume what works well in school (e.g. group structure) will work out-of-classroom.
Accept high levels of motivation (often manifested as noise and even giddiness).	Ignore the need to follow up an activity.

There is a tacit requirement for debriefing the children especially after residential visits of even two days duration. Once again planning is critically important and if this is done well it will facilitate both teachers and learners in making more sense of why the visit took place. An effective follow-up is not writing thank you letters as part of a literacy lesson. There is another time and place for such obvious tokenism; carefully planned wraparound teaching will be far more productive. We have seen that stark contrasts between the cultures of any outdoor setting and the classroom exist which, when combined with a strong tendency for teachers to quickly return to their dominant institutional identity, have the potential to result in a significant and arguably detrimental impact upon the pupils. The excitement, motivation and stimulation as a result of learning outside the classroom can be easily lost through falling back into the routine that this culture can demand if this is not actively managed by the classroom teacher. It takes a great deal of conscious effort on a teacher's part not to lose the potential in these situations and indeed to harness and sustain the positive impact of this novel learning experience.

Points for Reflection

Think about the activities that can be done to support the transition from the out-of-classroom context back into the traditional setting. How can the experience be used to support teaching and learning? Are there strategies you can employ to harness the enthusiasm from the visit? Is there a way of using some of the effective teaching strategies from the out-of-classroom experience to encourage, engage and motivate otherwise reluctant pupils?

Too often off-site visits are one-off events and few science learning opportunities are experienced serially outside of the classroom or with repeated visits to an educational venue. Serial visits to the same venue are more likely to result in greater and longer-term cognitive, personal and social benefits, although set against all this is the time cost of being away from school. Using science to enhance and support teaching in other areas of the curriculum and to develop transferable skills should counter such argument but this is reliant on accepting how time (and science) can be used across the primary curriculum.

This chapter assumes that the true purpose behind out-of-classroom visits is firmly located in being educative. 'Trips' out, though, are often referred to by teachers as rewards and treats and can be used to bargain with children in relation to behaviour goals. Whilst out-of-classroom visits should be enjoyable for pupils it is arguable that they will be far more rewarding if they are planned with learning as a central component. It is ironic that pupils are threatened with not being able to go on a trip if they do not behave when, as previously mentioned, trips are often so closely linked with the curriculum; if this is the case then why deny any pupil the opportunity to learn? Rarely are pupils faced with the sanction of not being able to attend a numeracy or literacy lesson for misbehaving.

Planning

- Identify where curricular links exist and what objectives are to be met with success criteria.
- Explore ways to teach this content – taking into account the new culture, discourse, objects and artefacts and the impact of these upon the behaviour and social interactions of pupils.
- Ensure that activities are structured and planned to actively promote learning and social interaction.
- Take care not to assume that what works in the classroom also works outside it – if the pupils, physical context and teachers change then so does the pedagogy.
- Plan time to debrief the children, something that becomes more important as the time spent offsite increases as on a residential visit.

Preparation

- Ensure that there is active management of the transition to the new learning environment and going back to the classroom.
- Take into account pupil history and the potential impact of novelty value.
- Determine to what extent pupils are anxious about this as opposed to it offering excitement.
- Accept that some teaching approaches used by staff at outdoor centres will be different from those seen in the classroom. Use this to seek opportunities to also expand your PCK.

We have seen that the use of outdoor settings for teaching and learning has the ability to create a very memorable learning experience for pupils. Pupils, many years on, will be able to share memories of trips which they took whilst at school, something they are much less likely to be able to do with classroom-based experiences. This highlights the educational potential of these often underused locations to have a significant impact on individuals and indicates that if teaching is planned and appropriate practice is adopted, there exists a powerful source for supporting learners and learning which is not being fully tapped into by primary teachers.

Summary

The most important point that this chapter has raised is that of not making assumptions – assumptions that all good practice is transferable without extension, that learning will happen, that planning is either unnecessary or constraining, that visits can function well as standalone events. It has challenged these views and suggests that teachers need to reflect upon their pedagogy and practice dependent upon the context and consciously embrace the need to manage transitions from one culture to another by first identifying that these different cultures do exist and then establishing what this means for the pupils and teachers involved.

References

Aikenhead, G.S. (1996) 'Science education: border crossing in to the subculture of science', *Studies in Science Education*, 72: 1–52.

Peacock, A. & Bowker, R. (2004) 'Learning to teach 'science' out of school: non-school placements as part of a Primary PGCE Programme', *Education and Training*, 46 (1): 24–32.

Rickinson, M., Dillon, J., Kelly, T., Morris, M., Young Choi, M., Sanders, D. & Benefield, P. (2004) *A Review of Research on Outdoor Learning*. London: National Foundation for Educational Research and Kings College, London.

Weblinks

Learning Outside the Classroom (n.d.) available at www.lotc.org.uk/

This government website is supportive of the rationale for undertaking work outside the classroom. It offers a range of resources and activities that can be carried out within the school grounds as well as advice for further afield and more adventurous activities.

ISAAA (n.d.) available at www.isaaa.co.uk/

This website was established for teachers in independent schools falling outside of the support offered through Local Authorities. It offers practical and general advice for any form of adventurous activities and general principles of safe practice which can be applied to an off-site visit.

The Rose Review (2009) available at http://publications.education.gov.uk/default. aspx?PageFunction=productdetails&PageMode=publications&ProductId=D CSF-00499-2009

A government commissioned review of the primary curriculum, published in 2009, and accepted by the then Labour government, but rejected by the Coalition in 2010.

TDA (2007) available at www.tda.gov.uk/teacher/developing-career/professional-standards-guidance.aspx

Further Reading

Dillon, J., Morris, M., Reid, A., Scott, W. & Rickinson, M. (2006) 'Education! Education! Out! Out! Out!', *Primary Science Review*, 91: 4–6.
A brief and readily accessible article examining what outdoor education involves, identifying the benefits, its relationship and value to the school curriculum and what are the most effective approaches.

Field Studies Council and Association for Science Education (2007) *Initial Teacher Education and the Outdoor Classroom: Standards for the Future. A report on the training of pre-service teachers to support the development of outdoor teaching in secondary science education*. Hatfield: ASE Publications.
Do not be put off by the 'secondary' emphasis as there is lots of content useful to anyone thinking about working beyond the classroom. This report is available as a PDF file from the FSC website as are a number of other relevant publications.

Peacock, A. & Dunne. M.J. (2005) 'Learning Science outside the Classroom'. In W. Harlen (ed.), *ASE Guide to Primary Science*. Hatfield: ASE.
This pragmatic chapter provides a useful rationale for this type of educational experience, the do's and don'ts of outdoor work and a wide range of exemplars of good practice. This publication provides a wide range of useful guidance for any teacher of primary science.

Waite, S. (ed.)(2011) *Children Learning Outside the Classroom from Birth to Eleven*. London: Sage.
This new text reviews recent research at both the Foundation/Early Years and Primary stages from a socio-cultural perspective, drawing lessons from this for your teaching.

CHAPTER 7

CHILDREN COMMUNICATING SCIENCE

Sarah Earle and Natasha Serret

Chapter Overview

This chapter begins with a discussion of the different types of classroom talk, and why these are important for children's development in cognitive, social and emotional terms. It highlights how such kinds of talk have been traditionally under-emphasised in the primary classroom and thus develops various frameworks for supporting the development of talk, including the planning of questioning, opportunities for debate and role-play, and providing learners with important things to talk about which will link discussion to ethical and moral issues in science. The chapter goes on to examine the importance of the teacher as a role model – as listener, enthusiast, creator of environments and provider of effective starting points. Examples of effective communication are then provided from the authors' own classroom, and the use of video is discussed as a means for learners to evaluate and peer assess their own activity.

Introduction

In a recent book, *Exploring Talk in School*, Mercer and Hodgkinson proposed that classroom talk, '… is the most important educational tool for guiding the development of understanding and for jointly constructing knowledge' (2008: xi). Yet talking seems such an instinctive and spontaneous activity do we really need to plan for it? Or teach it? Or assess it? Won't it just happen naturally anyway?

Considerable research, indeed over thirty years' worth, suggests we do. In this chapter we start with a brief theoretical overview that highlights some of the reasons why we need to consider talk and indicate how the quality of classroom talk could be improved. We then draw from these theoretical principles to explore, in subsequent sections, the teacher's role in improving communication in primary science, pedagogical approaches and the resources that will encourage children to communicate in science. Finally, we consider how classroom talk in primary science can provide some powerful and insightful assessment evidence of children's learning.

Student Perspectives

Our focus groups emphasised the importance of talk and discussion as a way of revealing children's misconceptions and curiosity about when (and when not) to use ICT in the communication process. We have tried to deal with these in what follows.

If the learning environment enables children to express what they really think about science, then their talk can be a rich source of evidence of their learning. In particular, it can reveal the alternative conceptions that they hold about key scientific ideas. This enables teachers to tailor their subsequent responses and further teaching to address these specific alternative concepts. In this chapter, we shall talk about the kind of learning environment needed to encourage this kind of talk and the kinds of teacher questions that can help prompt children to share what they think – not what feel they ought to say to keep the teacher happy.

The potential use of debates, discussions, role-plays and children communicating science to the world outside school is also examined.

Debates and role-plays are excellent creative opportunities that, when used within the context of primary science, can powerfully illustrate the reality of science beyond the classroom. There is therefore a whole section within this chapter that contains some practical and relevant examples that can be used as starting points for debates and role-plays. This section also begins to explore the ethical dimension of debates within science and how this way of teaching and learning can highlight how in science we will weigh up the scientific evidence and consider a range of perspectives before arriving at an informed opinion.

When ICT can Help and When it Gets in the Way of Science Talk

ICT can be a powerful way of stimulating and recording science talk. Children find its use very motivating, thus thoughtful discussions can be provoked by a video clip on an interactive whiteboard or by asking pupils to work together to create a PowerPoint presentation. The case study at the end of this chapter examines how video can be used to support children to discuss their own investigative work. The section on starting points highlights a number of resources, for example, virtual experiments which can be compared with a real class investigation and used to support understanding. ICT can also sometimes present technical demands which mean that the focus rests more on how to get something working rather than on the science involved. Nevertheless, as long as it is used in a focused way, ICT can complement rather than replace practical work.

What do we Know about Communication and Learning?

Talk is a tool for cognitive development

Vygotsky (1978, 1986) used a term called *semiotic mediation* to describe the processes we use to make and convey meaning. This emphasised the critical role of social interaction in cognitive development. Research into classroom talk often starts from this Vygotskian premise and his work can provide a good theoretical rationale as to why improving the quality of classroom talk is so fundamental to learning.

According to Vygotsky, we use psychological tools (or mediating artefacts) to construct understanding together. A key tool that is used in society is language. The triangle below explains how this works and the examples in brackets illustrate how this might translate in a primary science classroom:

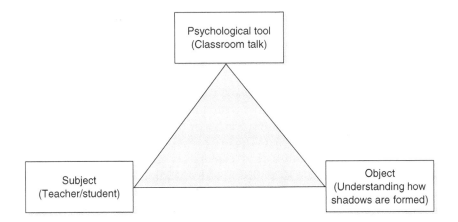

Figure 7.1   Vygotsky's mediational triangle

Constructing a scientific explanation of shadow formation is best supported through practical activity (e.g. making shadows in the playground, making shadow puppets, exploratory work with torches and transparent/opaque materials). However, this practical activity doesn't occur in a verbal vacuum. It is the language (the 'talk') used by the children as they share what they notice with each other, the questions they ask, and the skilful teacher's verbal and non-verbal (para-linguistic) interventions that will enable scientific understanding to arise from this experience.

There is more than one type of classroom talk. Different types of talk serve different educational purposes.

In his seminal (1976) book *From Communication to Curriculum*, Barnes drew from his longitudinal observations of classroom talk to suggest there are two distinct forms of talk used in the classroom. His *presentational* talk describes the verbal interactions that children use to demonstrate what they know. This talk is often directed through teacher questions that seek to check or communicate specific pieces of knowledge. His *exploratory* talk describes the kinds of talk that children use to think aloud. This is where the teacher creates opportunities and a learning environment where children ask questions (e.g. *'What if I ... ?'*) and provide tentative explanations (e.g. *'Maybe it is because ... '*). In these instances, children's talk can be spontaneous, messy, and partially formed.

Consequent research has developed this idea to suggest there are multiple forms of classroom talk, each serving a specific purpose. Mercer's (1996a, b) work helped to articulate the progression that children can make when talking together in small groups. In this context, children's talk starts from single-word utterances (*disputational talk*) and moves towards repeating and reinforcing ideas (*cumulative talk*) and ideally reaches a stage (*exploratory talk*) where longer utterances, signalled by phrases such as 'I think ... because ... ' are used to co-construct understanding through their talk. The kinds of groundrules and activities needed to encourage exploratory talk can be found in a teacher-friendly publication, *Thinking Together* (Dawes et al., 2000).

Alexander (2008) considers the entire oral repertoire available to a classroom teacher which acknowledges the place and purpose of more common oral teacher-led techniques: *rote* (using repetition to transmit facts), *recitation* (building knowledge by using questions to stimulate recall) and *instruction/exposition* (explaining information or instructions). All rely heavily on the teacher whose role is to provide knowledge. Alexander introduces a further facet to the teacher repertoire called *dialogic teaching*. Sharing many characteristics with Barnes' exploratory talk, *discussion* (students share ideas) and *scaffolded dialogue* (a common understanding achieved through cumulative discussion and questioning by students and the teacher) complete Alexander's oral repertoire.

The full learning potential of talk is often under-utilised in primary classrooms.

These frameworks, that help to characterise the different kinds of classroom talk, often stem from prior research that implies that there is an over-use of the kinds of talk used to transmit/reinforce knowledge and understanding and an insufficient use of talk that allows children to think aloud. This can be especially challenging in the primary science classroom, where teachers not only feel pressured to teach science as a body of knowledge but also want to promote science as a process of enquiry.

In order to readjust the balance between teacher-led and student-initiated talk within the context of science classrooms, Mortimer and Scott (2003) offer a way of looking – a 'communicative approach' – at a sequence of teacher-student interactions in two dimensions that each run along a continuum. One dimension (*non-interactive-interactive*) describes the degree of interaction between teacher and students. The other dimension (*authoritative-dialogic*) describes the extent to which student ideas are being accounted for in the talk. We will return to some of these theoretical ideas and explore how they might translate into classroom practice in the consequent sections.

How Can We, as Teachers, Improve Communication in Primary Science Classrooms?

There is a lot of good practice already in place in the primary science classroom. However, there are always opportunities to improve. The questions below may help to encourage and structure a reflection on your existing practice in relation to how talk is used in your primary science classroom.

Do I plan my questions? What kinds of questions do I use? Do I use a wide range of questions? What kinds of questions do I need to include more of?

Sometimes, especially when trying to plan for a science investigation, we can get so caught up with ensuring there are enough resources that there will be little time left to actually consider and write down some key questions. These are a critical part of the lesson as they can help to promote the conversations we have with the children, their own talk as they engage in practical or non-practical tasks and activities or as a whole class when they reflect on their findings. Furthermore, without planning for our questions, there is no guarantee that a range of questions (both open and closed) will be asked or that these will stimulate differentiated levels of higher order thinking. One useful framework is Bloom's Taxonomy (Anderson and Krathwohl, 2001: 67–68). Table 7.1 below

Table 7.1   Bloom's Taxonomy

Bloom's hierarchy of thinking skills	Suggested questions
Remembering: Retrieving, recognising, and recalling relevant knowledge from long-term memory.	*What can you say about … ?*
Understanding: Constructing meaning through interpreting, exemplifying, classifying, summarising, inferring, comparing, and explaining.	*How did you decide to sort … ?* *I'm not sure I understand, can you explain … ?*
Applying: Carrying out or using a procedure through executing or implementing.	*Does this remind you of anything we have done before?*
Analysing: Breaking material into its constituent parts, determining how the parts relate to one another and to an overall structure or purpose through differentiating, organising, and attributing.	*What were some of the problems with … ?* *Can you explain why … ?*
Evaluating: Making judgments based on criteria and standards through checking and critiquing.	*What changes would you recommend?* *Is this the only way to investigate…?*
Creating: Putting elements together to form a coherent or functional whole; reorganising elements into a new pattern or structure through generating, planning, or producing.	*I wonder what would happen if … ?*

offers ideas as to how different questions could address Bloom's hierarchy of thinking skills. You can also use this to do a self- or peer-audit of the kinds of questions you currently use. Some teachers conclude that while a lot of their questions encourage remembering and understanding, they need to plan more questions that will stimulate analysis, evaluation and creating. The questions in Table 7.1 are not just a tool for the teacher, they could also go up as a classroom display or be given out to groups to support and encourage children to ask both themselves and each other a range of questions.

Do I plan for creative opportunities where talk is a vital component of learning such as debates and role-plays?

As well as improving the quality of talk that we and children use in practical science investigations, we need to think about other, more creative, drama-based learning experiences that will not only provide the potential for children to develop their ability to talk but will also allow them to experience science through other contexts. Littledyke (2004) presents a range of cross-curricular ideas that meaningfully use science and drama to stimulate learning. In particular, he suggests real-life simulations such as children taking on the role of the 'expert' (e.g. teaching younger children, explaining our planet to aliens) or using an interview format or the role of a presenter on a TV or radio documentary (think David Attenborough or the BBC's *Springwatch*!) to create their own science show where they may communicate their understanding of a particular science topic.

Debates that consider the ethical, environmental and moral consequences of science-based issues – such as *'What are the economic consequences of whaling?', 'Which is more important – the trees that will need to be cut down or the new climbing frame for our school?', 'Should we rescue marine mammals that become stranded?'* and *'Why are plastics dangerous to wildlife?'* – are addressed practically and in depth in a whole issue of *Primary Science* (2008) devoted to science and ethics. The rationale for raising these kinds of dilemmas in a primary science classroom is clear: we live within a global community where, as citizens, we are constantly making choices. The choices we make will have an immediate and far-reaching impact on other people and our planet. If we can introduce the concept of a debate within a science context, we are helping our children to recognise that the world of science isn't always 'black and white' and that it is important to consider the evidence available and acknowledge a range of perspectives before reaching a well-informed conclusion. This type of engagement provides a super opportunity for an authentic way of linking this sort of work with primary citizenship (i.e. decision making and personal responsibility). Such work also actively encourages our learners to become even more scientifically literate.

For example, a class debate on the plight of the red squirrel could start with research into why their numbers have declined since the introduction of the grey squirrel. Teams could propose the grey squirrel should be culled (since it can eat unripe nuts which leaves none for the reds who must wait for the Summer ripening) or that the reds should be fed – or even that they should be left to become extinct since they are not as well adapted as the greys. Such a debate not only develops speaking and listening skills it also requires an understanding of ecosystems, food chains and evolution.

As well as simply having a classroom debate relevant contexts such as a 'question-time panel', a 'government or council meeting' or a 'law court' (Littledyke, 2004) can help children to step away from their opinion and see different dilemmas through other people's eyes, something which is highly relevant to good quality citizenship education. Debates and role-play situations are valuable opportunities for learning science through talk. They provide children with rich illustrations of how communication supports science in the 'real-world' that exists beyond the classroom. It prepares them so they can begin to actively engage with science communication outside of school through media such as local and national newspapers, the radio, TV and the internet. Debates and role-plays are also sensitive contexts that require support, time and a safe learning environment where children can learn to express their points of view and use science to provide reasons for their opinions (Bianchi et al., 2008).

A good example of a cross-curricular role play comes from *Rational Food* (Bird and Saunders 2007). Whilst studying rationing during the Second World War, children are asked to use their knowledge of healthy diets to decide who should be allowed to have extra rations. One way of setting up the debate is to ask pupils to take on the roles of people who are asking for extra rations (e.g. a pregnant woman, a mother of two, a recovering soldier) and to state their case in front of a panel of judges. Alternatively, the children can work in teams to present each case and then come out of the role to vote on the most deserving case.

What kind of role model am I?

A teacher can be a powerful model for children in terms of the subtle and informal behaviours and exchanges they have in the classroom. Teachers can promote the attitudes and characteristics of the enquiring scientist, not just in their actions but also in what they say. Investigate alongside the children and ask questions like, '*I wonder what would happen if …* ' or '*Is this the only way to investigate …* '? Model how important it is to back up scientific thinking with evidence by using phrases like, '*I think this because …* ' Create a climate where learning from others ('*You have changed my thinking …*'), asking questions ('*I wonder why …* '), taking risks, making mistakes and engaging in debate are all part of what it means to be a scientist.

Am I really listening to what the children are saying? How do I respond to what they are saying?

Armed with a set of planned questions, the next step is the follow-up exchanges in response to what the children have said. This is a critical aspect of communication in primary science because how we respond can influence what learners will say next as well as in consequent science lessons. In the initial theoretical section in this chapter we explored how research into classroom talk has suggested that there are many purposes and types of classroom talk. Using communication effectively can feel like a balancing act – trying to satisfy the learning objectives/outcomes, laid out in our science plans, within a limited time frame while also trying to give children the freedom, time and space to explore their ideas and think aloud. It may often feel like there is an overwhelming pressure to 'get through the curriculum'.

This can influence a teacher's perception of the purpose of primary science and their role within this. This in turn can block out our ability to listen to what children are actually saying. While they are trying to articulate their explanations, we may be thinking, '*What do they need to know … is what they are saying the right answer … what can I say next to ensure the whole class grasp the science objective?*'. As a result, the detail of children's talk that can make for meaningful assessments will get lost, teacher questions will become more closed and children will end up using their talk to play a game of

'Guess what is in the teacher's head'. In order to use communication effectively in primary science, we really need to block out these pressures and listen carefully to what learners are actually saying.

How can we Help Students to Communicate Better in Science?

Getting children talking

If we want to encourage children to participate in a science-based dialogue then we need each of the following:

- *Something to talk about*, e.g. a surprising stimulus, like a giant footprint or body outline on the floor, will immediately get children talking.
- *Time,* for the children to think, explore and clarify their ideas for the 'exploratory talk' discussed above.
- *Someone to talk to*, e.g. using talk partners or learning buddies.
- A *safe place to talk*, namely a classroom climate where talk is valued.

The first step in setting up a learning environment where it is safe to talk is to emphasise the importance of listening. Students will be more likely to share their ideas if they know they will be listened to, both by their teacher and their peers. We must make it clear that sharing ideas is not 'cheating' and that working collaboratively as a pair, a small group or class reflects how scientists work. It remains a popular myth that science is all about facts and hence answers are right or wrong; in actual fact scientists are much more hesitant, acknowledging unknowns and having tentative theories that can be disproved but never proven. As discussed in the previous section, in the classroom we need to create a climate where it is OK to be wrong or not to know – 'being stuck' is often where science starts. When the teacher thinks aloud and admits that they do not know everything, then the children are given permission to do the same. By careful teacher questioning we can actively encourage them to ask questions, to explain their thinking, and to offer opinions.

Starting points for stimulating science talk

Prompts which stimulate talking will also stimulate thinking, so many 'thinking skills' activities can be easily transferred to a science context. For example, de Bono's PMI activities (http://schoolnet.gov.mt/thinkingskills/thinkingtools.htm) are where children can list the **P**ositives, **M**inuses and **I**nteresting points of a particular situation, like a world with no friction or what life would be like if you had an ear in the middle of your hand (Coates and Wilson, 2003). Such open-ended discussions underline the importance of creative thought and applying and linking knowledge and emphasise that there are no right or wrong answers.

Concept cartoons (Naylor and Keogh, 2001) can provide a starting point for any class, but are particularly effective for those children who are hesitant to join in with discussions in case they are 'wrong'. Cartoon children provide people who can be agreed or disagreed with, which is a lot less scary than putting forward your own ideas. If these given viewpoints are presented by a puppet, then a real discussion can happen between the children and the teacher's hand! Using puppets in science is suitable for all ages and there is much support for getting started at www.puppetsproject.com. The puppet presents a problem which the children must help to solve, for example, how to find a cat in the dark. Children may talk directly to the puppet, which is less threatening for those who find it difficult to share their ideas. One of the puppets, Ricky, recently took part in an expedition to the Antarctic, and was supported by survival technique advice provided by children around the country.

Science talk can also begin with a topical news story, like the PDFs produced by Primary Upd8 (www.primaryupd8.org.uk). For example, 'Sorting out the oil spill' examines the effect of BP's offshore drilling disaster in the Gulf of Mexico. This real problem can lead to numerous avenues for discussion, from what is crude oil and why do we need it, to what is the impact on the environment, to how can we separate oil and sea water? Such context-based discussions provide opportunities for further research and discussions with parents.

Virtual experiments can prompt children to predict and explain. Since the results are instant they receive immediate feedback and can focus on any patterns which emerge. For example, in *Collins Virtual Experiments* (www.collinseducation.com) children can spot 'the larger the jar, the longer the candle flame burns' or 'the more sugar, the more the yeast grows, until there's too much sugar'. These discussions are the most meaningful when the children are comparing the virtual experiments to their own investigations: 'Did we find the same pattern?', 'Why are our results different?'.

The resources described above provide opportunities for focused and largely teacher-led discussions. However, arguably the most important science talk will happen when the children are investigating with peers. Sorting and classifying materials, creating their own test for electrical conductivity, timing the length of flight of paper aeroplanes … whichever practical task the children are engaged in will require them to communicate with those around them. Teachers can support these discussions to be more scientific by encouraging children to ask each other 'Why?' – Why do you think that? Why do you want to put that material in that group? Why should we repeat our test? Making the investigations open-ended and giving the children a choice, in equipment or variables, will not only show that you value their opinion, it will also make the sharing of conclusions more interesting since everyone will have approached the task differently.

How can we use communication in assessment for learning?

Every interaction between a pupil and teacher is an assessment opportunity, where we are asking questions which can elicit the child's current understanding. Elicitation activities and the ensuing discussions will provide the teacher with the information needed to plan the next learning opportunities in order that the child's learning is moved on. This can also be done using various techniques like those described in Active Assessment (Naylor and Keogh, 2004), for example KWL grids: what learners think they already **Know** about a topic, what they **Want** to know, then later on, what they have **Learnt** about the topic. (Assessment for Learning is discussed in more detail in Chapter 9.)

Using talk for peer- and self-assessment

In practice, it is very difficult to find the time for extended talk with individual children, meaning that most talk will be short 'checkups' or as part of a class or group discussion. However, learners can have very productive discussions where they reflect on their learning with their peers. Once groundrules for listening are in place, there are a number of frameworks which children can be given to guide the discussion. For example, 'three stars and a wish' involves them choosing three things that they like about their partner's work and one 'wish' for something that could be improved. This kind of structure is frequently used to peer-assess pieces of writing in Literacy, but it is equally valid for science written work or group investigations.

It is essential, however, that children know what good science work 'looks like'. Just as Literacy lessons will often start with developing the success criteria for a particular type of writing, science lessons could begin with a discussion about what will make a good science investigation. Often children will require a concrete example as a starting point for this discussion. With permission, you could show them some examples of a particular aspect of pupil investigative work (a group plan, a table of results, a bar graph, a description of findings or an evaluation). From this, quality indicators could then be developed relating to work in a group, how to carry out a fair test or how to collect and present accurate results. These indicators of quality could then be used by learners to structure their peer- and self-assessments within a discussion context.

The challenge for teachers is to initiate these discussions within a context that will encourage children to remember what they did and reflect on this in a purposeful way. Sometimes, simply asking them to recall what they did will not be enough and the danger will be that children will communicate superficial self- and peer-assessments (e.g. 'He was great at science today!'). One possible approach of stimulating and supporting purposeful pupil assessment discussions is described in the case study below.

Evaluating investigations by discussing video evidence

My Year 6 class would confidently plan and carry out fair tests and present their results, but were at best superficial when evaluating their investigations. When 'caught up' in the practical, the children failed to notice many of the things that were happening and would just say that their investigation was fair/accurate and need not be improved. I hoped that by watching themselves on video it would encourage them to stand back and critically reflect.

The *Popping Pots* investigation involved placing an effervescent vitamin C tablet in a film pot half-filled with water, quickly putting the lid on and waiting for it to pop off. The children chose to change variables such as temperature of water and amount of tablet, whilst they measured the time taken to pop or the distance for the pot lid to land. I videoed the children while they investigated and when they presented their findings to the rest of the class.

Watching clips of themselves definitely held their attention and when asked, the children themselves felt that the video *'helped them to look more closely'*. I used the video clips to stimulate focused, teacher-led discussion about how fair and accurate we could really be. Ordering the variables (on Post-Its) from least- to most-controlled supported the children's evaluations of how fair their investigations were.

The video also supported a discussion of which variables we were able to control (e.g. size of tablet) and which variables were very difficult to control (e.g. temperature of the water). It also helped them to spot variables which they had not considered when deciding on what to 'keep the same' (e.g. type of pot).

I found that video could also support judgements on the accuracy of measurement techniques. It prompted a discussion of reaction times and whether lid landing distance could be considered the same as flight distance.

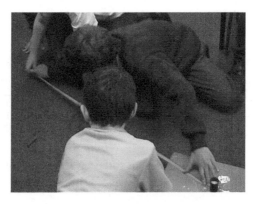

(Photo: the class watched the lids fly in a curve on the video and decided that the measurement along the floor did not accurately reflect how far the lid had travelled.)

Reflecting on investigations and evaluating evidence require 'higher order thinking skills' (see earlier section on Bloom's taxonomy) which involve children stepping back from the practical to look for patterns, to suggest explanations for their findings, and to judge the accuracy, reliability and value of their method (Goldsworthy, 1998). The skill of evaluation is an important component in Black's (2003) Assessment for Learning model; for a learner to make an accurate self-assessment and decide their next steps, they must be able evaluate their own performance. This requires both an ability to step back to judge their own performance, and knowledge of what good practice 'looks like'.

The child's ability to self-assess (like the teacher's ability to assess the child) depends on their knowledge of the subject. By watching and discussing their own investigations the children gained a deeper understanding of scientific enquiry.

Summary

We began the chapter by discussing the importance of classroom talk, in particular the kind of exploratory talk where children think aloud and teachers interact dialogically. In order to raise the quality of talk in this way, teachers need to plan and ask a variety of questions and then listen and respond to what children are saying. This kind of child-teacher interaction needs to be supported within an environment where learners feel safe enough to put their ideas forward. A number of ways of stimulating talk in science were discussed and opportunities for using talk in assessment for learning were also highlighted. By valuing and making time for talk in science we can enable children to develop higher order thinking skills which can be applied across the curriculum, such as we have seen with citizenship education.

References

Alexander, R. J. (2008). *Towards Dialogic Teaching: Rethinking Classroom Talk*. Cambridge: Dialogos.

Barnes, D. (1976). *From Communication to Curriculum.* Harmondsworth: Penguin

Bianchi, L., Bloom, S. & Robins, L. (2008) 'Making tough choices,' *Primary Science*, 104: 9–11.

Black, P. et al. (2003) *Assessment for Learning: Putting it into Practice.* Buckingham: Open University Press.

Coates, D. & Wilson, H. (2003) *Challenges in Primary Science: Meeting the Needs of Able Young Scientists at Key Stage Two*. London: NACE/ Fulton Publication.

Dawes, L., Mercer, N. & Wegerif, R. (2000) *Thinking Together: A Programme of Lessons and Activities*. Birmingham: Questions.

Goldsworthy, A. (1998) 'Learning to Investigate'. In, R. Sherrington (ed.), *ASE Guide to Primary Science Education*. Cheltenham: Stanley Thornes.

Littledyke, M. (2004) 'Drama and Science', *ASE Primary Science Journal,* 84: 14–16.

Mercer, N. (1996a) 'The quality of talk in children's collaborative activity in the classroom'. *Learning and Instruction,* 6 (4): 359–375.

Mercer (1996b) 'Sociocultural Perspectives and the Study of Classroom Discourse.' In C. Coll & D. Edwards (eds) *Discourse and Learning in the Classroom*. Madrid: Infancia and Aprendizaje. pp. 13–23.

Mercer, N. & Hodgkinson, S. (2008) *Exploring Talk in School: Inspired by the Work of Douglas Barnes*. London: Sage.

Mortimer, E.F. & Scott, P.H. (2003) *Meaning making in Secondary Science Classrooms*. Buckingham: OUP.

Naylor, S. & Keogh, B. (2001) *Concept Cartoons in Science Education*. Sandbach, Cheshire: Millgate House.

Naylor, S. & Keogh, B. (2004) *Active Assessment*. Sandbach, Cheshire: Millgate House.

Primary Science Journal (2008) *Focus on Science and Ethics,* No. 104.

Vygotsky, L.S. (1978) *Mind in Society*. Cambridge, MA: Harvard University Press.

Vygotsky, L.S. (1986) *Thought and Language*, (A. Kozulin, ed. and trans.). Cambridge, MA: MIT Press.

Further Reading

Millgate House Publishers will be the place to go for further ideas to stimulate children communicating in Science. This is the home of Concept Cartoons which can start discussions (available as a teacher book, or CDRom for interactive whiteboards or posters). Whilst stories from the Puppets Project present and extend the problems by placing them in context with Problem Pup (age 3–5), Discovery Dog (age 5–7) or in Spellbound Science (age 7–11). Active Assessment also contains a range of activities which could be used as the basis for science discussions.

http://millgatehouse.co.uk/resources/science.htm

Newton, D.B. (2002) *Talking Sense in Science*. London: RoutledgeFalmer.

The strapline to this book is 'Helping Children Understand Through Talk' as this is what is delivered. This is a very readable and practitioner-focused publication with 'science talk' right at the heart of its content.

CHAPTER 8

TRICKY TOPICS AND HOW TO TEACH THEM

Mick Dunne and Dave Howard

Chapter Overview

This chapter explores the practical application of analogies, metaphors, similes and models to help children engage with and understand difficult skills and concepts in science. There is an extended discussion of how these work, in terms of constructivist principles, and examples of how to help learners progress through increasingly complex levels of conceptual understanding, e.g. in areas such as electricity and the flow of current. The limitations of analogies and metaphors are discussed, with examples taken from the concepts relating to light, vision and the human eye. Research is alluded to that indicates how children generate their own models and metaphors, and this in turn leads to a discussion of the concept of Pedagogical Content Knowledge (PCK), which refers to a teacher's repertoire of ways to teach specific concept areas effectively.

Introduction

Science is an area of study that is full of challenging ideas, facts and concepts and particularly those of an abstract nature. Children often find many of these difficult to access as do many experienced teachers and student teachers. One beneficial pedagogical approach is to employ metaphors, similes, analogies and modelling as a means of representation that enables the construction of new meaning. Learners are able to connect what is unknown or poorly understood to something more meaningful; they help to make the invisible visible. It is in essence a scaffolding technique and in this way the new and unfamiliar can become more readily known and eventually understood.

It is important to consider the significance of building metaphors, analogies, similes and models into our teaching, as these are significant elements of a teacher's Pedagogical Content Knowledge (PCK: more about this later) that is often associated with highly effective teaching. Common analogies are unlikely to have a universal application and the classroom practitioner needs to take note of the context in which learners are located; this is likely to require careful modification or even a complete change of analogy. One point often ignored in the discussion about the use of analogies and metaphors is the significance of harnessing children's imagination and creativity. As Dewey wrote 'Every great advance in science has issued from a new audacity of imagination' (1930: 294). The move towards a more creative curriculum should in some way benefit children's capacity to understand and generate their own metaphors and analogies.

Key Ideas

This chapter will provide a clear explanation of what analogies, metaphors, similes and PCK are and their importance to the teaching of science. It will highlight the differences between physical and analogous models and provide examples of useful analogies, metaphors and similes that can assist with some of the 'hard to teach' concepts and topics in science. We shall address theoretical perspectives on why analogies work and provide a critical examination of their use in the teaching of electricity as one key example that has been extensively researched. The chapter will conclude by examining some of the limitations of the use of analogies, metaphors and similes in a primary science context.

Analogies

The term is derived from the original Greek word *analogia* meaning proportionality.

Traditional analogies used by the teacher in science include dandelion seed and parachute; eye and camera; food and fuel; brain and computer; energy and money; electrical current and the flow of water; heart and pump; ribs and cage; and electrical switch and gate. Such analogies are relatively well known but a teacher needs to remember that learners themselves will often create their own.

Many of us were taught using analogous models and indeed such use has a very long history. Johannes Kepler imagined planetary motion as analogous to the workings and movements of a clock. William Harvey struggled to understand blood circulation and resorted to making connections to pumps, sponges and swamps as a means of communicating his discovery. Darwin's evolutionary ideas were presented conceptually as a *tree of life* that visually modelled interconnections between different species. These three examples illustrate the need to utilise familiar objects or words in order to communicate new ideas to a learned audience and we should not be surprised that exactly the same principles will apply to all learners at whatever level.

Models are physical representations of something e.g. a simple bulb. Compare Figure 8.1 with Figure 8.2. Both are representations of a simple filament bulb. Which is most suitable for KS1/2 learners? Is Figure 8.2 unhelpful? The first figures are of physical

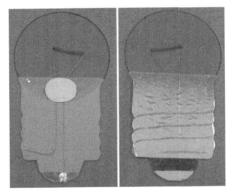

Figure 8.1

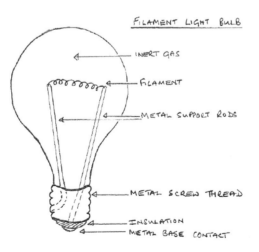

Figure 8.2

models that can be used both by teachers and pupils. What is the electrical symbol of a simple bulb? Does such symbolism help or hinder the learner?

Analogous models are often employed as a physical means of explaining a scientific idea, concept or theory whereas the scientific theory is how it really is (or is imagined to be!). Quite a range of these types of models is used in the teaching of simple electrical circuits to primary-aged children. Electricity has been adopted to exemplify the use of analogies, due to the difficulties often associated with teaching and learning this area of science. Examples here include the water circuit model; the rope model; the railway model; the bicycle chain model; the marble run model; the tin of beans model; and the sack of coal model. We have not the space here to discuss the relative merits of each model, but the fact that seven exist to explain the theory behind simple circuits confirms the importance of modelling scientific phenomena analogously.

Points for Reflection

Many teachers tend to have their preferred analogous model of the simple circuit, however the rope analogy is often seen as the best way to represent this.

- Why do you think this is so?
- What are the advantages and limitations of the seven models identified above?
- Can one be better than the other?

Metaphors

We have seen that using analogies can provide a model of teaching that will enable children to make links between prior knowledge and understanding and the target learning outcomes. Whilst similar in the way they work, metaphors tend to have more direct connections to the concept (i.e. there will be a statement of the form that 'X' is 'Y' whereas in analogies the relationship can be expressed as 'W is to X as Y is to Z'). For example, one definition of a simple circuit is 'a continuous path along which electricity flows'. The use of path is metaphorical and suggests the conductor (i.e. metal wire) is a 'path'. Electrons 'live' in the wire is another example, as is the metaphor 'push' to introduce the concept of voltage (e.g. the electricity is 'pushed' around the circuit by the battery/cell). A metaphor used by children to describe dissolving is 'disappear' and it is easy to see how some teachers can be drawn into using this metaphor too. However, its use reinforces or directs children into a serious misconception about this type of physical change. Powerful analogies, metaphors and similes can become *de facto* scientific descriptions; for example the heart is universally perceived as a pump (in the mechanical sense).

Similes

It is worthwhile to briefly mention similes whose use is very common in science work with all ages. Imagine you are using the water circuit model (this model uses things like tubing, water and a pump, etc. connected in a continuous path to represent wire, electrical current and a cell in an electrical circuit respectively). Stating that the hose or tubing that you are using is *like* a wire makes a comparison without stating that it actually is a wire, which of course it is not. Science has an abundance of examples that utilise similes.

Theoretical Perspectives

The use of analogy is firmly rooted in the notion of scaffolding as a means of enabling learners to make progress. Analogies can help children link existing knowledge and understanding with new ideas within their 'zone of proximal development' (ZPD: Vygotsky, 1978: 86). Indeed they can be seen right at the heart of Ausubel's view that there is a need to 'start from what the learner already knows'. Analogies are significant elements of teaching models. The choice of analogy is determined by the social and cultural context of the learners, the subject and pedagogical knowledge of the teacher (PCK – see below), and accuracy of assessment judgements of children's starting points. This is represented diagrammatically in Figure 8.3 below from the perspective of the teacher leading the learning within a social constructivist paradigm. It is not only teachers who employ analogies: research has shown that self-created analogies also exist and may be more effective than those imposed by the teacher (Gunning, 1996).

Children are more than capable of generating their own analogies in different ways, for example through mind mapping, role play and creative writing. A very strong pedagogical argument exists that learners will embed their understanding better if they themselves *construct* the links. Bob Kibble (2002) wrote about how children pictured electricity moving through a conductor and some of their images were very similar to those produced by Year 2 BEd student teachers! He also suggests that a typical 9 year-old is capable of grasping moving particle models but their teachers first need to have the confidence to teach it.

Figure 8.3 identifies the inter-relationships between teaching, a teacher's PCK and learning. It assumes that a teacher's PCK enables him or her to match their choice of analogy with the readiness of the learner to progress.

The modelling of a scientific concept can often be a social experience. Take for example modelling simple circuits through a water circuit model, the rope model, or the bicycle chain analogy. This often involves a collaborative approach in order to derive meaning. Children communicating and sharing their scientific ideas with others provides an opportunity for them to become modified, extended or even completely rejected. It is not unreasonable to conclude that given the personalised nature of learning the use of analogies requires a differentiated and individualised approach. One

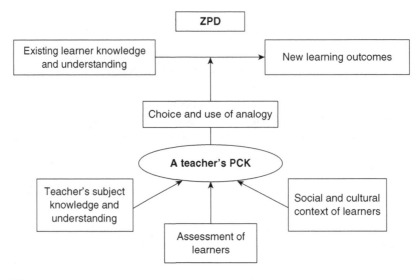

Figure 8.3

analogy may work particularly well for one group of learners (e.g. the movement of particles being likened to a football crowd contrasted with the movement of particles associated with the movement of people at a disco). This has serious implications for a teacher who will need to be able to call on an extensive repertoire of appropriate analogies and role-play techniques which will be dependent on a secure subject knowledge and understanding.

When should we use a simile, metaphor or analogy? We should not be surprised that children's capacity to use or understand similes, metaphors and analogies depends on their level of language acquisition. Harlen and Qualter (2009: 87) identify several characteristic patterns of progression in children's ideas; ideas move from *description* to *explanation*, from *small* to *big ideas* and from *personal* to *shared ideas*. Using their simple model and taking the main areas for teaching electricity in KS1 and KS2 as defined in the National Curriculum (QCDA, online) we have attempted to map when these language tools (metaphors, similes and analogies) are likely to be observed in use.

- *Finding electrical appliances*   This is essentially a phase of learning that focuses on recognition, naming, and simple sorting. Children generally have naive language development and an egocentric approach to learning. The use of analogies is unlikely but such young learners will meet similes in the form A is *like* B e.g. the torch is *like* a light.
- *Electrical safety*   This is a continuation of the previous phase but begins to locate the learner with the topic. Children generally have immature linguistic knowledge and skills and so this is still likely to be a pre-analogous stage. There is little or no use of analogies but some use of both similes and metaphors.

- *Using batteries and making connections*   This is the small ideas phase. There is familiarity and a direct engagement with scientific apparatus and the start of collaborative working, experimenting, observing and simple explanations. It is likely to be a first use of analogies. Metaphor and simile use mainly by the teacher increases to embed simple understanding at an individual level. Some simple physical modelling e.g. model of a simple bulb, battery and wire (see Figure 8.1) is included.
- *Making a circuit*   Here small ideas continue to develop, a pre-requisite for moving to explanations based on identifying outcomes. Extended use by teacher of simple simile-based analogies such as 'a circuit is like a continuous <u>path</u> or <u>track</u>' is employed. Children begin to generate simple analogies of their own and start to model scientific concepts. There is a move to shared understanding.
- *Investigating different circuits*   There is now an application of prior learning and the adoption of analogies to explain the outcomes of scientific investigations. Shared understanding and negotiated meaning-making appear (analogies are very important here, because they enable the learner to communicate their scientific knowledge and understanding by using commonly recognised words. For example, a simple bulb is brighter with two cells rather than one because two cells give greater *push* than one).
- *Making useful circuits*   Big ideas now become better understood within a context of shared discourse and experimentation. This leads to the development of secure science subject knowledge. Ideas are challenged by the use of words (more sophisticated analogies and metaphors by teacher). Learners become more able to generate models, metaphors and similes.

What this progressive pattern strongly indicates is that teachers of science must be sensitive to the linguistic capabilities of the children they are working with. The timing of a use of metaphors and analogies is important. Clearly very young children in the nursery and lower KS1 will struggle with many analogies, but will find similes – and to some extent metaphors – a useful means of accessing scientific ideas and concepts.

More Theoretical Thoughts

A constructivist view is that children have responsibility for their own learning and it is the teacher who must variously function as a facilitator, enabler, manager … Learners throughout their education continually strive to make personal sense of their experience and to give meaning to what they observe and hear. Often there will be cognitive dissonance (conflict) between what they have seen and/or heard and the teacher's scientific explanation. Such a misconception can be introduced when children hear that electrons 'live' in a wire. Why shouldn't children believe that electricity is 'used up' by a bulb or the reason a bulb lights up is because electricity travelling one way round a simple circuit happens to meet electricity travelling the other way round the same circuit (a common misconception called the Clashing Current Model)? Both of these ideas have intuitive merit but are not scientifically correct. Not only are metaphors and analogies important as language tools assisting in eliciting children's ideas, but they also provide a means to both identify and challenge misconceptions; unfortunately they can also lead to children creating their own misconceptions too! An important tenet of Constructivism is that children arrive at a learning situation with their own pre-existing ideas and the teacher needs to recognise this. Analogies are often the bridge between what children already know and what it is the teacher wants them to know, but they can also be used to identify what they have learned as well. Asking them to produce an annotated model of a simple bulb, battery, wire or simple circuit once they have spent time studying these things provides useful assessment information but also assists the teacher in reflecting on and evaluating their teaching too.

Limitations

We have presented a strong case for the use of metaphors, similes and analogies but these are not without their problems …

Asoko and de Boo (2001) were concerned that analogies could over-complicate rather than clarify the phenomena which they were trying to explain through introducing irrelevant or misleading features or creating an idea that was more complex than the original scientific one. Only a teacher can judge the suitability of the match between a chosen analogy and children's existing knowledge, understanding and capacity to imagine.

Teachers can identify analogies that they believe are sufficiently familiar to learners but in reality this may not be the case. Take the idea of pairing food with fuel. The concept of fuel might be understood by the teacher to mean a source of energy that makes different things work but most children will not have the same level of acquaintance with this word. How many children would be genuinely comfortable with a parachute and what it does when describing some seed types and dispersal?

 Points for Reflection

List all the ways in which energy is like money: e.g. one form of money (£) can be changed into another form of money ($).

Word familiarity becomes an even greater problem with EAL children. For example, simple bulbs can be referred to as light bulbs. The word 'light' however has multiple meanings in Urdu (*halka, roshni, halka karna, roshan karna* and *jalaana* – the only noun) and 'bulb' will not translate into that language at all. Using analogies with second language users requires additional sensitivity on behalf of the teacher that considers cultural and social relevance as well as any prerequisite language demands.

Some analogies are also time sensitive. Take the pairing of the camera with the eye, something routinely done with both KS2 and KS3 children. Given today's technological

Table 8.1 Comparison of the human eye, optical camera and digital camera

Feature	Eye	Optical Camera	Digital Camera
Changes in light intensity	Pupil size varies with brightness	Mechanical variable aperture	Automatic sensor
Image capture	Image on retina sent to the brain	Image recorded on the film	Image recorded electronically
Reduction of internal reflection	Black lining to the eye (choroid layer)	Black lining to the camera	Not applicable
Focusing image	Lens shape changes	Lens moves forward or backwards	Not applicable
Binocular vision	Two images used	No binocular vision	No binocular vision

advances is this still appropriate? How many children or their parents will use optical cameras? Can a useful comparison be made between a digital camera and the eye? What about an i-phone and the eye? There is a danger of teachers passively adopting well-known and established analogous models without due regard to their current relevance. The table above illustrates the importance of selecting the appropriate analogue concept to pair with the target concept.

Analogies can often be over-extended beyond their relevance. For example, our earlier description of the water circuit analogy to represent the flow of electricity around a simple circuit can become strained when a teacher uses it for purposes it cannot meet. It works well with respect to explaining current flow (the water flowing through a pipe/hose, electrical resistance when the hose is squeezed causing the water to move through it more quickly, and even the functioning of the battery – the pump that moves the water around the circuit). However, it is hard to demonstrate what it is that causes a bulb to illuminate (increased resistance modelled by squeezing the hosepipe is not enough). Equally the water model does not help when discussing a broken circuit as electricity cannot leak like water.

Vignette 1

This is taken from a Y5 class that explored the purpose of the battery (a single cell), the wire and a bulb. The student teacher working with the children had chosen to use the water circuit model to explain how a simple circuit works.

Ch 1.   So the pump is like a battery.

Student   Which bit represents the bulb?

Ch 1.   Where the hosepipe is squeezed but why isn't it hot? Is it because the water's cooling it down.

Student.   No. This is just a model to show you how the electricity flows through the bulb.

This demonstrates a possible problem where the analogy has become mixed up with the science (water from the analogy cooling the bulb in the actual investigation) – an interesting circumstance of different worlds combining!

Pedagogical Content Knowledge (PCK)

Throughout this chapter and at earlier points in this book reference has been made to a teacher's PCK but what is this exactly? The concept of PCK as first proposed by Shulman (1986) describes the 'knowledge' possessed by teachers operating at an expert level of practice that is developed and continues to develop over time. Such knowledge involves subject knowledge and understanding and subject-specific pedagogical expertise extending to all aspects of professional practice. PCK encompasses a variety of aspects or attributes, the number of which will depend on the model being described. It is generally agreed that secure content or subject knowledge is critical to the development of PCK followed closely by a teacher's knowledge of his/her teaching group. It is on this foundation that teachers will apply their knowledge of the curriculum, socioculturalism, pedagogy, the context and assessment. Shulman's work on PCK was often focused on the notion of the 'expert', however the student teacher also has PCK – it is naïve and grows as their professional development proceeds. If we compare the student teacher with the NQT it will be the latter who is typically better able to communicate science to learners, who is able to draw on a range of teaching approaches, who is likely to have a deeper understanding of social, cultural and other contextual factors, and who recognises both the advantages and disadvantages of the educational context in which they are located.

All student teachers in England have to teach science (whether or not it is called science) as part of their placement experience. Some may feel threatened by this subject, most likely because of the way they were taught and/or because of a lack of confidence in their subject knowledge. However, whether a science enthusiast or not, teaching this subject will require them to extend and expand their 'expertise' in order to operate effectively in whatever educational context they are located – something that is not always easy to attain. More experienced teachers may have greater content knowledge but their effectiveness at delivery is likely to be context-dependent. For example, they may function extremely successfully when planning, organising, delivering and assessing some aspects of the curriculum but also display a lack of contextual knowledge associated with aspects of primary science. Good classroom practice in one subject is not simply transferable across all subjects as the PCK associated with science teaching will contrast to PCK associated with other subject teaching. The active continuous development of a practitioner's PCK is at the heart of being a professional educator – being able to identify appropriate similes, metaphors and analogies for science education which are meaningful to the learner context and using these effectively is a very important aspect of teaching.

Teaching electricity is difficult. The concepts involved are often abstract and can challenge many adults let alone primary-aged children. A good tip for anyone faced with teaching this topic is that whatever it is you want the children to do you will need to do it yourself first. If they only ever meet simple bulbs when they are in bulb holders then it is hardly surprising that they would never find out that the bulb itself has to be connected at two different points to the circuit. And this is where your choice of model is important – your choice of analogous model and/or metaphor needs to have been carefully considered. Try not to become distracted by *why* things are happening and focus instead on what is happening and how things are working. It is far more important for the children to have some knowledge about how a bulb, wire and battery might work than about why these do work.

Summary

- Contextualising and personalising the use of analogies is essential in order that they become genuine learning tools that are fit for purpose rather than clichéd 'off the shelf' resources.
- Analogies will inevitably change with time.
- A good analogy choice reduces the possibility of conceptual errors.
- Children generating their own analogies is very beneficial to the development of their scientific understanding.
- The use of analogies, metaphors and similes is inextricably bound up with a practitioner's own pedagogy (PCK) and professional development.

References

Asoko, H. & de Boo, M. (2001) *Analogies and Illustrations: Representing Ideas in Primary Science*. Hatfield: ASE.
A readable publication that explains the importance of recognising children's pre-existing ideas. It looks at how scientific concepts can be introduced in different ways such as through models and analogies.

Dewey, J. (1930) *The Quest for Certainty: A Study of the Relation of Knowledge and Action*. London: Allen and Unwin.
Glynn, S.M. (2007) 'Methods and strategies: the Teaching-With-Analogies Model', *Science and Children*, 44 (8): 52–55.
A brief article describing how analogies can enable young learners to make connections between what is familiar and what is new, such as an electric circuit. It also identifies the six step 'Teaching with Analogies Model' and how it can be used.

Gunning, T.G. (1996) *Creating Reading Instruction for All Children* (2nd edition). Boston, MA: Allyn and Bacon.

Harlen, W. & Qualter, A. (2009) *The Teaching of Science in Primary Schools* (5th edition). Abingdon, Oxon: Routledge.

This book does not explicitly address the subject of this chapter yet readers will discover throughout the text implicit reference to models and analogies. Chapter 5's focus on children's ideas is particularly valuable not least for the way children's drawings are considered to be powerful tools in identifying how they are 'modelling' mental images of scientific concepts.

Kibble, B. (2002) 'How do you picture electricity?', *Primary Science Review*, 74: 28–30.
This is a very short but accessible article describing some common models that learners use to help them conceptualise electricity. It also considers how to help them move towards a better understanding of the 'moving particle' model of a simple circuit that not everyone agrees is possible.

Shulman, L.S. (1986) 'Those who understand: knowledge growth in teaching', *Educational Researcher*, 15 (2): 4–14.
An important academic paper in which Shulman introduced the phrase 'pedagogical content knowledge', useful for anyone wishing to know more about this theoretical model of the teacher.

Vygotsky, L.S. (1978) *Mind and Society: The Development of Psychological Processes.* Cambridge, MA: Harvard University Press.

Further Reading

Howe, A., Davies, D., McMahan, K., Towler, L. & Scott, T. (2005) *Science 5–11: A Guide for Teachers.* London: Fulton.
This is a very useful book to any beginning teacher but of particular relevance to this chapter is its Chapter 5 which addresses teaching electricity. The authors provide an expert examination of the use of different analogies and models in the teaching of electricity.

Newton, D.P. (2002) *Talking Sense in Science: Helping Children Understand Through Talk.* London: RoutledgeFalmer.
This is a very readable book that focuses on helping children to acquire science knowledge and understanding through conversation and other forms of talk. Scaffolding learning by employing analogies and models, introduced through talk, is explored in some detail.

Osborne, J.F., Black, P.J., Smith, M. & Meadows, J. (1991) *Science Prosesses and Concepts Exploration Research Report: Electricity.* Liverpool: Liverpool University Press.
Do not be put off by the date this work was carried out. Russell and Watt's report provides a fascinating insight into children's knowledge and understanding of electricity. They also describe the research procedures undertaken which those undertaking a dissertation might find invaluable.

CHAPTER 9

PLANNING FOR ASSESSMENT FOR LEARNING

Tara Mawby and Mick Dunne

Chapter Overview

This chapter presents a comprehensive overview of the development of a variety of assessment procedures up to the current day. It begins by distinguishing between types of assessment, notably Assessment for Learning (AfL) – sometimes referred to as formative assessment – and Assessment of Learning (AoL) – known as summative assessment. The evolution of more sophisticated assessment methods since the 1988 Education Act embodying statutory testing is discussed, with attention given to the current requirements of the assessment process in England, leading to an outline of ten major principles of AfL.

The second half of the chapter discusses the linking of assessment to planning for daily, termly and yearly science programmes, and explores the importance of performance language for the statement of learning objectives in terms of observable behaviour, in order to make these easier to assess by teachers. This leads on to a survey of a variety

(Continued)

(Continued)

of techniques to facilitate assessment, including effective questioning; oral and written feedback to learners; linking assessment to targets and progression; the use of digital forms of assessment (e.g. electronic voting), and a final consideration of peer- and self-assessment by the learners themselves.

Key Ideas

'I'm doing an AfL lesson this afternoon, what are you teaching?'

An overheard snippet of conversation from a staffroom reveals this misconception about what AfL is. We've all heard the phrase '*Assessment for Learning*' and many people when asked will say that they know about it and its principles. But how much of this is because the phrase has been used a great deal and we are now too scared to ask what it *really* means and how we should teach it?

During this chapter we will not only look at Assessment *for* learning, we will also consider it alongside Assessment *of* learning and the National Requirements for assessment and reporting arrangements. You may well have heard some of this previously, but before you turn to the next chapter, ask yourself whether you can list all ten principles of AfL? Then ask yourself whether you can explain why the quote above is a misconception and unpick how you make sure it doesn't happen to you! And be honest. Do you know what sort of statutory assessment you have to provide and where to find out about it if you don't?

We will not only explore the principles of AfL but also identify and evaluate some of the innovative ways you can use AfL techniques linked to today's technology, which is key in this age of iPads, tweeting, Facebook and blogs – all of which have a place in today's and tomorrow's teaching of science. Some of your students may well be ahead of you with these web-based technologies, so we will provide some ideas and tips on how to work with them on this.

Student Perspectives

The focus group discussion focused on the importance of linking assessment to planning, the need to trust in teachers' professionalism, and the fairness of various assessment systems. Unsurprisingly, trainees were concerned about the added pressures of assessing in composite classes and how best to utilise ICT in the assessment process. They made clear that they needed help with understanding the different approaches to assessment in the classroom.

What is Assessment?

Before considering the concerns mentioned above, let's look at 'assessment' in general – namely what and who is it for and why do it? Historically there has been a strong tendency to consider 'assessment' as just another term or word for 'test', which has in turn conjured up all sorts of connotational meanings, concerns, and even fears. Assessment shouldn't create such negativity: it isn't only about tests and examinations and it shouldn't be about being put on the spot. Typical dictionary definitions of the word 'assessment' would be:

> When you judge or decide the amount, value, quality or importance of something, or the judgment or decision that is made. (Cambridge Dictionary)

or

> The process of making a judgement or forming an opinion, after considering something or someone carefully. (Macmillian Dictionary)

Such definitions illustrate that assessment is an information-gathering *process* that informs a judgment; it is not synonymous with testing or examining. Critically it is about being informed about the progress a learner is making and not just measuring them.

One major problem is that over the past few decades (in fact since 1988) the teaching profession has had its professional status steadily compromised, sometimes overtly as when the Secretary of State for Education (2010) described teaching as a 'craft' or through the imposition of Standard Assessment Tests (SATs) – these are just a few of the significant consequences of political intervention in the teaching profession. The shift of emphasis away from 'education' towards 'training' (Ofsted's description of student teachers as 'trainees' is not an accident!) has accompanied a move away from qualitative information about pupils, with the result that huge importance is now being placed on quantitative data which has resulted in league tables, sink schools, and so on. Testing has become a major part of school-based assessment, but before you begin to think that 'test' is a dirty word, be reassured that tests do have their time and place but are only one form of assessment, just as a thematic approach is not the only way to deliver a creative curriculum. This chapter will make explicit the value that tests have but also show they are only part of the assessment process.

Assessment *of* or *for* Learning?

Assessment of learning (AoL) is also known as 'summative' assessment. This is because it is usually based on a test that will typically come at the end of a lesson, a topic or Key Stage which will normally result in a measurable outcome (a number, grade …) that can be used quantifiably often as a performance indicator. It may measure the current stage

Pupils
Teachers
Resources
Rules
Tests

Better results
More
knowledgeable
pupils
Exhausted
teachers

"Teachers need to know about their pupils' progress ...so they can adapt their work to meet their needs"

Figure 9.1

of a pupil's learning but critically this is a one-way process, when the teacher gathers data about a pupil using a snapshot in time of their performance.

Assessment for learning (AfL) is also known as 'formative' assessment – formative because it 'informs' and is used to support further steps. Significantly this is a two-way process whereby the teacher not only gathers information about a pupil but also provides feedback that will directly support their further development.

AoL and AfL are often seen as two very distinct and separate processes, however summative assessment can also be employed formatively as when an end of topic test informs the teacher about future learning goals that need to be planned for.

Black and Wiliam (1998) summed this up well when they produced *Inside the Black Box*. The 'black box' they referred to was the classroom: all the hard work that teachers and pupils were doing was designed to produce good results … but no one considered *how* these were being produced. They saw Assessment *for* learning as a valid means of providing focused diagnostic and formative support for what went on in the classroom rather than simply concentrating on the final 'number' or grade. To slightly misquote an old saying, Black and Wiliam recognised it was about '*fattening the pig rather that weighing it*'!

Assessment and the Planning Cycle

There are several key things to consider when carrying out assessment and where it fits into the planning cycle as well as your lesson planning on a more personal level. It may help to consider the following points in Figure 9.2 below.

Assessment needs to be planned for carefully, so that each of these stages is addressed at appropriate times within the school year. Effective assessment should

Daily:
This is detailed assessment, part of AfL. It involves:

- Learning outcomes being shared with pupils.
- Peer- and self-assessment.
- Immediate feedback and next steps for pupils.

Half termly/termly:
Periodic assessment. It involves:

- Both AfL and AoL (APP or Active Assessment).
- Gaps in the learning being identified.
- Identifying a broader view of progress (both pupil and teacher).
- Use of national standards in the classroom.
- Identifying improvements to curriculum planning.

End of Year:
This is terminal assessment. It involves:

- Reporting the outcomes of assessment to parents and Nationally.
- Formal recognition of attainment and achievement.
- Reporting to parents/carers and next teacher/school.
- Possible use of moderated and validated tests/tasks.

Figure 9.2

capture each learner's best performance, seeking out what they *can* do much more than what they can't!

National Curriculum Assessment (England)

There are clear assessment requirements in relation to delivering a National Curriculum. Currently, there is a need to provide teacher assessment at the end of the Foundation Stage and at the end of each key stage. The nature of teacher assessment will be discussed later in the chapter, however all such assessment outcomes are reported around the end of June.

EY practitioners assess their children in the final term against all 13 profiles of the Foundation Stage Curriculum and provide an overall score. This final judgement is based on continual observation over the course of the year, with these regular observations being carried out by a Key Worker with responsibility for up to eight children. Key Stage 1 teachers assess reading, writing, speaking and listening and provide a sublevel for each but only if the pupil is working within the 'Level 2 range'. They also provide an overall level for mathematics using the same principle as for the literacy. A range of tasks and tests are employed to support teacher judgments for numeracy, reading and writing.

Assessment for science is slightly different because science has a weighting towards scientific enquiry. At KS1, Sc1 has a weighting of 3 due to the 50:50 balance between conceptual development and scientific enquiry respectively. The formula for calculating the final level is given below and the final level is entered as a whole number, by rounding up or down, and not as a sublevel:

(3 × (Level for Sc1)) + (1 × (Level for Sc2)) + (1 × (Level for Sc3)) + (1 × (Level for Sc4)) = Total ÷ 6 = Overall Level for Science

A similar process, return and reporting dates will apply to levelling in Key Stage 2. Optional testing materials are available for years 3, 4 and 5, although these have not been reprinted from 2010. Year 6 SATs are generally held during the second week in May. One obvious difference here is that the weighting for Sc1 is reduced to a value of 2 rather than 3 so the total is then divided by 5 instead of 6, which is again recorded as a whole number and not as a sublevel.

How do you arrive at these judgements?

There are several ways by which you can level a pupil including them carrying out a test, of which there are many published (e.g. Rising Stars, Mini SATs and NFER). These can provide snapshot judgments often related to whether or not the pupil performs well in test situations and lead to a false picture of attainment.

More formative systems are also available like Assessing Pupil's Progress (APP) which provides a series of progressive statements in various aspects of scientific enquiry. Other materials of a similar nature, such as Assessing Progress in Science produce by the QCA (as it was then), provide a range of activities for KS1 and 2 and levelled criteria (these are useful benchmarks and can even support agreement trials), allow an assessment judgement to be made.

Tracking

A huge amount of time and energy is invested by teachers in tracking pupil progress. Assessment information obtained systematically (via AfL tools) and at timely intervals is used to monitor the progress learners make over time. Identifying over- or underachievement in relation to expected progress targets produces valuable data. Every pupil is expected to make a certain minimum level of progress (i.e. 6 points in EY, to Level 2 in KS1 and to Level 4 in KS2). This broadly equates to children progressing one level per year in KS1 and half a level per year in KS2. However as we are all aware each child is different, so a more complex calculation can be carried out which is provided by the Fischer Family Trust (FFT). These data are sent to each school in about October of each year so that pupils can be tracked and their progress monitored against their expected end of year attainment. Having this information enables teachers to better tailor teaching and learning expectations.

Assessment for Learning

We have seen the importance of being able to track pupil progress and how AfL has an important role in this process but what is effective AfL? The best AfL needs to be:

- Part of an effective planning for teaching and learning.
- Focused on how students learn.
- Recognised as being central to classroom practice.
- Regarded as a key professional skill for teachers.
- Sensitive and constructive because any assessment will have an emotional impact.
- Take account of the importance of learner motivation.
- Promote a commitment to learning goals and a shared understanding of the criteria by which these are assessed.
- Provide learners with constructive guidance about how to improve.
- Develop learners' capacity for self-assessment so they can become reflective and self-managing.
- Recognise the full range of achievements of all learners.

(Assessment Reform Group, 2002)

In practical terms these ten principles can be effectively addressed through a clear professional knowledge of the value of:

- Objective-led lessons.
- Questioning.
- Feedback.
- Curricular target setting and progression.
- Peer- and self-assessment.
- Formative use of summative assessment.

Objective-led Lessons

Whilst you may use the terminology, what does it *actually* mean? Learning is a journey and setting a clear objective means that you have a clear idea of the journey you are going on. We will rarely get in a car and drive aimlessly (not unless we've had a stressful day!); there is usually a clear purpose with an identified destination and typically you would normally share this with your passengers. (Have you ever tried to take someone on a 'mystery tour'? How did they react?)

The same rules apply to lesson planning. Have a clear destination in mind (e.g. by the end of the lesson you will … '*be able to explain how to keep ice pops cold for our picnic*', or '*today we are going to … learn how to draw a scientific image of our results*') and this is particularly effective if there are clearly communicated reasons for 'going on the journey' (e.g. '*Let's learn more about the properties of materials*'). The main point is to share this with the learners in their vocabulary, so as to eliminate any sense of being on a 'mystery tour' and the concomitant stress this can generate.

Note that no mention of *learning objectives* (some teachers prefer to use learning purposes or goals or intentions) was made in the previous paragraph. Learning objectives are what the teacher identifies that the children will learn and are often based on the National Curriculum (NC), the National Strategies materials (NS), or the QCA scheme of work. Learning objectives are often written in terms of learners, such as 'The children will know the meaning of transparent, translucent and opaque' or 'The children will be able to sort out materials according to whether they are transparent, translucent or opaque'. Note the following in this regard:

- It is usual to have no more than three learning objectives for any one teaching session.
- The balance between identifying a learning objective related to the development of conceptual knowledge (Sc2-4) and another that relates to Sc1.
- The use of performance verbs in each learning objective such as 'sort' and 'know'. Other good performance verbs include 'draw', 'group', 'label', 'record', 'conclude', 'identify', 'recognise' and 'sequence', and there are many others. Avoid the use of 'appreciate' and 'understand' because good performance verbs are measurable or observable and can therefore be assessed as something that cannot be done with terms like 'appreciate' or 'understand';
- Always share the learning objectives with the children but avoid insisting that they write them down. Objectives do not need to be ritualistically shared at the beginning of a lesson and neither should they waste time copying them down. Yes, the children *must* know what they are expected to learn and the teacher should share this with them at several points during the session. They need to employ a range of strategies (e.g. questioning to reassure themselves that the children know what is expected of them). It is particularly useful at the end of a teaching session to reflect with learners what they have achieved in relation to the learning objectives.
- Learning is never restricted to the learning objectives. One of the great delights of teaching, and especially teaching science, is that it frequently generates unexpected learning opportunities and these should not be dismissed because they are not part of the original lesson plan.

It is quite obvious that all children are patently different and consequently it is inappropriate to expect each one to complete the same learning journey in the same amount of time. It is for this reason that teachers will employ differentiation strategies based on either outcomes or expectations. It is also becoming more common to see *Learning Outcomes* identified in planning documentation and these are the intermediate learning steps towards achieving the whole learning objective. It may be too ambitious for a learner to sort out a collection of materials into those that are transparent, opaque and translucent but they may be able to separate them into 'see-through' and not 'see-through'. This is a perfectly acceptable learning outcome that represents genuine progress in learning and is theoretically related to Vygotsky's ideas about scaffolding learning as learning is located within the zone of proximal development. AfL techniques can inform the teacher about progress against both learning objectives and learning outcomes.

So how can a teacher know that their pupils have arrived at the end of this bit of the learning journey? How will they know they have been successful? And what will pupils have to do, say or show to demonstrate they have reached their destination? Clearly well written learning objectives and learning outcomes will help hugely here.

What might this look like in practice?

Learning Objective: How can I keep my coffee hot on playground duty when it's snowing?

Learning Outcomes:

- State which material kept the coffee hottest (loosely pitched at Level 2).
- Explain simply which material kept the coffee hottest (ditto, Level 3).
- Explain why the material that was 'best' worked well, using key vocab (ditto Level 4).

This process is the same whether you have a subject knowledge (Sc2, Sc3 or Sc4) objective or an enquiry specific objective (Sc1) in that the teacher is required to have a clear knowledge of the levelness and progression embedded, for example:

Learning Objective: What 'rules' do we need to carry out our experiment about keeping my coffee hot so that it is a fair test?

Learning Outcomes:

- State whether the test was 'fair' or not.
- Keep at least one variable the same.
- Decide which variables to change and which to measure and keep these the same.

EY practitioners will approach this differently in that they will plan more retrospectively. They will focus on the interests and the learning taking place rather than on what the child needs to be taught. This does not however reduce the need for detailed planning or identifying clear expectations for learning.

We have seen that having clear expectations and sharing these with learners is very important, but as the lesson progresses, how can a teacher manage to monitor an individual's progress or that of the class? There are two fundamental parts to this. The first is 'questioning' and the second is about providing carefully considered feedback to the student.

Questioning

Children's natural curiosity and inquisitiveness will often emerge in science activities and tasks and they can ask a huge number of questions. However, it is teacher questioning that lies right at the heart of effective AfL and therefore it is one of the most important pedagogical skills for any teacher to develop. It is through careful and purposeful planning for a learning journey that a teacher will know where they wish to take learners. It is most often through questioning that they will be able to maintain frequent feedback about pupil progress towards the intended learning outcomes.

There are many types of questions with the commonest being open and closed questions, pupil-centred questions and subject-centred questions, but all can have an assessment purpose; we are not considering here those questions that are used for control and management purposes or indeed the plethora of questions generated by children themselves, which also provide a valuable insight into what they are thinking. Unfortunately the range of questions employed by teachers, and not just in a science context, tends to be narrow and dominated by the closed subject-centred type. Closed ones are appropriate in order to check key points and to gather rapid feedback from a wider sample of children; they are often seen as important for maintaining a 'good pace' and will have a 'right' answer. Open questions can provide opportunities to the student to show their developing knowledge in so much as there is no single correct answer.

We would suggest that there are four additional points worthy of consideration when questioning children. Firstly, give them time to answer. Research informs us that teachers are prepared to wait for about four seconds before they ask another child the same answer or answer the question themselves – we need to practise being silent. Secondly, we should not always rely on a hands-up approach. Why not invite a child by name (not all children will be comfortable with this but to a large extent this depends on the classroom ethos that has been developed) to respond to a question? Then ask if a second child agrees with the first child's response. Teachers should not take total responsibility for providing the answer to every question. Thirdly, not all questions need to be answered immediately. Have part of a display board with 'Science Questions of the Week' which can be used to record a question which can be attended to at a more appropriate time; here the children will be able see their questions being valued which in turn will encourage them to ask more. These are important insights into learners' thinking and they will often reveal such things as alternative frameworks and misconceptions which represent valuable assessment data. Finally, remember that a child's question is most often best answered by a teacher using another question – something that demands considerable skill. The teacher's subsidiary question when employed is designed to scaffold the learning experience such that whereas the answer to the first question may have been out of the child's reach the subsequent question has been carefully crafted to enable that child to progress.

Language can be an inhibiting factor in answering a question. Compare the following two forms of the same question – 'Explain the process of fertilisation in plants' and 'How does a flower produce seeds?'. What is the purpose of each question? If we want children to demonstrate an understanding of fertilisation in plants then they can do so without recourse to technical terms; the specific scientific language involved may be best provided at a later stage. We also need to be sensitive to the language we use while recognising the need for children to become more conversant with scientific terminology.

Feedback

At some point questions will be answered and such feedback can provide assessment-related information about how well a child is doing and what they need to do next to improve. Other means of providing feedback could include short conversations with children as they are working in class or a comment written down in their books.

Oral feedback

Providing encouragement, praise and other positive forms of feedback to learners is often an accepted part of a teacher's role. Less obvious is the benefit of doing this with specific AfL principles in mind. It is important for non-spontaneous feedback to be planned in advance or additional opportunities for formative guidance may be missed. Some tips for this include:

- Making it specific to the point being discussed, i.e. relate the questions or comments to the learning objectives and outcomes. Rather than saying '*Great bar chart Fred*' tell 'Fred' why his bar chart is 'great', e.g. '*You've labelled your axes very clearly Fred, well done.*'
- Even better, encourage the learner to think of the next step for themselves e.g. '*How do I know what this bar chart is about? What do we need to add?*'
- Once again allow children enough time to respond to your feedback.

Written feedback

Generally written feedback should be in the form of comment-only marking. Research strongly suggests that learners will make little progress when their work is marked with grades or numbers, even if these are accompanied by a comment (Black and Wiliam, 1998). Mark schemes that produce these grades are rarely shared and are often demotivating if the marks are low. This is particularly so for most AoL methods when there is no formative gain from the 'test' result.

Some tips about written feedback:

- DO make time for learners to act on your comments in their books, otherwise you may as well not have bothered.

- DON'T just write 'well done' or 'try harder' or use a rubber stamp.
- DON'T write just 'L.O. met' – this is meaningless.
- DO write either a next steps statement (sometimes called 'next steps marking' or 'close the gap marking') or a question for the pupil to answer. Try two stars and a wish – two things that the pupil did well or achieved from the lesson or previous targets, and one thing they could do to improve; these would be based on the lesson's learning outcomes.
- DO relate your feedback to the learning objectives and the outcomes of the lesson.
- DO provide comments and targets for students from a summative assessment.
- DON'T over-comment.

Effective feedback will result in new targets being identified for the learner which leads us nicely into the next aspect of AfL.

Curricular Target Setting and Progression

Providing next steps comments either verbally or written down should directly help with maintaining progression. By setting and sharing clearly formulated learning objectives and outcomes both teacher and pupils know the expectations of the session and these in turn can provide the basis for feedback and helping students progress. Carefully integrated into such a framework are appropriately selected AfL instruments such as questioning, observation checklists, observation comment slips, portfolios and general marking.

Providing variety in the way learners are enabled to 'apply' their learning is highly necessary. 'Reporting' in science can be depressingly limited but by presenting this in more imaginative ways children can have a greater opportunity to evidence what they have learnt. Card sorts, cartoon strip sequences, concept cartoons, consumer reports, deliberate mistakes, annotated drawings, games, KWL grids, odd one out, and sales pitches are just some of the assessment techniques promoted by Naylor and Keogh (2005). How these can be used is up to the teacher but the real strength of using such a variety of assessment methods is that these are good teaching resources in their own right – they can be easily incorporated within the lesson (not as a bolt-on) and help to sustain learner interest.

Peer- and self-assessment

There is considerable evidence to show that children from the age of 5 upwards are more than capable of assisting in reviewing and assessing both their own and their peer's work and can also provide supportive and developmental feedback. However, they can only do this when they are absolutely clear about the intended learning targets which despite the emphasis on sharing learning objectives with them, they may not have. Self- or peer-assessment needs to be phased in and it is unreasonable to expect children to be able to do this without support.

Let's use the example of writing a conclusion. Consider the value of identifying an explicit list of criteria and/or some question prompts that will enable 'good' conclusions to be produced.

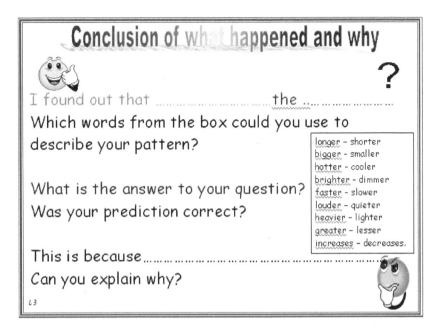

Figure 9.3

Figure 9.3 illustrates one approach that can be helpful but it also provides a clear framework for writing conclusions. From this the teacher would be able to model a WAGOLL (**W**hat **A** **G**ood **O**ne **L**ooks **L**ike) so that children can quickly learn what is required. Clearly communicating what is being assessed assists pupils in becoming better able to independently assess their own work and that of others. This can easily be extended by producing teacher examples with deliberate mistakes as children particularly enjoy pointing out their teacher's mistakes!

Technology and Assessment

The pace of technological change is impressive with more and more of this is entering the classroom and some of these new devices can have a very positive impact on assessment.

Electronic voting

Instead of traditional quizzes where pupils use pencil and paper to write their answers, which are handed in, why not try some of voting pods? These not only make a quiz more fun they also allow for analysis of the responses through the simple graphs they produce. While the teacher knows which student is using a handset this isn't obvious to the latter. A traffic light system can also be used to assess learner confidence related to lesson outcomes.

Wikis

The word *'wiki'* is Hawaiian for 'hurry' or 'quick' and so a website can be a wiki if it allows for quick editing by a range of people. Start your own wiki at school simply by using part of your on-line environment. For example, pupil might post a piece of work such as the findings to an Sc1 investigation. Other pupils are then invited to comment on this, so that over a period of time it becomes a WAGOLL. This allows for a library of WAGOLLs to be produced that will match different age groups and abilities.

Blogs

Blogs can be used for students to make 'diary' entries. Consider a project about healthy living and learners providing their own entries into the blog. These could then be used as additional evidence for assessment and also transferred to a wiki and further developed.

Videos

Recording students' activities as video or still picture can capture valuable assessment data. If these are then uploaded, other pupils can add their comments. This provides clear evidence of students' conceptual and procedural knowledge and skills. Still pictures can be turned into movies by using Photostory 3 or Movie Maker, both of which are free to download from the internet. These could 'tell the story' of an investigation by turning it into *'Where is the worst place to keep an ice-cube?'*

Summary

- All good classroom practitioners should recognise the value of AfL, not least in enabling learners to think about their own learning. Such metacognition needs to be actively promoted by teachers.
- Children must be actively involved in their own assessment if their learning needs are to be effectively met.
- The most effective forms of assessment are often invisible to the learner but also an integral aspect of the learning process.
- The greater the diversity of assessment approaches employed by the teacher, the more complete the picture of achievement and attainment is likely to be.
- Remember: *'Not everything that counts can be counted'* (attributed to Albert Einstein).

References

Black, P. & Wiliam, D. (1998) *Inside the Black Box*. London: NFER Wilson.
The *Black Box* series of books, including *Science Inside the Black Box* and *Inside the Primary Black Box*, have a range of tips and cases studies as well as theory. They are pamphlet- or booklet-sized, therefore an easy and short read. These can be purchased from the ASE and GL Assessment.

MovieMaker, available at www.microsoft.com/windowsxp/downloads/updates/moviemaker2. mspx (accessed July 2010).
Naylor, S. & Keogh, B. (2005) *Active Assessment: Thinking, Learning and Assessment in Science*. Sandbach: Millgate House.
If there is one book that you buy this should be it, as not only does it provide the ideas but also the reasons that the ideas and activities work so you can then produce your own.

Photostory 3, available at www.microsoft.com/windowsxp/using/digitalphotography/ photostory/default.mspx (accessed July 2010).
QCDA Assessing Pupil's Progress, available at http://nationalstrategies.standards.dcsf.gov. uk/primary/assessment/assessingpupilsprogressapp (accessed July 2010).
QCDA Assessment and Reporting Arrangements, available at www.qcda.gov.uk/ assessment/3871.aspx (accessed July 2010).
Sets out the details for assessment at the end of each key stage. You can download this and read it on line, or a hard copy is sent to the headteacher of every school each year.

Russell, T. & McGuigan, L. (2003) *Assessing Progress in Science KS1, KS2 & KS3*. London: QCA.

Further Reading

Harrison, C. & Howard, S. (2010) 'Issues in primary assessment: assessment purposes', *Primary Science*, 115: 5–7.
This is the first of a three-part series (all three articles are well worth reading) that focuses on a range of assessment matters. This article addresses the interface of AfL and AoL and considers their interrelationship and different purposes. The usefulness of both approaches is examined from both a teacher and pupil perspective.

Hodgson, C. (2010) 'Assessment for Learning in Science: what works well?', *Primary Science*, 115: 14–16.
This is another highly readable but brief article. Its value lies in the discussion about peer-assessment, self-assessment, provision of good quality feedback to pupils, the use of questioning including different types of questions and the influence of the acquisition of scientific language.

CHAPTER 10

TRANSITIONS IN SCIENCE EDUCATION

Leigh Hoath and Tanya Shields

Chapter Overview

Transitions occur at various a stages in a child's education, including from home to school and across the boundaries at the end of each key stage. Particularly crucial is the transition from primary school to secondary (Y6 to Y7 in most cases) where research has shown evidence of a dip in learners' enthusiasm and attainment where science is concerned. This chapter therefore emphasises ways of ensuring continuity and progression across this interface, whilst also considering the specific problems at other boundaries.

Use is made of the 2010 Royal Society report, which asserts that pupils in Y7 are repeating things they have done in primary school and are not being sufficiently challenged in lower secondary science work. The need to improve mechanisms for passing on information from primary to secondary schools and the adoption of some primary practice in lower secondary school are emphasised, including the importance of enquiry-based teaching. Examples of good practice are outlined, including those where Y7 and Y6 learners can work together and those where use of more sophisticated digital technology is applied. The chapter ends with a discussion of the importance of planning for micro-transitions, i.e. those from one lesson or sequence of lessons to the next.

Key Ideas

This chapter focuses upon transition which has been viewed traditionally as a primary-secondary interface issue. Readers will see that this is only one dimension, as transition also applies at all stages of educational development, including from the Early Years Foundation Stage (EYFS) to Key Stage 1 (KS1) and KS1 to KS2. In addition we also refer to 'micro-transition'; something important both to recognise and plan for as teaching sequences develop to ensure an effective progression in pupils' learning experience from one set of activities to another.

Historically, research into transition has focused on that of the primary to secondary age phases, fuelled by the apparent dip in science attitudes and educational achievement at that stage – an issue highlighted in the 2010 Royal Society report on science education for 5–14 year-olds. It is reasonable to suggest that a greater liaison between primary and secondary has gone some way to address the challenges and 'post-transfer regression' (Royal Society, 2010: 75). There is a clear distinction in the perception of science in primary and secondary schools, especially in terms of what constitutes 'proper' science. This chapter identifies and explores strategies for bridging the gap between the predominantly enquiry-led approach in primary education and the content-driven focus that is so characteristic of secondary education. It also considers strategies designed to help primary teachers effectively manage classroom transitions and suggests particular techniques to address issues relating to the cross phase transition.

For many subjects the structure of any activity is dominated by specific pedagogical approaches and pupil behaviours. There are predetermined expectations for certain subjects – for example, PE may have a less formal approach with pupils having the freedom to move outside of the classroom, while written tasks are usually associated with a more formal classroom environment and limited pupil mobility. Good primary science teaching combines formal and informal approaches to develop all aspects of scientific enquiry as well as subject knowledge and understanding. The facilitation of micro-transitions – the movement between formal and informal approaches – demands careful planning and preparation to ensure pupils develop the skills and attitudes to become successful scientists. Pupils must also be made aware of expected outcomes and appropriate behaviours in each situation for them to successfully meet the intended learning outcomes.

Student Perspectives

Trainees' main concerns were that all key stage transitions were important and that they needed some suggestions about how to minimise the gaps between practice on each side of the transition boundary. Practical examples of what works, in terms of ways of approaching science learning and different teaching styles, were seen to be particularly helpful here, especially as many would be teaching in year groups at one or other transition boundaries.

Enquiry and Transition

It is widely accepted that there are distinct teaching styles associated with each educational phase. In order to manage transition effectively, these differences must be considered and best practice identified. Possibly the most noticeable difference is the level of emphasis placed on developing enquiry-based skills. The term 'enquiry', as earlier chapters have shown, encompasses all the processes associated with generating and investigating questions and analysing the results. Enquiry-based learning tends to be more prominent in the primary phase (4–11 years-old), with teachers developing pupils' knowledge of the world through hands-on exploration and investigations. The term 'enquiry' is less frequently used in secondary schools where pupils are more likely to find themselves engaging in practical 'experimental' work in order to make specific observations related to a particular concept or aspect of the curriculum or develop particular scientific skills.

Points for Reflection

Enquiry is the process of asking questions that can then be investigated. Within the Early Years Foundation Stage pupils are observed on a daily basis making independent discoveries about the world in which they live. When playing in the sandpit children will quickly recognise that wet sand makes better sandcastles than dry sand. Whilst this observation may not be overtly communicated, their conceptual development can be observed through a pupil's behaviour and actions. E.g. Pupils add water to the sand and repeating the same task to test ideas/theories and improve their output.

Pupils investigating chemical reactions in KS3 may be asked to carry out a series of steps to observe outcomes. E.g. Place a strip of Magnesium (Mg) into a test tube then add a small amount of hydrochloric acid (HCl). Observe the reaction and collect the gas produced. To identify the gas pupils are then directed to place a naked flame within the gas upon which they will observe a 'popping' sound – this indicates the presence of hydrogen gas (H_2).

There is also general agreement that the content of practical science in both primary and secondary education involves some form of investigation as reported by the Science Community Representing Education (SCORE, 2008). However, the purpose for carrying out such work differs greatly between the two phases. The most significant difference is the purpose for carrying out practical investigations. In KS3 there is a strong emphasis on developing the skills and techniques to observe phenomena or on using specific pieces of equipment such as light boxes and prisms to demonstrate the refraction of light. Whilst this technique is not completely absent in the primary phase, here there is a much stronger emphasis placed on exploration and investigation. Independent exploration (play with a purpose) is facilitated most effectively in the EYFS where teachers can provide hands-on, minds-on opportunities for pupils to make sense of the world around them. This practice is formalised as children progress through Key Stage 1 and 2, developing techniques traditionally associated with working scientifically such as fair testing and problem solving.

The Royal Society 2010 report suggests that supporting the transition between KS2 and KS3 occurs at a pastoral level and is rarely to *promote continuity and progression in relation to subject programmes and pedagogy'* (p. 71). The shift in focus from an enquiry-led to a more content-driven approach requires support to enable pupils to manage the fundamental changes 'both in terms of the formal content of the curriculum and the manner in which it is taught' (p. 63).

Pupils' Enthusiasm for Science

Early science experiences are met with great enthusiasm by the majority of pupils. This is evident throughout the Foundation Stage where pupils will ask questions about the world around them. As they move through KS1, one area they will begin to explore is the difference between living and non-living things. This continues into KS2 when working on such aspects as piecing together the ecology of an ecosystem. They will generally remain keen both to share their enjoyment of science and embrace the learning opportunities presented to them. Their high level of interest in science is likely to be rooted in their being encouraged to think about what they are doing, the use of meaningful contexts, their own contributions being valued (they are often encouraged to make their own decisions) and actively sought, and being used to an educational regime in which learning objectives are consistently shared with them. They will take this through to the secondary setting with the anticipation of new but even more exciting science. The reality would appear to be, however, that the Year 7 science curriculum *'was not sufficiently challenging or different from that the pupils experienced in Year 6'* (Royal Society, 2010: 68). Galton (2009: 26) identified this repetition as one of the major themes accounting for regression in Year 7. He also identified the culture of learning as another key issue (see Chapter 6 for a further discussion of culture brokerage) and the importance of recognising and valuing prior learning.

> ## Points for Reflection
>
> Stringer (2003) suggests that the move to secondary school represents a distinct rite of passage for many children. With this transition it is accepted that there will be changes and unfamiliar experiences and in many cases pupils will look forward to this step forward and thrive on the challenges that lie ahead.
>
> Consider the ways in which stronger links can be established between your class and their future science setting – what can they take with them to KS3? How can you help support the transition from one culture of teaching to another? How can you support the pupils in their transition from one key stage to the next? What role is there for cross Key Stage planning in science teaching? What value is actually placed upon recognition or prior and future learning in the transition from one Key Stage to the next?

Pupils' prior learning can be explored using a graphic organiser such as the KWL grid in Table 10.1 below. The grid allows children to record what they *Know*, what they *Want* to know and what they have *Learnt*. Teachers can then use this information to identify misconceptions and areas of interest and in turn plan lessons that are interesting and appropriate to pupil ability. The final column provides learners with opportunities to self-assess and identify the progress they have made throughout a topic.

A fourth area Galton raises is that of assessment and the trust that can be placed in it. Rose (2008) indicated that '*too little regard appears to be paid by many secondary schools to the reliable information on primary children's academic progress that now*

Table 10.1

The Earth and its Axis		
Know...	Want to know...	Learnt...
The Earth is at an angle – Sarah	How fast the Earth spins – Louis	
The axis is at the bottom of the Earth – James	Why the planets don't crash into each other – Shelby	
The Earth spins on its own axis – Matthew	If there is oxygen in the sun's atmosphere – Scott	
There is life on Earth – Evie	If there are really aliens on other planets – Sam	
The Earth doesn't produce light – Louise	What an axis is – Chloe	
The Earth is a planet – Hannah		
The Earth is made mainly of water – Callum		

exists' and that potentially there is not enough value placed upon the data accompanying the pupil into KS3, but also that there are '*longstanding concerns about the accuracy of information received from primary schools*' (Rose, 2009). The abolition of the science SATs is an issue for debate in its own right: however, the shift to Assessing Pupils Progress (APP) and Assessment for Learning (AfL) across the primary and secondary age phases should support pupils in their transition. The DCSF document '*Strengthening transfers and partnerships: partnerships for progress*' (2008: 11) suggests that one strategy for managing an effective transition is for there to be a '*shared understanding of effective teaching and learning and a strengthening of the use of assessment information including pupils tracking and AfL*'.

The spiral nature of the science curriculum should enable pupils to revisit familiar subjects and extend their knowledge and conceptual understanding. However, where teachers do not address progression from the lower key stages and adopt a 'clean slate' approach, pupils can be found to be repeating work with insufficient challenge or scope for creativity. Their natural curiosity and interest in science leaves them with such great enthusiasm for the most simplistic of 'practical' exercises such as lighting a Bunsen burner. Unfortunately, by the end of KS3, teenage pupils are treating science in a more functional way. For a significant number, science becomes a subject they *have* to do rather than *want* to do. It may be that their natural curiosity is suppressed through the content-driven approach of the secondary curriculum, that they are less active (make fewer decisions), experience a greater emphasis being placed on following instructions and routines and have greater difficulty in relating what they are doing to themselves. Of course what is happening to their views of science teaching and learning is also likely to be significantly influenced by the sociological factors relating to adolescence.

Recent years have therefore witnessed a growing shift towards a more primary approach to teaching Year 7 pupils within their secondary setting. The introduction of bridging or transfer tasks and the collaboration between primary and secondary teachers have moved some way in addressing differences in teacher expectations and the 'Transition Plans' which formalise these strategies are commonplace in Welsh schools (Royal Society, 2010: 76). The use of bridging units also goes a long way to addressing curriculum continuity with pupils beginning a project in Year 6 and completing it in Year 7. For many this provides the opportunity for cultural adjustment. However whilst this is helpful in reducing learner anxiety, it should not be seen as the primary aim. For bridging units to work successfully, teachers from both key stages must play an active role in the implementation of work. This not only ensures shared expectations against standardised levels but also provides opportunities to share teaching practice and pedagogical approaches. Having two teachers from different classes or even schools working together can support the mediation of pupils transiting from one class or school to another. This level of collaboration also often facilitates the development of professional trust between two distinctly different organisations.

Transition in Action

Eleanor Brodie has actively tacked the issue of managing transition between KS2 and KS3 and produced resources which are for use across Year 6 and Year 7: these are flexible enough to be used formally within the curriculum or in a more informal way. The project aimed to *develop self-confidence and personal skills of year 7 pupils by enabling them to work collaboratively with their teachers in running cross-curricular science and history activities* (Brodie, 2010: 25). Entitled 'Double Crossed', the project made explicit links between history and science (see Figure 10.1 below). It also encouraged pupils to undertake activities which could promote progression and learning in these areas by using topics that were familiar to pupils.

Example 1: Time Raiders – Death of the Mummy

Pupils take on the role of archaeologists working in small groups to examine and excavate the mummy of an Egyptian king. The aim of the excavation is to learn as much as possible about the subject and to interpret all available evidence from the tomb to determine the cause of death. Who was this? How did they live? How did they die?

Working in small groups the pupils develop team-working, communication and interpersonal skills, culminating in putting together a report and presenting their findings to the rest of the class at the end of the activity. The activity also involved investigative skills and linked directly to science, the human body and history.

Example 2: Vanished! A Blitz Mystery

Pupils take on the role of young air-raid wardens in order to solve a mystery that takes place after an air raid in the Second World War. The scene of the mystery is an abandoned wartime house in Coventry at the time of the Blitz. The aim of the investigation is to find out what happened to the family that used to live there. The scene is set with a montage of evocative photographs showing the damage caused by bombing and the aeroplanes used.

The activity involves investigative skills and links directly to science (flammable liquids) and history. The activity includes a final group presentation which focuses on both the scientific evidence and the pupils' own thoughts on how the family involved would have felt.

The outcomes of this project are encouraging and can serve as a positive indicator that managing transition is beneficial. The pupils involved spoke of being less nervous, more confident and more able to work well with others as a direct result of the work they undertook in this project. The most interesting aspect of this work is the use of Year 7 learners to deliver some of the activities to Year 6 pupils and 87 per cent of the Year 6s involved stated they felt huge benefits of working with the Year 7s in this way, whilst the teachers who were involved also found benefits in working together. For example, they felt free to focus more on their questions, to develop an argument, question evidence and apply their thinking and reasoning skills. By using this common

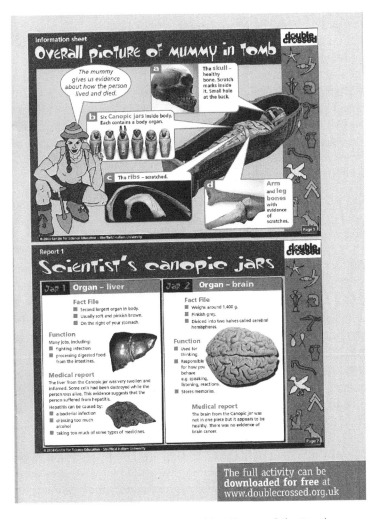

Figure 10.1 (supported by the Astra Zeneca Teaching Trust and the Trust)

theme teachers were able to support pupils in developing skills and learning that they had previously considered mutually exclusive.

This case study offers a real, practical example of effective transition management and further information can be found in the article (Brodie, 2010) as well on on the website supporting this project (www.doublecrossed.org.uk).

Pedagogy and Practice

You have read in Chapter 6 about how different educational spaces will talk in different ways, they will communicate the rules within that space. The expectations in Physical Education are that pupils will be able to move freely, whether it is in a large indoor space or outside of the classroom. In an extended writing task they are relatively inactive and expected to remain seated at a desk for the majority of the lesson. Science too has its own set of rules and it is these conventions that a teacher must establish and maintain for pupils to engage successfully with a subject. In primary science learning contexts pupils will expect practical work, exploration, investigation and experimentation. They will need to work collaboratively, spend time at a desk, and often move around the classroom. They may also have to 'behave' as they do in the other subject areas – sit at their desks, work individually, and read in silence. Science not only has its own rules but also draws upon those from other subject areas as well.

﹏﹏   Points for Reflection

Think about a typical primary science teaching session. What are the expected conventions of such a lesson? Would you expect different conventions to exist say compared to a history session or a literacy session? Would such conventions vary if the children were being taught by a science specialist rather than a general primary practitioner? How important is it for the novice teacher to develop their professional knowledge in this way and how would they address this? How do children acquire knowledge and understanding of expected conventions? What might hinder/assist their acquisition and how might this impact on their learning? Aikenhead's work (1996, 2000) unravels this in more detail.

There is also a need to ensure effective learning and the progression of pupils' knowledge and understanding. Learners are often distracted by 'what' they are doing rather than engaging with the 'whys' and 'hows' of the science underpinning the work. The expectation of a pupil 'doing' science is that they will have fun (*'Are we doing something fun today Miss?'*), something that is strongly associated with practical work. It is the teacher who must skilfully harness such enthusiasm and use it to engage their minds and further develop pupils' scientific knowledge and understanding. The pedagogical challenge for that teacher is managing this and ensuring pupils do not simply engage at a superficial level. They must do so in order that key learning outcomes are addressed; this highlights the hands-on to minds-on aspect of transition which requires careful planning and consideration.

Points for Reflection

Children can easily explore the effects of air resistance by increasing and decreasing the surface area using a variety of objects e.g. large sheets of card, kites and umbrellas. This investigation enables them to experience the effects of an unseen force. The teacher must then ensure that the concept of air resistance is developed and consolidated. If this is not done children are most likely to focus on the activity itself and consequently will fail to develop any scientific knowledge and understanding of forces. Some teachers are also guilty of doing scientific activities simply because 'It is science therefore I have to do a practical activity.'

How do you manage the transition from relevant practical experience to the development of relevant scientific knowledge and understanding? How does this support your self-evaluation of your teaching? If the pupils didn't learn what you wanted them to learn, how 'fit for purpose' was the practical activity?

Micro-transitions

A teacher must utilise a wide range of pedagogical approaches and management strategies to teach science successfully (see Chapter 8 on Pedagogical Content Knowledge). Teaching science involves engaging pupils in a wide range of activities which will vary from lesson to lesson. The opportunity to include such variation is one of the strengths of science but it also presents a significant challenge. It is key for classroom practitioners to recognise the importance of managing the moves between different phases of a learning experience whether this is from introduction to development activities, from core tasks to plenary, from practical work to a class discussion. Most of this professional development will occur through experience – in other words what worked well or, most likely, what didn't work well. It is wrong for teachers to assume such short-term changes do not present problems but that they actually need to be carefully considered. This expansion of PCK allows student-teachers and teachers to facilitate pupil learning and manage the micro-transitions from practical activities to class/group discussion or even individual work. In doing so, learners are better able and also more likely to develop an holistic knowledge and understanding of science.

                    Points for Reflection

Whilst carrying out an investigation to find the noisiest part of the school, the class teacher manages a series of micro-transitions. The initial input requires the KS2 pupils to adopt more formal pedagogical behaviours with a series of listening, discussion and questioning activities. Once pupils have formulated their questions and planned methods to collect evidence/data, they will adopt informal pedagogical behaviours. The process of collecting data outside the classroom boundaries demands a significant level of pupil motivation and task management. On returning to the classroom the pupils will combine both formal and informal behaviours to compile their evidence and discuss conclusions with peers.

In this example, think about the transitions the pupils make (and you should facilitate!). These may be physical – where are the pupils in the room, do they move around, are there materials they need in different parts of the room, are you taking them outside? They may be cognitive – how do you support the pupils in thinking about links between the practical activity and the concept it is supporting the development of? How do you ensure the minds-on as well as hands-on aspects of your lesson? They may also be affective – how do you support the pupil who is unable to share, work co-operatively or is unfamiliar with the rules of engagement?

Supporting Learning

When identifying best practice within our science teaching it is essential to consider those motivational factors which aid learning. There is strong evidence to suggest a direct correlation exists between engagement and enjoyment, both of which are greater at primary school. Why this is the case is subject to considerable speculation, with contributing factors such as the style of teaching, increased difficulty, parental influence, gender factors and social perceptions all playing a significant role. It is therefore worth considering the barriers created by external factors, such as parental and social perceptions.

Parents and other adults will often negatively convey their experiences of science education. Stories of failed experiments, gory dissections and general boredom from science lessons in the past are handed down between generations and can contribute to the creation of a generally negative view of science. The stereotypical image of a scientist or science student continues to persist and is influenced further through social factors such as the media. Society's fascination with science focuses predominantly on the negative impact reported by the press, as with the speculated link between autism and the MMR vaccinations or the effects of genetically modified crops on human growth. If children are to develop an understanding of the scientific world they must be given opportunities to discuss, consider and reflect on the evidence presented to them. Providing learners with meaningful contexts for their investigations is particularly useful when raising the profile of science within the real world has already been identified as being important.

A context-based approach to the teaching of science therefore not only increases pupil enjoyment but also increases pupil engagement with the subject. Teachers within the EYFS and KS1 will actively involve children with investigations designed to find a solution to a problem that is presented within a familiar story. This pedagogic strategy not only often promotes pupil creativity but also generates a sense of purpose in the learner.

Points for Reflection

Consider resources that are not typically 'science' and you will find that science is everywhere and allows work to be set in a context that is familiar and will then further support a cross-curricular or thematic approach to teaching. For example, 'The Lighthouse Keepers Lunch' by David Armitage provides the perfect context for exploring materials. Children could be asked to investigate which material will keep the lighthouse keeper's lunch warm. Alternatively they could explore the type of materials that could be used to keep him dry during a storm. Are there other areas of scientific knowledge that this story might contextualise?

What other stories do you use throughout the Key Stages? Next time try to read these with a science 'hat' on in order to support expanding the range of sources being used in science teaching.

Finding a story that will engage and motivate children will vary greatly from one class to another and therefore needs careful consideration. As pupils progress from KS1 into KS2 and beyond so the use of stories as a context for investigations declines as teachers opt for real-life contexts as an alternative. This should not be seen as a distinct point of transition between the imaginary world and the real world. Instead it is an acknowledgement that as children mature, their ability and willingness to engage with fictitious settings can decrease. In some instances this transition may not occur until the later stages of KS2 whereas in other setting pupils may prefer real-life contexts at a much earlier stage.

Using established pedagogical approaches teachers can facilitate pupil work within primary science. Building upon small group work allows children to take active roles in the science tasks they are doing. For example, within a group of no more than four each child could be given a specific role/area of work – recording results, collecting/selecting equipment, measuring/timing evidence, communicating evidence/conclusions. Ensuring that pupils have a role to fulfil and must understand what they have to do in order to achieve this presents the teacher with an opportunity to differentiate the practical skills developed. When planning investigations it is important to consider pupils' practical abilities. If a child does not have a secure understanding of how to read graduated scales they will be unable to measure volumes of liquid, force and mass or temperature accurately. This highlights a fundamental aspect of teaching science. Whilst it is important to develop pupil knowledge, the prerequisite skills to develop this knowledge must also be developed.

Closely related to the success of any science lesson and arguably a fundamental part of this is planning and preparation. The focus of many lesson plans is the intended learning outcomes and the specification of the activities. Often a superficial consideration of resources and equipment will be made when planning science lessons. Careful consideration of the resources and equipment used in science is an important part of curriculum progression. Children need opportunities to explore and use a range of scientific equipment and build on their previous experiences.

 Points for Reflection

When making detailed observations of objects or minibeasts, pupils must have the skill to use specific pieces of equipment. For example, be clear about why the following represents the progression in magnification equipment:

Tripod table-top magnifier ⟶ magnifying glass ⟶ hand lens ⟶ digital microscope ⟶ light microscope

Consider other examples of where pupils can make progress in using equipment. Challenge ideas about equipment which 'belongs' in a certain Key Stage e.g. using digital microscopes in Early Years settings as opposed to traditionally KS2 (see Chapter 4).

It is also worthwhile to consider social issues that do not directly link to progression within the curriculum. We have discussed how the transition from one class or school to another can be unsettling and teachers and schools going to great lengths to limit the perceived changes. However, we must also recognise each child's desire to become more independent and 'grown up' and consider how to meet the expectations of pupils as they take the next step to becoming young adults.

Striking a balance between age-related expectations and curriculum progression requires lines of communication to be opened between teachers from one year to the next. In order to achieve curriculum continuity all teachers involved in the end of key stage transition must establish an accurate understanding of the curriculum and children's attainment when moving into their class/school.

Summary

We have seen that when it is unpicked transition is a complex issue and broadly there are two layers associated with it. Transition at the macro level (from home to an Early Years setting, to primary school, through key stages, to secondary school) requires careful management. At each step the various moves can cause problems as children do not necessarily respond to such changes positively. These issues can be ameliorated by recognising that learners need to understand their new context and supporting them in doing so. It is the teacher's role to enable children to do this. An effective inter-professional dialogue (e.g. between Year 6 and Year 7 teachers) is imperative for managing the transitions on this level.

Transitions described between activities at a micro level require equal attention. The dangers of assumptions being made by teachers have been discussed. Effective practice is characterised by a recognition of these micro-transitions, planning to support children at the interfaces and drawing threads through the learning sequence to create effective lessons. Teachers are generally good at planning coherent sequences of learning but not necessarily for the transition between them. An evaluation of lessons must move beyond 'what worked well' and there is a need to draw upon reflections on your own pedagogical approaches and practice in order to determine the extent to which you, as the classroom teacher, are supporting pupils in managing the transitions they encounter.

References

Aikenhead, G.S. (1996) 'Science education: border crossing into the subculture of Science', *Studies in Science Education,* 27: 1–52.

Aikenhead, G.S. (2000) 'Renegotiating the Culture of School Science'. In R. Millar, J. Leech and J. Osborne (eds), *Improving Science Education: The Contribution of Research*. Buckingham: Open University Press.

Brodie, E. (2010) 'Learning science through history', *Primary Science*, 111: 25–27.

DCSF (2008) *Strengthening Transfers and Partnerships: Partnerships for Progress*. Available at http://nationalstrategies.standards.dcsf.gov.uk/node/88183

This publication explores seven key principles upon which effective transition should be based. Its aims were to support motivation and attainment and develop strategies which prevented the post-transfer regression often seen. There are a number of sound ideas reported to which strong partnership between schools is pivotal. This work begins to explore the notion of the teacher as a 'culture broker' facilitating the transition from one context to another. The principles of this role can be applied at both micro- and macro-transition level and will support teachers in helping pupils make sense of the boundaries they must cross within their educational lives.

Galton M. (2009) 'Moving to secondary school: initial encounters and their effects', *Perspectives on Education 2 (Primary-secondary Transfer in Science)*: 5–21. See www.wellcome.ac.uk/perspectives

Galton, M., Gray, G. and Rudduck, J. (2003) *Transfer and Transitions in the Middle Years of Schooling, 7–14: Continuities and Discontinuities in Learning*. Nottingham: Department for Education and Skills.

Rose J. (2008) *Independent Review of the Primary Curriculum: Interim Report*. London: HMSO.

Rose J. (2009) *Independent Review of the Primary Curriculum: Final Report*. London: HMSO.

Royal Society (2010) *Science and Mathematics Education, 5–14: A 'State of the Nation' Report*. London: The Royal Society.

This report considers issues arising from the teaching and learning of science and mathematics in the 5–14 age phase. There is a chapter addressing the transition between Key Stage 2 and 3 which offers an account of previous research and current projects as well as aims and objectives and good practice in order to achieve an effective move from primary to secondary school. A summary version of the document is also available.

Stringer, J. (2003) 'We've all done this before', *Primary Science Review*, 80: 4–6.

This article considers the history of transition in science education and identifies some of the issues associated with it.

CHAPTER 11

EFFECTIVE INCLUSION PRACTICE IN PRIMARY SCIENCE

Dave Howard and Ashlee Perry

Chapter Overview

This chapter focuses on the diversity of primary classrooms in terms of the characteristics of all learners (gender, culture, language, attendance, attitude, ability, disability) and considers the dangers of labelling children inappropriately. It goes on to provide practical examples of science activities and how these can best be differentiated so as to maximise opportunities to learn. Although some of the case studies or examples may appear extreme, teachers are likely to encounter pupils with a range of different needs. Ultimately, a good teacher must provide opportunities for each individual learner to achieve, enjoy and be positive about themselves. Science, as a learning context, enables each learner, facilitated by the teacher, to explore their understanding of the world in the company of others.

Key Ideas

By the end of this chapter you should be clearer about some of the approaches to addressing pupils' diverse needs in a range of settings with a specific reference to science. Obviously many of the considerations addressed in this chapter could also refer to other subjects. Practical examples will be provided which demonstrate classroom-based science activities that may be used from early years up to KS3 (Y7) to meet individual needs. This chapter is shaped by pedagogical and practitioner considerations rather than by formal curriculum or assessment imperatives.

 Student Perspectives

Inclusion is a topic that was not part of the original chapter structure for this book, yet it was clear from our focus group discussions that it needed to be dealt with. Their concerns overlapped with some of those arising within earlier chapters, particularly in relation to the increasingly diverse range of learners' needs, the emphasis on assessment for learning and the growing acceptance of the needs of gifted and talented children, as well as those with learning difficulties or disabilities.

Our Starting Point

> The myth of the average learner has been shattered and teachers are recognizing the need to individualize and honor [sic] the unique profiles of all students. (Kluth et al., 2003: 19)

This demonstrates the point that for most practitioners class groups are considered as a collection of individuals rather than as an homogeneous cohort. It is now widely accepted – through the experience of Initial Teacher Education courses with their emphasis on meeting individual needs, through Continuing Professional Development, and through legislation – that one size does not fit all. In Britain the Special Educational Needs and Disabilities Act (2001), the Disability Discrimination Act (2005) and the Equality Act (2010) all seek to ensure the right of all pupils to access the curriculum.

Teachers need to be well informed about the pupils in their classroom regarding a range of factors. These might include background and culture though beyond simply applying labels such as 'deprived', 'free school meals', 'from single parent families', or 'SEN'. The other key presupposition is that if teachers do have this information they also have the knowledge, skills and appropriate teaching skills to use it to inform learning and teaching. This will most often include working as part of a team to address the holistic needs of each pupil as an individual and a learner.

Discussion of the Issues: Linking Together Key Ideas

We have identified seven characteristics for *all* learners which will drive them. These will affect pupils in many areas including educational achievement and attainment, employment successes or failures, relationships, and personal ambitions and aspirations. In the classroom such characteristics will impact pupil access to education in its broadest sense, e.g. the formal and informal curriculum, the planned and the received curriculum, and the hidden and explicit curriculum.

Points for Reflection

What is meant by the formal science curriculum? Kelly defines this as the 'activities for which the timetable of the school allocates specific periods of teaching time' (2006: 7). However, what is meant by the:

- Informal science curriculum?
- Planned science curriculum?
- Received science curriculum?
- Hidden science curriculum?
- Explicit science curriculum?

How do these differ in status? would you emphasise one above another? Which of these types of curriculum does the ethos of your school support?

Labelling any individual can create potential barriers and discrimination. The term 'Special Educational Needs' (SEN) carries with it a large amount of baggage which can result in a self-fulfilling prophecy being implemented in practice for both the pupil and others. The same applies to someone categorised as Gifted and Talented (G&T) in science, where the expectations are created due to the label rather than the actual accomplishments or talents of that individual. Indeed the label itself is an assessment – it can predispose a teacher not to reach their own professional judgments based on evidence and knowledge of the pupil.

Our characteristics are also labels but have been designed to create a model to demonstrate the thesis that there are several performance drivers that impact on individuals. The categories are not mutually exclusive. For example, a person's

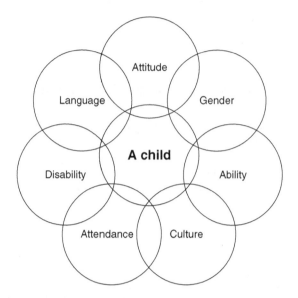

Figure 11.1   Representation of individual drivers

linguistic competence *could* be related to their ethnicity or a girl's attitude towards science *might* be affected by peer pressure and the view that science is a male domain.

Each category will be addressed through an exploration of the underlying ideas and, in some cases, specific science activities and approaches that can be employed when teaching pupils.

Gender

Is the argument that girls are less interested in science a myth? Believing this, whether it is true or not, can determine how a teacher conducts a lesson and how the pupils receive it. What matters however is the belief system of a teacher who values equality, access to the curriculum and meeting the needs of every pupil. Positive actions to meet these needs can include such approaches as:

- The promotion of successful female scientists (role models), e.g. Diane Fossey (gorillas); Susan Greenfield (the brain); Rosalind Franklin (DNA).
- The use of media-positive images, e.g. Dora the Explorer, Charlotte Uhlenbroek.
- Gender-neutral or female-biased scientific themes, e.g. materials in the fashion industry; the science of cosmetics and animal testing.
- Grouping – mixed *vs.* single sex. Considerations of engagement and passivity. For example, do boys really get asked more questions in science than girls?

Points for Reflection

How many female scientists, real or fictional, can you name? Try this with any group of friends and the list is likely to be surprisingly small. Now consider your own practice when teaching science to girls in your classroom. What messages, conscious or subliminal, are you giving? This could be easily extended to cover science as it is portrayed in the media or in textbooks.

What language are you using? Do you refer to a scientist as 'he'? Do you explore the science of medicine when discussing health professionals, e.g. nurses?

Culture

We are using the term 'culture' here to embrace a person's situation in a plurality of contexts which will include language, ethnicity, socio-economic class, religious beliefs, shared prior experiences and general belief systems. As part of your assessment of pupils you will need to be able to identify the significant cultural aspects that can impact on learners. You will also need to make sensitive judgments about how your approaches will be received by them. Positive actions to address such approaches are:

- The use of examples or resources that can enhance an understanding of different cultures rather than relying on Anglo-centric or other mono-cultural examples or resources.
- The identification of scientists across and beyond socio-economic class groups, e.g. food scientists working in large factories; builders understanding loads and materials; chefs recognising the science of food preparation and storage.
- A discussion of scientists' responsibility for their discoveries/inventions, e.g. the development of weapons; vivisection.
- A discussion of the links between religion and science, beliefs about the origin of the universe, evolution, and an after-life.

Points for Reflection

If you are teaching a topic on food groups, why not bring in an oyster or a squid or some sauerkraut as alternatives to apples, pizza or chocolate? Using resources that are their unfamiliar to pupils can broaden both the expectations and experiences.

(Continued)

> *(Continued)*
>
> Have a multicultural day with pupils bringing in food stuffs (and their parents) from their own cultures and classifying the relevant food groups. This can value individuals' identities and help encourage ALL pupils to make equal contributions. An engaging, cross-curricular topic on vivisection raises moral considerations, an awareness of the outcomes of such experiments, and emotional responses to the feelings of others.

Language

In this section 'linguistic competence' refers to the range of language and linguistic skills pupils possess. Consider the use of the mother tongue, bi-lingual learners, pupils with delayed language development and other specific language difficulties. Science offers a vocabulary-rich context which can be very exciting and challenging but can also be a barrier to learning. Science achievement and attainment can be compromised by an inability to access the teaching or express ideas in the 'normal' form. Positive actions to address such approaches are:

- The use of displays in languages that are relevant to the pupils, created by themselves.
- Clear modelling of the key terms or phrases pupils will need with supportive pictures, signs, etc. that they can build up for themselves.
- The use of a range of question types including closed questions to build confidence, engagement and achievement.
- The use of writing frames to support recording and reporting (either bilingual or with key words to incorporate in the text).
- The use of diagrams rather than spoken or written instructions.
- Resources, e.g. keyword cards/displays, worksheets that can be accessed by ALL pupils at appropriate reading levels; also, the use of published schemes or materials that pay close attention to the linguistic needs of diverse pupils.
- The use of other adults or peers to help mediate the work, e.g. as 'expert' others or for language support.
- Avoiding a simple translation of words for EAL learners; use the scientific term in context to provide meaning.

Below is an example of a partial writing frame for the life-cycle of a butterfly. The mother tongue (Russian) is written beneath the English.

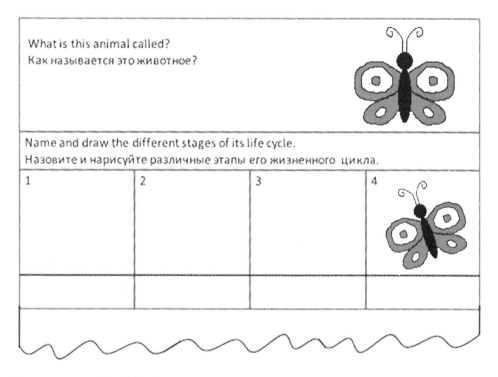

What is this animal called?
Как называется это животное?

Name and draw the different stages of its life cycle.
Назовите и нарисуйте различные этапы его жизненного цикла.

1	2	3	4

Figure 11.2   Partial writing frame

Attendance

> There is a strong correlation between the amount of absence in a school and the qualifications that its pupils achieve. (School Attendance Matters, 2007)

The question of attendance and getting pupils to school is multi-faceted. Factors such as parental attitudes, pupils' attitude to school, mobility, health (parent/carer and pupil), school response and initiatives, LA interventions and culture can all affect an individual pupil's attendance (and punctuality). A teacher may feel detached and distant from concerns about attendance but – as part of the ECM agenda and individuals' roles within multi-disciplinary teams – each can play a part. Positive actions to address attendance issues are:

- Planning and teaching engaging, meaningful and innovative lessons which will enable pupils to experience the 'Wow' factor.
- Relating familiar contexts as starting points for science experiments and investigations (using pupils' hobbies and interests).

- Pitching work to meet individual needs so that pupils can experience a sense of success and achievement.
- Building in opportunities for re-visiting key concepts and skills for those whose attendance is intermittent (a willingness by the teacher and school to commit to pupils).
- Sending work home (where applicable) with support coming from those at home.

 Points for Reflection

A focus on scientific process skills would enable pupils to access learning even if their attendance was variable. Through creating the right classroom climate and ethos, they could engage with the scientific skills and develop their understanding of concepts via these skills. This presupposes a shift away from a teacher-led, content-based curriculum towards a skills-driven curriculum as espoused, for example, by 'How Science Works'. The pupils would not be as disadvantaged as their peers whose attendance is more consistent.

Some aspects of attendance are beyond a teacher's control, but at a classroom level, providing exciting learning opportunities which will enable pupils to progress and succeed can encourage them, if possible, to mitigate the external factors. For example, a pupil can use their 'voice' to state what they want even if other factors are creating barriers to their attendance. There will, of course, be both LA and school policies on attendance and punctuality which will impact on individual teachers' response.

Attitude

By 'attitude' we mean a pupil's beliefs about a subject which will affect their approach and demeanour. The impacts of pupils' attitudes include a willingness to engage as well as their motivation, desire to learn, effort and perseverance. When the attitude is good, positive outcomes can ensue, e.g. higher achievement and attainment, positive responses from others (peers, parents and teachers), an increase in self-esteem, and greater enjoyment in the educational process generally. A virtuous circle is thus constructed.

 Points for Reflection

The teacher has a significant role to play in creating an environment that is conducive to a positive approach to learning science. You can model your own positive enjoyment of and engagement in science. Where the opportunities arise you should convey a willingness 'to have a go'. For example, when measuring speed, you could be timed covering 10m. Or you can also demonstrate your fallibility and 'not knowing'. Or you can model researching information, possibly there and then on the IWB, based on your own curiosity to find out.

If pupil attitude is poor, negative outcomes will ensue, e.g. a negative attitude towards science per se could result in a learner 'switching off' throughout a lesson, not knowing what is occurring and self-fulfilling views about one's own capability. These can manifest both in performance and in behaviour – being distracted, disrupting others and being told off. A vicious circle is the result.

Central to Figure 11.3 is the quality of science teaching. This is created by the teacher using such pedagogical skills as praise, differentiation, a use of effective resources, a dynamic delivery, enthusiasm, management and organisation, and engaging all pupils. In primary school many pupils are keen to learn and will want to contribute to lessons. They have not reached, nor hopefully will reach, the age of cynicism.

Science lessons can be used to generate excitement and harness curiosity through a careful choice of a wide range of activities. These could include investigations, observations, demonstrations, use of resources and visits/visitors. It could also be the case that those pupils who are already engaged can be turned off by undertaking dull, repetitive and meaningless activities.

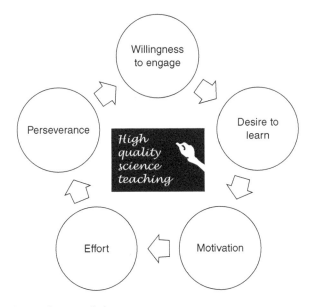

Figure 11.3   Creating a virtuous circle

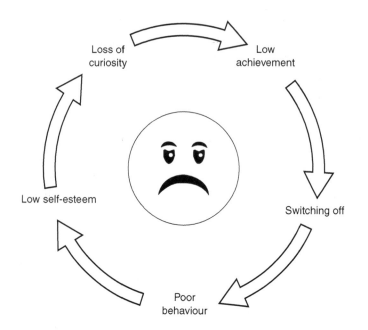

Figure 11.4   Addressing a vicious circle

In a science lesson on light, for example, a teacher or the pupils themselves can generate ideas about fundamental properties of light, such as travelling in straight lines and being emitted from an energy source. The teacher or pupils can then project shadows of interesting, unseen objects onto the wall (a toy, a child's hand, Javanese shadow puppets) so that learners can begin to create their own hypotheses about light which can be subsequently tested. Differentiated activities can be planned by getting them to direct a beam of light around an obstacle course using mirrors and/or reflectors. Eventually all pupils could experience a sense of achievement by designing and constructing a periscope. Environmental consequences can be explored and developed in turn such as using the sun to generate heat and electricity. Links could also be made to renewable energy, sustainability, global warming and applications in the home.

Disability

We are adopting the term 'disability' as it is used in the Disability Discrimination Act (2005) that defines a disabled person as someone who has '*A physical or mental impartment which has a substantial and long term adverse effect on his or her ability to carry out normal day to day activities*'. This covers categories relating to mobility, physical co-ordination, continence, speech, hearing or eyesight, memory or the ability to concentrate, learn or understand, and the perception of physical risk. Extra consideration will often be needed to meet the needs of a disabled pupil in terms of planning, resources preparation, risk assessments and, in some cases, parental consultation. This is particularly important when planning practical work or engaging in science activities in non-traditional settings.

As far as possible the intention should be to include a disabled pupil in all planned activities in order not to treat them less favourably and to avoid putting them at a substantial disadvantage. In practice, we assume that the school will have met their legal duty to have accessibility plans that will enable pupils to access the curriculum. It is essential that class teachers are involved in producing individual education or behaviour plans (IEPs and IBPs) and that these are shared with other adults working in the classroom and also with the child, as far as they are able to know and understand the content of the plans. While science should not be seen as a special case, we need to recognise that this subject can present particular challenges to non-specialist support staff. Communicating with parents, previous teachers and any support workers is vital in order to focus on the needs of each child.

For example, in science lessons some immediate concerns will become apparent such as moving around (inside the classroom or outside), using resources such as viewers, manipulating data-loggers and digital microscopes, conducting investigations requiring working with others, and recording and presenting results. Other less obvious barriers could include group dynamics, the role of the TA, the teacher's knowledge of the specific disability, or the teacher's reluctance to 'challenge' a disabled learner. Sometimes there will be a desire to over-support a disabled pupil which can actually impede can any possible learning and progress. We will exemplify a variety of approaches for three commonly encountered types of disability: these are pupils with Attention Deficit Hyperactivity Disorder (ADHD), those with mobility difficulties, and those diagnosed as being on the autistic spectrum.

Pupils with ADHD

Pupils with ADHD can present significant challenges to teachers. ADHD is a common behavioral disorder that affects an estimated 10 per cent of school-age pupils. Recent research suggests that there are both genetic and environmental causes and that environmental factors are many. Boys are approximately three times more likely than girls to be diagnosed with this but the research evidence is inconclusive as to why this is so. Pupils diagnosed with ADHD will often act without thinking, be hyperactive, will not learn from their mistakes, will have trouble focusing and concentrating, and experience difficulties with their short-term memory. They may understand what's expected of them but will also have difficulty keeping on task because they find it hard to sit still and pay attention to detail.

Certain practical scientific activities are particularly suited to meeting the needs of pupils with ADHD. These can be categorised in terms of science content and scientific processes. Take for example sorting and classifying materials within 'Materials and their Properties'. Pupils could role-play the properties assigned to them such as 'I am steel' – pulling a hard face or taking up a body-builder pose. For rubber, the pupils could walk in a floppy manner or speak in a languid, relaxed, drawn-out voice. For nutrition within 'Life Processes and Living Things' (AT2) pupils could draw on paper plates the foods they had consumed the previous day and be judged on their nutritional value (with a nod towards *The X Factor*).

For manipulating equipment as well as collecting raw data they could be shown how to use pooters, starting with collecting and sorting plastic insects in the classroom as a means of understanding how they work. The pupils would then apply the skills in the playground or field, carefully collecting the insects before observing them and recording their findings.

~ **Points for Reflection**

What these activities have in common includes the following; hands-on tasks, short, easily understood instructions, the use of interesting equipment, and managed group work. There is also a fun and novelty element, a sense of discovery, and a sense of achievement. In terms of practice teachers should consider 'chunking' which, although relevant in many lessons, would aid those students with more limited concentration spans. Questions should also be carefully planned and targeted. The activities can be completed within a single session rather than being protracted.

Do your science lessons conform to a regular, routine pattern of delivery, activities and types of question? What impact might this have on a pupil with ADHD?

Pupils with limited mobility

Pupils with limited mobility can present challenges to teachers due to the range of such difficulties, e.g. from some difficulty in walking to being wheelchair-bound. The range impacts hugely on how a teacher might respond to addressing individual need. It is possible to be seduced by the label of disability that creates a barrier between the person who is disabled and the rest of us. Some disabled pupils learn to manage their reduced mobility without the need of any intervention or adjustments being made; for them it is essential that they manage their difficulties as this empowers them, enabling them to develop sets of skills and problem solve. For a teacher to over-support in this case would be doing a disservice to the pupil. For others support will be needed. Teachers need to find a happy medium between meeting specific needs and challenging each child. This will be determined by the teacher's experience, expertise, perception and judgement.

There are some obvious immediate practical considerations for learners with mobility difficulties:

- *The physical environment* Some schools are well designed to cater for children with a range of mobility. If this is not the case, despite recent legislation, then teachers must make the best of what does exist. Tables and chairs can be re-arranged and spaces between items of furniture can be enlarged to create pathways. Particularly pertinent to science sessions is when floors become wet, sandy, or littered with various materials which then creates obstacles or hazards, especially for those with limited mobility.
- *Resources* One important aspect of AT1 in science is children selecting and collecting their own resources. If a pupil feels able or wants to do this it may be the case that

they can transport the equipment in different ways; e.g. placing items in a bag for carrying; using a trolley; writing down what they want for someone else to collect. It might be sensible that such children obtain the equipment either before or after others to avoid the busyness of the normal primary classroom.

- *Participation in some activities* Some science activities may not be possible for children to undertake, for example, running to check pulse rates before and after exercise or collecting mini-beasts from uneven ground. If a child cannot run there are other ways to raise their heart rate, such as by raising their arms in the air, bouncing a ball, squeezing a stress ball, moving their wheelchair along a course – in fact, rather than running all the children could do these alternative activities. For collecting mini-beasts, a similar environment to that which is found outdoors could be re-created in a tray or terrarium.

Pupils with autistic spectrum disorder (ASD)

Pupils on the autistic spectrum can present slight to significant challenges to teachers depending on where they are on the spectrum, the support available in school, their prior experiences in school and home environments, and their coping strategies. Autism

Table 11.1

Aspects of ASD	Teaching Strategies

Adapting to change (both daily routines and unexpected events)	• Visual timetables.
	• Communicating explicitly about:
	  o the session, its structure, duration and time constraints
	  o anticipated changes
	  o who is working with them (adult and/or children) and where
	  o equipment/resources to be used
	  o choices they can make.
	• 'Chunking' instructions and tasks.
	• Continuity of staff (where possible).

Social communication	• Unambiguous instructions, messages, explanations. • Use of repetition. • Sufficient response time to answer questions: o if many questions are asked re-processing occurs. • Visual cues can be used to ask and answer questions. • Be sensitive to a pupil's non-verbal communication (NVC) markers (gestures, facial expressions, demeanour). • Appreciate the pupil's difficulty in reading other people's NVC.

Social interactions	• Structure group work appropriately
	  o make-up of group
	  o model and encourage turn taking
	  o assign roles – measurer, recorder, resource gatherer
	  o targeted questions for pupils to ask and answer.
	• Appropriate responses to pupil's inappropriate comments, e.g. 'You are really old and ugly'.
	• Managing the pupil's response to others.

is usually characterised by individuals having difficulties with social communication, inter-action, and their flexibility to adapt to change. Our experience suggests this can manifest itself in poor behaviour, disengagement, and varying levels of achievement. Many famous scientists are thought to have been autistic; examples include Sir Isaac Newton and Albert Einstein. Certainly the logical, left brain thought processes that are useful in science could result in the autistic child engaging more fully in subjects like science or maths.

This is how an autistic child might feel when confronted with change. The teacher had planned an outing to an outdoor centre to study pond life. To manage Barry's anxiety she informed Barry and his carers about the trip several weeks in advance both by letter and personal contact. She regularly mentioned the trip to all the children and undertook much pre-visit work including using the school grounds for a dummy run. She displayed on the IWB photographs of the centre, its grounds, and the people who will host the visit. Barry had been given a timed itinerary of the day and his mother accompanied them on the trip. Barry was made responsible for the box of magni-fying glasses which served both as a focus for the activities and as a distraction if needed.

In terms of communicating with others Saima tended to respond very literally to instructions. On one occasion, when the class was discussing electric circuits, she was asked to pretend that she was a light bulb and told that when another pupil passed by her she was to smile as if she had been illuminated. Initially Saima looked confused and did not respond. The teacher realised his mistake and proceeded to give her precise, simple, step-by-step instructions:

1. Saima, you are pretending to be the light bulb in this circuit.
2. The other pupils are pretending to be the electric current.
3. You are 'off' at present.
4. When a pupil goes by you become lit up.
5. You are now 'on'.
6. To show you are 'on' you can give a big smile and put your arms in the air.

Callum prefers to work on his own, which the teacher allows much of the time; however, he also believes that Callum should experi-ence working with others as a life skill and one that he will need to develop further. In the science session the pupils were investigat-ing insulation and the properties of various materials. The teacher selected the groups and communicated this at the start of the lesson, supported by the TA who worked on a 1:1 basis with Callum. His group was given a limited number of resources to use and instructed that each person was to have a role – measurer, recorder, or resource gatherer. Callum was given the task of recorder. One pupil complained, after a while, that they couldn't read Callum's handwriting. Callum took offence and stormed off. The TA managed to get him back on task by re-directing him to compare the insulating materials and support the 'measurer' in taking temperature readings. The previous insult was forgotten. The teacher decided not to follow up either the initial slur on Callum's writing or his subsequent response.

There is a fine line, as can be seen from the above, between supporting and over-supporting so that often other pupils will want to do the work for the child with a disability rather than facilitating them to do it. There is still, in some quarters, a perceived link between physical and mental disability – hence the dreadful spectacle of a person raising their voice or speaking slowly when speaking to someone in a wheelchair. The disability itself could be a focus for scientific investigation where opportunities arise and where the pupil does not feel threatened or singled out. For example, in discussing the functions of the eye, a pupil with a visual impairment may elaborate on their own circumstance. This could be seen to be no different than a pupil from a certain culture discussing their place of worship, their special books, or their specific kind of foods. This has to be handled very sensitively and with communication between home and school but could prove very fruitful for all concerned. It could also be argued that by not explicitly acknowledging differences in terms of disability in their classroom they are maintaining the status quo whereby a disability is either ignored or marginalised.

Ability

We are using the term 'ability' to refer to all pupils' natural competence in any given subject – it can comprise achievement and attainment. For the purpose of this chapter we will consider the most able pupils (Gifted & Talented) and those designated least able (Below Average – BA). Most teachers will already be differentiating tasks to about three levels of ability, however it is our experience that some will use a small range of preferred approaches which may limit their effectiveness and learners' ceiling of achievement and attainment. The boxes below address some strategies for differentiation that are especially suited to the science content for the same learning objective (Knowledge and Understanding of the World: KUW) within the Early Years Foundation Stage ELG 2.14, which states that by the end of the EYFS children should '*Find out about, and identify, some features of living things, objects and events they observe*'. The context is a walk around the local environment close to the school where there is a range of flora and mini-beasts.

If we link differentiation to effective inclusive practice so that, in attempting to include all, we are making specific provision we may end up excluding the majority. The specific provision for all pupils should still involve challenges and the raising of attainment and achievement; the intention is to work to the highest common factor and not the lowest common denominator.

Examples of different forms of differentiation

These are set out below.

1. *Task* – Differentiation by task means giving different activities to individuals/groups based on prior attainment. These may be simply modifications of an existing task or specifically designed. For example:

〰 Points for Reflection

G & T – pupils could be presented with a variety of habitats in which to locate the mini-beasts found on their walk, offering explanations for their placement. Samples of the flora and fauna could be compared to information sources, including digital photographs captured on the walk, and parts identified.

BA – Pupils are given a limited range of habitats with clear descriptions. They are then asked closed questions to help place the mini-beasts in the appropriate environment. Picture cues are used with word cards to help identify body parts.

---

2. *Support* – Pupils will work on a common task but receive additional support in a variety of ways from an adult. For example:

〰 Points for Reflection

G & T – Before the walk pupils could be given time to plan what they will do and how; for example, predicting what mini-beasts they might see, where and how to collect them. The pupils could also use data-loggers on the walk to collect a range of data to process back in the classroom.

BA – Pupils are shown some of the resources used to help collect the mini-beasts and asked which instrument is most useful for which type of animal, e.g. pooters, aerated jars, nets and trays. On a walk to collect mini-beasts the adult will model and explain how they will use the resource before the pupils have a go.

---

3. *Resource* – Pupils will work on a common task but will be able to use different resources to support their learning.
4. *Pace* – Pupils will work on a common task but the time allocated for its completion will be determined by an assessment of prior attainment. We also use this term to indicate the speed and momentum of input/delivery. The key element is pupil engagement which is often achieved by self-management and organisation.

Points for Reflection

G & T – Pupils can be given a deadline for task completion; also, tasks could be extended to be worked on at home or completed over a number of days. Pupils could be given brief but detailed input about the task with the expectation that they will 'join the dots' in terms of the various staged needed to accomplish the task.

BA – Pupils will receive a longer, more scaffolded type of input with smaller, more manageable 'chunks' of both task and time, e.g. five minutes to choose a habitat and then another five minutes to identify three mini-beasts within it.

Summary

In conclusion, effective inclusive practice is about trying to meet the needs of all pupils. Although some of the case studies or examples may appear extreme, teachers are likely to encounter pupils with a range of different needs. Ultimately, a good teacher must provide opportunities for each individual learner to achieve, enjoy, and be positive about themselves. Science, as a learning context, will enable the pupil, facilitated by a teacher, to explore their understanding of the world in the company of others.

References

Booth, T., Ainscow, M., Vaughan, M. & Greenhill, S. (2002) *Index for Inclusion: Developing Learning and Participation in Schools*. CSIE: Bristol.

DfES (2005) *Leading on Inclusion*. London: DfES.

Great Britain (2001) *Special Educational Needs and Disability Act 2001*. London: TSO.

Great Britain (2005) *Disability Discrimination Act 2005*. London: TSO.

Great Britain (2010) *The Equality Act 2010*. London: TSO.

Kelly, A.V. (2006) *The Curriculum Theory and Practice* (5th edition). Sage: London.

Kluth, P., Straut, D.M. & Biklen, D.P. (eds) (2003) *Access to Academics for All Students: Critical Approaches to Inclusive Curriculum, Instruction, and Policy*. Mahwah, NJ: Erlbaum.

School Attendance Matters (2007) *Guidance on Policy, Practice and Matters that Impact on School Attendance* (April). Bracknell: Education, Children's Services & Libraries, Bracknell Forest Borough Council.

Weblinks

http://www.csie.org.uk/inclusionuk/
This is a website that links to four key organisations concerned with inclusion in education and contains a wealth of information for a range of stakeholders.

http://inclusion.ngfl.gov.uk/
This site supports individual learning needs, providing information and links to resources. There is also an online section for seeking help and guidance.

http://inclusiontips.webs.com/inclusionwebsites.htm
This website links to a range of other websites within the field of inclusion to address individual needs.

Further Reading

DfES (2004) *Removing Barriers to Achievement*. London: DfES.
This is a government publication that espouses the need for effective early intervention, the philosophy of inclusion and raising expectations and achievement. The content underpins effective practice.

Knowles, G. (ed.) (2006) *Supporting Inclusive Practice*. London: David Fulton.
This is a collection of chapters addressing different individual needs in accessible, pragmatic and helpful ways. It includes case studies, suggested activities and bibliographies for each chapter.

Spooner, W. (2006) *The SEN Handbook for Trainee Teachers, NQTs and Teaching Assistants*. London: David Fulton.
This is a useful guide for a range of stakeholders providing easy-to-find information, case studies and useful further reading on specific topics such as asthma, cystic fibrosis, etc.

CHAPTER 12

A WAY FORWARD

Alan Peacock and Mick Dunne

What Have the Previous Chapters Told Us about Where We Are Now?

The Royal Society's report, referred to in various chapters above, brings us up to date with the state of play in late 2010. But for you, as a trainee or novice teacher, or as one of the many non-science specialists wishing to engage more productively with science, it raises several important questions about your attitudes to policy, its likely implementation, and how it can help you develop good professional practice. One of the characteristics of being a good professional is the capacity to engage with change but not to do so unquestioningly. Top-down change is likely to continue to focus primarily on the 'what' and perhaps less so on the 'when' but not on the 'how', as those charged with policy making will often have little or no experience of practical classroom teaching. Your own personal decisions about how to implement prescriptions should therefore be guided by the principle of their appropriateness in your own specific classroom and school context.

Yet we are not Luddites. All the authors of this book accept and welcome the dynamic nature of education in general and science education in particular. We hope that by sharing and taking on new ideas you will see that change can be engineered effectively without a consequent loss of quality in educational provision. The authors have placed a strong emphasis on not providing you with a 'ready reckoner' or 'tips for teachers' for science learning, but with a resource that will encourage you to think, to not to be afraid to exercise your professional judgement, and to know what is high quality science education for our younger learners.

Having other countries admire our pioneering approach has been a double-edged sword – it has led to a sense of confidence amongst science educators, whilst generating a reluctance, especially in England, to accept that much could be learned from elsewhere. That is now changing as practice in the home countries diverges following devolution and as collaboration within Europe becomes more prevalent. The change of government in 2010 has also thrown what looked like a new approach based on 'areas of understanding' back into the melting-pot. So new teachers like yourselves will have to keep an open mind and faith in your skills and knowledge in order to seek out whatever ideas and resources are available and then accept the challenge of taking responsibility for being creative, enquiring teachers that can in turn inspire children to find science exciting.

Various chapters have emphasised how planning plays a pivotal role in the quality and depth of children's learning experiences. Several models have been identified, ranging from subject-based through to fully integrated thematic work. Whatever vehicle a school chooses to adopt to deliver learning experiences, the evidence has indicated that any effective planning needs to provide relevance and contextualisation, to utilise assessment for learning principles, to match knowledge and skills objectives closely to learners' needs, and to deliver focused science enquiry skills. These taken together can allow learners to experience a range of ways of enquiring into issues that will make them curious and into problems they will find fascinating.

Relevant cross-curricular opportunities have been strongly emphasised and we have also argued for maximum use to be made of environments outside the classroom. From a teaching perspective, setting science learning in the wider curriculum has been shown to benefit children in developing their understanding across subjects through the use of meaningful real-life contexts and a genuine engagement, exploiting their natural curiosity and stimulating their imagination. It enables teachers to plan learning experiences based on children's needs, the curriculum's demands and flexibility. And whether schemes of work are subject-based or integrated, teachers need to focus more time on planning for diagnostic and formative assessment opportunities without which effective learning is unlikely to take place.

The use of ICT in science has been emphasised because of its potential to promote a better learning of science. Given the rapidity of change in this field, an adaptability and readiness to trial new applications will be crucial as will be the need to avoid a tokenistic engagement. The overwhelming amount of information and assistance available through the internet is already beginning to transform attitudes to knowledge acquisition and will also contribute multiple opportunities for supporting science literacy, taking this to be the capacity to make sense of the world around us in order to be enabled to make informed decisions. Evidence from many contexts, including societies in remoter parts of the world, also highlights the ability to share ideas and concerns as crucial to raising the confidence and professionalism of primary teachers – especially where science is concerned. And it is the knowledge and skills which you and your pupils have acquired through your first-hand experience of the world around you that is most resilient. Such knowledge is context specific and personal and it also provides a key way of understanding and respecting ourselves and the environment on which we all depend.

Your learners, of course, come to you from elsewhere and leave you to work with other teachers who may not share your philosophy or approach. Your views will be challenged and you will need to reflect upon your practice and participate in managing transitions from one stage (and possibly culture) to another. Identifying that these different cultures do exist, what they are like and what this means for the pupils represents a starting point for understanding and effectively managing transitions, in a subject where practice on either side of the interface between stages is markedly different. Teachers are generally good at planning coherent sequences of learning but not necessarily that adept at making plans for the transition between them. You need to draw upon reflections of your own pedagogical approaches and practice in order to determine the extent to which you, as the classroom teacher, are supporting pupils to manage the transitions they encounter.

Learners' talk and communication between each other and their teachers is therefore a crucial element in science learning. This kind of child-child, child-teacher, and teacher-child interaction needs to be supported within an environment where children feel safe to put their ideas forward but also one in which an institutional and inspection culture exists that promotes and values pacey lessons. A number of ways of stimulating talk in science have been discussed and opportunities for using talk in Assessment for Learning were highlighted. By valuing and making time for talk in science, we can enable children to develop higher order thinking skills which can be applied across the curriculum, such as we have seen with citizenship education. Scientists are more hesitant in their conclusions, acknowledging unknowns and having tentative theories that can be disproved but never proven; teachers and children in turn have to feel safe with this kind of uncertainty.

There are always, of course, going to be some 'tricky topics' to teach, as we have called them. These tend to arise within the same concept areas – for example, energy, forces, electricity, Earth and beyond. Fortunately, over the years, effective strategies have been developed which can help both teachers and learners cope with these, involving the use of analogies, metaphors, models and role-play scenarios. Utilising such strategies is inextricably bound up with each practitioner's specialist teaching knowledge for science – what has been called, somewhat unfortunately we feel, their Pedagogical Content Knowledge (PCK). PCK is a complex concept but one, we would argue, that shapes a teacher's pedagogical literacy: their capacity to make sense of particular teaching and learning contexts when identifying those educational strategies that apply most effectively to specific content areas. Contextualising and personalising your use of analogies in enabling learners to access scientific concepts and processes is essential, so that they become learning tools that are a key part of your repertoire as fit for your purpose rather than 'off the shelf' resources. Children's creation of their own analogies is also very beneficial to the development of their scientific understanding.

Finally, effective inclusive practice is about trying to meet the needs of all pupils. Although some of the case studies or examples may appear extreme, teachers continue to encounter pupils with a range of different needs. Ultimately, a good teacher will provide opportunities for each individual learner to achieve, to enjoy, and to be positive about themselves. Science, as a learning context, enables each pupil, facilitated by a teacher, to explore their understanding of the world in the company of others.

The next two final sections of this book look at some things to consider when looking ahead to how you might generate and sustain good practice in your science teaching.

A Way Forward?

'*What science concept would improve everybody's cognitive toolkit?*' This question, recently put to an invited group of eminent scientists, philosophers and artists, threw up some highly relevant responses (Jha, 2011), common amongst which was the idea, summed up in the article's title, that '*the only real truth is that there's doubt*'. Some of the suggestions included offerings such as, 'a good scientist is never certain …' and, 'uncertainty is a central component of what makes science successful' or, 'the most common misunderstanding about science is that scientists seek and find truth. They don't; they make and test models'.

This has to be taken seriously by all of us who teach science, even though historically it has been far from the accepted view of science teaching in school. For generations science has been about facts and laws and the standard testing of science over the past twenty or more years has only served to institutionalise this view, even at the primary phase. A couple of years ago, when the discussion about ending compulsory science SATs was at its height, one teacher wrote to the *TES* saying 'if there weren't SATs, how would I know what to teach?' Yet all the home countries except England have done so and signs of greater curiosity and creativity have emerged in these regions. But it is one thing to emphasise something as elusive or uncertain as a teaching goal and another to operationalise this in our teaching strategies. So what might be the kind of science teaching approach that would bring this about? And would it be possible in practice for the average, non-specialist primary teacher?

Before going on to look at our principles of good teaching, though, let's answer the second question first: it is possible, without doubt. Between them the authors contributing to this book have taught or observed science lessons in hundreds of classrooms over several decades, across the UK and elsewhere. And we have all seen how this real development of children who can think like scientists is happening, as in the example below.

〰 **Points for Reflection**

One of the best examples of true science teaching comes from an untrained teacher in a rural primary school in Kenya, which had no running water or electricity. His strategy was to let his pupils investigate problems identified by themselves: each afternoon, after their practical work was over, the groups came together, taking turns to explain where their investigation had got to, always concluding with a request for help from the whole class; *'our problem now is … '*. This led to class discussion and suggestion of ways forward for the following day's investigations. These children not only out-performed those in other schools in science in the primary leaving exams, they also out-performed them in English and Maths too. (Githinji, 1992)

So what are our principles of good science pedagogy? First and foremost is the generating and sustaining of excitement and curiosity amongst children about the world around them. And this comes from being excited and curious yourself, as a role model. Don't be afraid to allow your class to work on things that crop up unpredictably – and there will be plenty of such opportunities relating to the weather, health, diet, technological innovations, TV programmes, etc. For example, only recently there has been media controversy about whether or not breast milk is best for babies, so who has done the research? Might the article you are reading be biased for some reason? Does it tell us where the original data are from? Who funded the research? How can we judge it? What do the mothers think?

Second, you can enable children to be independent learners and not consumers of memorisable trivia. A classroom visited a year or two ago had a large display on one wall headed, *'Posh science words you need to know'*. About 20 words were listed, the first being 'photosynthesis'. But what did 'know' mean in this context? Did that teacher simply expect pupils to be able to say and spell the word? Or parrot a definition? Or understand the process and apply it to plants (e.g. how might your answer explain why some plants are evergreen and others deciduous?)? When children are first released from learning and regurgitating science facts they will often lack the confidence to accept that there are not necessarily any 'right answers': hence this self-confidence has to be cultivated gradually by accepting their suggestions, exploring them and postponing a judgement, as the eminent scientists indicated above.

For you as a teacher though, you will also have to deal effectively with a rapidly changing system that continues to make demands on the way you teach science – demands which may be at odds with what you believe is right. It is here that sharing and solidarity with colleagues become important. In response to Michael Gove's recent ideas about emphasising the teaching of facts, one *Times* reader responded by pointing out that, whilst not having a science degree, he now does his own plumbing and re-wiring and services his own car. He put this down to three things: the ability to read a book and extract the detail; the ability to ask the right people the right questions; and an enquiring mind – thanks to the help of wise and diligent teachers.

Asking the right questions is crucial here and children will only do so in an ethos that is conducive to these questions being listened to, respected, and followed through. You are on the right track to be 'wise and diligent' if your pupils see science as a process of tackling problems which may not have simple answers; convince them that science *begins* when we get stuck. You really and truly don't need to know all the answers and it's OK to admit this! As environmental and health problems become more intractable, this increasingly implies taking the longer view, understanding the implications of data, and not jumping to conclusions, all the while exploring the issue alongside your pupils.

A good example here was the data from the Spring Bulbs Project described above in Chapter 3. As data were accumulated from across the country year on year, this emphasised the need for caution in interpreting what these told us. After two or three years, for example, one might have concluded from the evidence that bulbs were definitely flowering earlier; yet after four and five years, and two hard winters, the opposite might be concluded. Thus being tentative and not certain is an important lesson to learn about science – which is not easy when the tabloid press consistently want to sell papers by offering us lurid and often distorted stories about what 'scientists have discovered'. You need to have confidence in yourself as a science teacher and linking up with other novice teachers in the same boat is one good way to engender this.

A final point here relates to the importance of 'cultivating' your headteacher. This may sound manipulative but it simply means working in order to have the support of the head for what you are trying to do, for example by publicising success and engaging parents and the community. The journal *Primary Science* has in recent years publicised numerous school garden and environmental projects that have engaged the support not only of other teachers and parents but also of local people, industry, universities, science centres and garden centres. Almost without exception, and for good reason, these projects will receive glowing endorsements from the headteachers concerned – a platform from which you as a teacher can move further forward in the ways you believe in.

What Works and Why?

It is fitting in a book of this nature to finish with the authors' strongly held views of the characteristics and features of what works and why this is so. We have read persuasive arguments about the significance of effective planning and assessment strategies, the significance of meaningful real-world contexts, the conflict between the need for a right answer and the nature of science, employing relevant ICT, and of escaping the insularity of a prescribed and narrow view of what is primary science – but have we left anything out?

Much has been claimed about harnessing children's natural inquisitiveness and curiosity. Setting out to provide opportunities where there isn't a right answer might sound reckless but consider the 'mystery box'. An object only known to the teacher is placed in a catering size coffee tin, the only opening being a small hole in the lid so small learners cannot see the object in the mystery box. The task is to identify any features of the contained object with direct, first-hand contact. All information is gleaned indirectly by gently rotating the tin, by shaking the tin, by listening to the sounds made as the object moves, by having a sense of the object's mass, material, odour composition and so on. The object's identity is not the goal – more important here are the learners' ideas and thought processes. To reveal its identity destroys this task's purpose and it takes a strong teacher to hold the line of not revealing the identity of the object. Science is full of examples where our knowledge of something (e.g. the structure of matter) has been gained through indirect evidence. It is not unreasonable for a child to ask *'How do you know what an atom looks like if no one has ever seen it?'*

A strong emphasis is frequently made about the need for a teacher to employ effective questioning but less is said about the need to create and maintain a questioning ethos. Such an ethos encourages children to ask questions, values their questions, and is not founded on a teacher's capacity to provide the right answer. We would not underestimate the difficulty this may present, but if as an effective teacher of science you accept and are comfortable with the premise that it is unreasonable to expect you to have all answers to all questions, then this can be highly productive. Children's questions can provide insights on their individualised knowledge and understanding; they can also reveal misconceptions, inform and direct the next step for learning, provide an incentive for further work, and stimulate further talk and discussion. The insightful teacher will often harness such questions to shape lessons such that what appears to be done has, in effect, been directed by the children which in turn can create a powerful sense of ownership of learning. In a remote school in East Africa, a pupil aged around 10 asked the student teacher in his class, *'How do I measure how far I can see?'*. How would you have responded to this?

Ofsted have observed that primary science is often characterised by good scientific investigations but these are often dominated by the 'fair-testing' form of enquiry. Practical work in science is so much more than this. Field work, surveys, explorations, pattern seeking, illustrative activities and tasks, observation-based work, demonstrations, drama, role-play, simulations, hot seating, debates … these can all be used if, and only if, they are fit for purpose. ITE students will often relish the idea of using role-play, perhaps to illustrate basic particle theory or how heat will move through a conductor and not through an insulator, but they will rarely do so during their teaching practice. We suspect that schools often adopt quite narrow pedagogic views and prefer a 'play safe' approach. Yes, there maybe CPD implications, and yes, there may be a certain amount of risk involved, but you will know whether or not such novel approaches will work in your own context. The predictable teacher delivering predictable lessons is anathema to the very essence of what we consider to constitute high quality science provision. Assuming that fitness for purpose is uppermost in a teacher's pedagogy then surely it is indisputable that a *variety of experiences is the educational spice of life*.

We should never underestimate the power of science in creating a huge sense of awe and wonder. Whether it is causing a balloon to stick to a wall, redirecting a smooth flow of water from a tap using a 'rubbed' plastic comb, or bringing a salamander into class, children will – if the presentation is appropriate – respond with genuine enthusiasm, delight and interest. Just try stopping them asking questions! Too often this will require the teacher to move a little from that which is approved but we should remind ourselves that the National Curriculum is a minimum entitlement and not the be all and end all of science. These are fun activities yet they can also help children to make connections and generate more 'joined-up' thinking.

A central aim of science education is to enable children to make better sense of their world. Being limited to and restricted by any approved curriculum, whether this is perceived or not, risks those charged with educating our young people to underestimate both what these young people need to know and children's capacity to learn. We do not need to provide all the right answers, but we should always be prepared to challenge our learners. Off you go! Inspire them!

References

Githinji, S. (1992) 'Using the environment for science teaching: a teacher's view from Kenya', *Perspectives*, 45: 105–123.
This article, based on work which won a Commonwealth Prize, is discussed in more detail in Peacock A. (1997) *Opportunities for Science in the Primary School*. Stoke-on-Trent: Trentham.

Jha, A. (2011) '"The only real truth is that there's doubt", say scientists' *The Guardian*, 15 January.

INDEX